Dedication

Walking with the Wise is dedicated
to anyone who has the desire
to be successful in business
and to experience a life
of prosperity with peace.

WALKING WITH THE WISE™

ISBN 0-9729875-0-9

Printed in the United States of America

10 9 8 7 6 5 4 3 2 1

Published by MENTORS Publications, Inc.
3540 W. Sahara Ave. Suite 202
Las Vegas, NV 89102

This book is available at quantity discounts for bulk purchases and for branding by businesses and organizations. For further information, or to learn more about Mentors magazine™, mentorsmagazine.com™, Walking with the Wise™ *and other products and services of Mentors Publications, Inc, contact:*

MENTORS Publications, Inc.
10755-F Scripps Poway Pkwy. #530
San Diego, CA 92131
Telephone: (858) 277-9700
e-mail: publications@mentorsmagazine.com
Web: www.mentorsmagazine.com

Cover Design, page composition and typography by Kim Muslusky, KimCo. Graphics, Poway, CA

The publisher would like to acknowledge the many publishers and individuals who granted us permission to reprint their cited material or have written specifically for this book.

What I've Noticed About Life

By Jim Rohn

It is an incredible honor to be part of *Walking with the Wise*. This book is a massive collaborative effort involving a multitude of successful individuals from all over the world who have banded together to offer their secrets for prosperity. But it's up to you, the reader, to apply them.

I have been here on this earth over 70 years and have spent a large majority of them studying the habits of people who obtain prosperity. This is a small part of what I've observed:

Life is about constant, predictable patterns of change. For the six thousand years of recorded history, as humans have entered this world, received parental instruction, classroom instruction, and gathered the experience of life, many have set for themselves ambitious goals and dreamed lofty dreams. As the wheel of life continues its constant turning, all human emotions appear, disappear, and appear once again.

A major challenge faced by us all is that we must learn to experience the changing of life's cycles without being changed by them; to make a constant and conscious effort to improve ourselves in the face of changing circumstances.

That is why I believe in the power and value of attitude. As I read and ponder, and speculate about people, their deeds and their destiny, I become more deeply convinced that it is our natural destiny to grow, to succeed, to prosper, and to find happiness while we are here.

By our attitude, we decide to read or not to read. By our attitude, we decide to try or give up. By our attitude, we blame ourselves for our failure or we blame others. Our attitude determines whether we tell the truth or lie, act or procrastinate, advance or recede, and by our own attitude we and we alone actually decide whether to succeed or fail.

Attitude determines choice, and choice determines results. All that we are and all that we can become has indeed been left unto us. For as long as you continue to draw breath, you have the chance to complete the work in and for the earth and for yourself that God has begun for you. In the cycles and seasons of life, attitude is everything!

Any day we wish, we can discipline ourselves to change it all. Any day we wish, we can open the book that will open our mind to new knowledge. Any day we wish, we can start a new activity. Any day we wish, we can start the process of life change. We can do it immediately, or next week, or next month, or next year.

We can also do nothing. We can pretend rather than perform. And if the idea of having to change ourselves makes us uncomfortable, we can remain as we are. We can choose rest over labor, entertainment over education, delusion over truth, and doubt over confidence. The choices are ours to make. But while we curse the effect, we continue to nourish the cause. As Shakespeare uniquely observed, "The fault is not in the stars, but in ourselves." We created our circumstances by our past choices. We have both the ability and the responsibility to make better choices beginning today. Those who are in search of the good life do not need more answers or more time to think things over to reach better conclusions. They need the truth. They need the whole truth. And they need nothing but the truth.

We cannot allow our errors in judgment, repeated every day, to lead us down the wrong path. We must keep coming back to those basics that make the biggest difference in how our life works out. And then we must make the very choices that will bring life, happiness and joy into our daily lives. And if I may be so bold to offer my last piece of advice for someone seeking and needing to make changes in their life: If you don't like how things are, change it! You're not a tree. You have the ability to totally transform every area in your life – and it all begins with your very own power of choice.

To Your Success,

Jim Rohn

Jim Rohn is considered to be America's Foremost Business Philosopher. To subscribe to the free *Jim Rohn Weekly E-zine* send a blank email to *subscribe@jimrohn.com* or visit *www.jimrohn.com* and also receive 20-60% off on all audios, books and tapes. Review the complete Jim Rohn archive of articles, vitamins for the mind and Q and A. © 2003 Jim Rohn International. All rights reserved worldwide.

TABLE OF CONTENTS

SECTION I – HOW TO OVERCOME OBSTACLES ON YOUR JOURNEY TO PROSPERITY

"Successful Individuals Share their Personal Stories, Inspiration and Guidance."

Section II – How You Think Determines Your Life

"Prosperity Thinking, Belief and Spiritual Wisdom Produce Prosperity Results."

SECTION III – BUSINESS TIPS FOR SUCCESS

"Business Secrets From the Masters."

Section IV – Keep Your Health to Keep Your Abundance

"Nutrition, Exercise, Lifestyle and Health Management for Optimal Living."

Section V – Remember Your Family!

"Remembering Your Spouse, Children and Parents on Your Journey to Prosperity Will Help You Keep it When You Arrive."

Section VI – Surprise Bonus Section

"Rare Exclusive Interview with Brian Tracy."

Acknowledgements

And Many Thanks...

Dawn Holman - For mentor scouting and recommending some of the contributors to this book. Thank you for editing articles, hosting teleseminars and being a trusted friend.

Patsy Lowry - For being my mentor and patiently guiding me in the right direction. Thank you for standing by me, even in the dark times. You always believed in me!

Nina Martinson - For being my life-long friend who I have always looked up to, even when we were only three years old. Thank you for being there for me when I needed you most. You're my soul sister.

Jay LeBeau - For providing both heart and brains to the company. Thank you for your design and editing contributions, and for using your business management, financial and planning genius to help make everything come together in a BIG way!

Eric Lofholm - For having terrific confidence that we both were going to live our dreams and be an inspiration to many people. Thankyou for helping me overcome the past and build a great future!

Mike Littman - For sharing your great ideas, and working to build me up. You've helped many times to recommend terrific people and I've learned much from your networking talents.

Denise Michaels - For living your dream and helping me with mine. Thank you for being a loyal friend.

Dan Kennedy - For taking the time from your very busy schedule to support and guide me. You've taught me so much and are a constant source of inspiration. I will always cherish our friendship.

Kim Muslusky - For having the patience of a saint. You've stood by me through thick and thin as we've created this book. Thank you for your immense contribution and for supporting me as we worked together.

Yvonne Stovall - For being my mother and first mentor. Thank you for your loving guidance and belief in me. You have made the ultimate difference in my life!

Tiffany Frank - For being the most wonderful daughter that a mom could ask for. Your approach to life inspires me and you've been a terrific help with this book.

Jason Wright - For being the most wonderful son that a mom could ask for. I love your sense of humor and zest for life.

Janet Attwood - For being a beautiful and faithful friend, and my model of what it means to be enlightened. Thank you for your support and encouragement.

Judy Hoffman - Thank you for all of your contributions since the inception of MENTORS magazine, and for donating your time to this book. You're the best copy editor ever, and we couldn't have done it without you!

Brian Smithies & Bryan Davis - For working with MENTORS magazine to help make it a huge success in the U.K. Your advice and know-how have expanded our horizons more than we thought possible.

Brad King - For being an all-around cool guy, and organizing the book tour for the *Walking with the Wise* contributors. Your contribution to the success of the book will be forever appreciated.

Introduction

WALKING WITH THE WISE

By Linda Forsythe

It happened again. Three months before I conceptualized this book, I was approached by a reader of MENTORS magazine asking me to tell her the secrets of how to get rich, *fast*. I remember sighing to myself and shaking my head. So many people want to know how to become millionaires without understanding what true prosperity is and what is required for that life style. We've all heard of individuals who have won a large sum of money, only to lose it and be in worse shape than when they started.

I listened to the passionate story of this young lady and learned that she was a single mom struggling to support herself and three children on welfare. My heart went out to her because I certainly had been in her shoes. I've known poverty, and have been a single mom for many years.

When I mentioned this, she seemed quite surprised. "How is that possible? You've built a huge business, started a successful magazine and lead such a prosperous life! Did you win the lottery or inherit some money?" I laughed and told her, "Not by a long shot. In fact I started this business without any money at all." Now that I had her attention completely, I went on to tell her my secret.

The day my life changed for the better was when I became absolutely fed up with living in desperation. I was sick of being evicted from my home because I couldn't pay rent. I was tired of never having enough for even the bare essentials. I was exhausted from living in fear all the time. My health was starting to deteriorate and my children were starting to show the effects of my not being able to provide well for them. Three marriages and divorces added to my emotional drain. The last straw came when I became homeless yet again because of another failed relationship. I was just plain sick and tired of being sick and tired. I came to the point inside myself that it simply wasn't an option to look for charity any more. There *had* to be a better way - and darn it, I was going to find it!

My journey toward prosperity most certainly wasn't quick and easy, but I had taken a very important first step. I was committed to finding a way to lead a better life for my children and myself. Without realizing it, I automatically took another step that I later found out was absolutely essential. *I CHANGED THE WAY I THOUGHT*. I didn't want to spend time going into therapy to find out why I made bad choices or did the things I had done before. I certainly knew what didn't work. To heck with my past, because I wasn't that person anymore. I was going to reinvent myself and start a totally new existence.

I didn't allow any draining or negative people to stay in my life. I searched for and found a mentor who lived the life that I wanted to live, and became an eager student. (Her name is Patsy Lowry and she still contacts me on a regular basis in order to lovingly check up on me.) As my thinking changed, the circumstances and situations surrounding me also started to change accordingly. This may sound simplistic, but it isn't. It took major on-going work to constantly keep control of my new way of thinking.

I acquired a voracious appetite for words of wisdom to learn about how to live a life of prosperity, and I fed myself large portions daily. Many of them came from the Bible. I also read words written by wise people from various cultures throughout history. This was my foundation, because I felt that real wisdom is truth and will therefore stand the test of time. From this basic foundation, I learned what words to listen to from today's mentors. I learned how to humble myself and take good advice. Most importantly, I applied the concept of the golden rule: *"Do Unto Others as You Would Have Them Do Unto You"* and adopted the very necessary component of loving myself. You don't hurt the one you love.

As my newfound friend sat and listened, I sensed a certain amount of disappointment. She looked at me and said, "That still doesn't explain how you did it." I smiled, "Yes, actually, it does." Then we spent more time together discussing the steps she needed to start taking.

It was after our discussion that I realized that someone should create a book filled with words of wisdom from respected and loved mentors. I also wanted the guidance to be geared specifically toward entrepreneurs because these are a group of people who are motivated to achieve a larger than average life. They are the trail blazers.

This *Walking With the Wise* book project turned into something more than I could have ever imagined or planned for. After putting the message out that we were looking for individuals with a proven history of success, the word spread and I received responses from all over the world. Many of the contributors have readily recognizable names. Every person who has contributed to this book has gone through various life-learning experiences to reach the position they are in right now.

The contributors to the first section tell about their personal trials and how they overcame obstacles. They also provide information and inspiration to you about how you can do this in your own life. You will find that at first glance quite a few of the obstacles these mentors experienced have the appearance of being insurmountable. I personally read this section with amazement because – knowing these people now – I never would have guessed what some of them had gone through.

The second section discusses how changing your thinking can change your life. You might want to search for some common threads as you read the words of each author.

The third section is full of guidance about how to become successful in business. These tried-and-true strategic methods have proven to be invaluable for many people just like you.

The next section features the writing of well-known consultants and coaches in the health field. We chose to include this section because keeping your health is an essential key for keeping your prosperity. I have seen so many individuals become wealthy, only to spend all of their hard-earned money trying to get back the health they lost in their quest for riches.

The fifth section, *Remember Your Family!* – is closest to me personally. The individuals who share their stories here help you to realize what prosperity truly is. I think we all have heard of someone who became very wealthy but was miserable because they didn't pay attention to nurturing or being nurtured by their family. The repercussions can be devastating.

The 70 contributors to *Walking with the Wise* are well-paid coaches, consultants and mentors in the area that they specialize. As a result, this book contains literally millions of dollars of advice from successful people with a wide variety of perspectives. You'll find the practical advice from their own learning experiences invaluable. The only question is, *How will you apply this in your own life, and when will you start?*

At the last minute we added a final section to this book. MENTORS magazine recently conducted a rare and exclusive cover story interview with Brian Tracy. The words of wisdom he shares are most appropriate for the readers of *Walking with the Wise*, so we're including it as a special bonus to you.

The members of our Advisory Board decided that *Walking with the Wise* should present many points of view. We believe we've accomplished this, and so you'll get good advice from many perspectives. It will therefore, be just a matter of finding what resonates best with you and your circumstances. Remember to refer to this book often. You'll get something new each time, even by reading the same article as time passes because of life changes.

As a final note: I've had a number of inquiries as to why we have used a caricature of Moses on the cover and throughout the pages of this book. The answer is simple. Moses was a great mentor and leader. He learned from his many mistakes and moved forth with boldness on his divine purpose. He became wise. Using his strong spiritual connection, Moses ultimately led his people to the land of milk and honey (prosperity). As you conduct research on your own journey toward success, you may find it interesting to note that many successful people have a strong spiritual belief and apply spiritual principles to their daily actions. I encourage you to explore and develop your own spirituality as part of your path to prosperity.

It is my most sincere desire that you find something within these pages that will improve your life and, as a result, the lives of those around you.

These words of wisdom by mentors from all over the globe is our gift to help you live a more fulfilling life. Learn from the authors and live the life you were meant to live.

**MOVE FORWARD WITH BOLDNESS ON YOUR QUEST
AND MIGHTY FORCES WILL COME TO YOUR AID.**

Linda Forsythe is the Founder and Editor-in-Chief of *MENTORS* magazine.
She has dedicated herself to helping others lead a life of true abundance
and prosperity. Her desire to learn, combined with excellent networking
skills, and a passion for empowering others has led her to create
magazines, books, teleseminars, conferences, workshops and Web
sites. She also has appeared in print, television, radio and
electronic media. She would love to hear from you via
e-mail at *Linda@mentorsmagazine.com*.

Dear Reader

By Kim Muslusky

Being the designer, illustrator and pre-press production coordinator for MENTORS magazine has been a two-year odyssey toward positive thinking and life-changing attitudes for me. Working in the same capacity for *Walking with the Wise* has provided me the opportunity to interact with marvelous mentors in both publications. By silently observing how these great people live their lives, I have expanded my horizons and created a more positive perspective to what once appeared to be a low point in my life.

In late summer 2001, we lost my husband's mother after three years of serious illness. At the same time, our youngest daughter experienced grave difficulties with the birth of our grandchild. The terrorist attack of September 11th brought yet another incredible jolt. Two days later, our home was robbed and all our important possessions were gone forever. My once serene life was shattered; my world turned upside-down.

Like many entrepreneurs, September 11th was also a turning point for my business. I had been a freelance artist for over 25 years, but within a few weeks of the attack, my clients either went out of business or stopped hiring. Everything came to a standstill – both on an emotional and business level. I felt as though I had been broadsided and was unable to think, function, or move forward.

Then one day the phone rang, and Linda Forsythe, Editor-in-Chief of MENTORS magazine blasted into my life! (If you knew her, you would understand what I mean here...) Anyway, I believe that things happen for a reason, and I'm sure that Linda and I were meant to connect on that day.

Linda and I speak continually about how it is possible for anyone to change his or her life – especially with the inspiration and help of a mentor. The personal and working relationships that we formed while creating *Walking with the Wise* have been powerful influences for me. My emotional and business life are now back in order. I am thriving once again.

I can't say my journey has been easy these past two years. There certainly have been several bumps in the road. Somewhere along the way, I began to more fully understand the path I had been seeking all my life. After reading all the MENTORS magazine articles, and the articles that appear in this book, (a nice perk when it is your job), I found the common thread. We all struggle through life; experiencing the good and bad. If you have a dream, you must stay true to yourself and somehow make it happen, despite what life throws at you. The results are in direct proportion to the effort you have given.

All the contributors to this anthology have worked diligently to share something of value with you. Like the others, this has been a labor of love for me. It is my hope that my small part in it will make a difference in your life's journey.

Kim Muslusky is a designer/illustrator with over 25 years experience in the fine art, publishing, advertising, and TV/video/film industries. You may contact her at *858-693-7380* or *kimcog@cts.com*.

Section 1

How to Overcome Obstacles on Your Journey to Prosperity

© 2003 Kim Muslusky

How To Kick
Adversity In The Butt
By Dan S. Kennedy

I have lived an interesting life so far. And if you ever want to lay a blessing and a curse on someone simultaneously, just tell them: "May you live an interesting life." Allow me to explain what I mean by giving a few brief resume' items, prerequisite to my thoughts about dealing with adversity.

I had the unique childhood experience of having entrepreneurial parents who were quite successful and very prosperous until my teens, when they became quite unsuccessful and very broke. I saw and experienced shiny new cars every year and then had old, rotting, broken down, bad cars. I began life in a mansion that resembled the one on "Joe Millionaire" and then moved onto a house in a rural area where we couldn't afford heating oil. I learned to sleep in clothes and blankets huddled near the dining room fireplace.

By the time I was an adult, I'd lived the Totie Fields quote: "I've been broke and I've been rich, and rich is better." Since my experience was backwards from most, I started my adult life broke. I stayed broke for quite a while. Later, I went both business and personally bankrupt in a messy and humiliating way. Along the way, my early business mentor and closest friend made a sequence of very poor decisions that put him in the state penitentiary for five years.

I have only actually had one job my whole life. Right out of high school, I spent one year as a territory sales rep. Near the end of the year, my sales manager and I both agreed that I needed to be entrepreneurial by virtue of the fact that I was "unemployable."

On nine different occasions, I have been confronted with severe, epic, giant adversities. In addition there were a zillion incidents of lesser significance, each of which seemed like a mountainous challenge or crisis at the moment.

In my earliest years in business, bank loans were called, I was sued, was wrongfully thrown out of a professional association and had to sue to get reinstated, had two cars repossessed in the same year, and occasionally went hungry. I have had to start all over again from scratch – with no scratch – more than once.

18

At certain times I noted a remarkable absence of friends and encouragers. (Former President Nixon once gave this sage advice: "Don't count your friends when you are on top of the world. Count them when the world is on top of you.")

There were times when I seriously questioned my own sanity. For some years, I had a serious drinking problem bordering on alcoholism. (I am fortunate to have been able to quit cold turkey). I've had a few other personal problems too. I am delighted to tell you (knock on wood) that for more than a decade now I have been sober and successful in my entrepreneurial ventures.

In total, I've gone belly-up and bust in three businesses. But the final good news is I have since developed very successful businesses and significant wealth. While not yet 50 years old, I have no need to earn even one more dollar to live comfortably the rest of my life. Instead of working, I get to put a lot of time into my race horses. (This does not qualify me for any kind of investing wizard credential. After all, they are an investment that "eat while I sleep.")

"I Kicked Adversity in the Butt."

I stuttered nearly uncontrollably for several years, and continued to have a stuttering problem well into my adulthood. Yet I still managed to become a very prominent, popular professional speaker. For nine years I was on international tour with many of the best-known business, sales and motivational speakers of our time – Zig Ziglar, Jim Rohn, Tom Hopkins and Brian Tracy – as well as a Who's Who list of former U.S. Presidents and world leaders, athletes and coaches, authors and Hollywood celebrities. I've addressed audiences as large as 35,000 people and spoken at specialized-topic "boot camps" costing as much as $ 10,000.00 per person to attend.

When I was a young man, there was no way I could afford college. There would have been zero assistance from my family; in fact, I needed to immediately start earning enough money to help my parents financially. So I never attended college, let alone get any initials to plunk down after my name, (MBA or others). Nevertheless, I have developed a thriving consulting practice working almost exclusively with millionaire and multi-millionaire entrepreneurs, along with a few Fortune 500 companies. My highest level coaching program, "The Kennedy Platinum Inner Circle," includes 18 individuals, each running large information publishing and marketing businesses, generating well over $150-million annually. As of this writing, I am routinely paid $8,300.00 per day for consulting, and turn down twice as many engagements as I accept.

I've had no formal training, apprenticeship, mentorship or even employment in advertising; yet I've become one of the highest paid freelance advertising copywriters in America. (For example, my current fees to write a client's direct-mail campaign range from $28,000.00 to $70,000.00 plus a royalty on all the gross revenues that result from its use.)

In other words... "I kicked adversity in the butt."

This doesn't mean, however, that I have lived or live a life free of adversity. It only means that I've developed some skill in handling it properly. There is, after all, only one population possibly free of problems... A number of years ago, I was driven to their place of residence – it's the cemetery.

I'd like to share with you the three principles I've lived by in the hope that they can be helpful to you whenever you are confronted with calamities:

Principle #1:
Nothing is ever as bad – or as good –
as it first appears.

Principle #2:
Most adversities conceal and provide
new, better opportunities,
and a temporary vacuum is
not necessarily a bad thing.

Principle #3:
I do not just want to cope with adversity.
I want to kick it in the butt, smack it around,
grab it by its throat and force it to divulge its hidden benefits,
subjugate it as my servant, and profit from it enormously.
(I kind of have an attitude about this.)

If you examine my life in this context, each disappointment, frustration, failure and calamity has directly led to and made possible something of greater benefit that would not have occurred otherwise. For example, I was for a while the CEO of a small custom cassette production company. Our terrible financial straits led me to sell its manufacturing division to a competing firm, owned by Bill Guthy. Bill invited me to work on Guthy-Renker Corporation's first TV infomercial, *Think And Grow Rich*. That, in turn, led to a 15-year consulting relationship with Guthy-Renker that was lucrative by itself and established me as an expert in infomercials. This led to many other successful independent projects. I have independently produced infomercials generating more than $100 million in revenue. As a consultant I have been integrally involved with infomercials generating more than $2 billion combined. This probably would never have occurred had I not been CEO of a company sinking like the *Titanic,* desperate for a cash infusion.

I have diagrammed this for my whole life documenting each incident that, at the moment, appeared to be tragic, and describing the opportunity it subsequently provided.

The benefits of what appears at first glance to be adversity are many and varied e.g., liberation from a situation or relationship that might have been a prison for you. It is better to find out sooner rather than later. Another benefit might be making a discovery about yourself that empowers you in a new way that yields enormous subsequent profit. Another might be a move to a new place, a new business, a new career, which will better enable you to achieve your major goals and objectives.

I've experienced all of these many times, at both relatively trivial as well as relatively serious levels. I've come to realize that I am not good at managing people. That audio product publishing company had 40 employees and would have had hundreds. For many years now, I've been much happier operating with one person in the company. My bankruptcy also revolutionized my entire attitude toward money, and soon provided a new kind of confidence. I thought it would be fatal. To my surprise, it was barely a minor inconvenience.

In one year, I had several short stories and two novels rejected by over 40 different publishers. As a result, I turned my attention to non-fiction. I've enjoyed considerable success, including nine different books published and sold in bookstores. Two have been on bookstore shelves continuously since 1991. My non-fiction writing has brought me prominence in two different fields, a steady flow of consulting clients and speaking engagements, and, overall, has served my purposes far better than having a novel published.

By the 18th year of my speaking career, the extensive travel was literally killing me. I hated it. I was eating poorly, way overweight, stressed out, irritable and unhappy. I went from a high of 70 engagements a year to about a dozen. After nine consecutive years, I walked away from the *Success Events* tour which required 20-25 all-day events. My income dropped dramatically and I lost my chief means of acquiring new customers for my "inner circle" newsletter, information and seminar business. A huge "money vacuum" was created. I have since replaced that revenue stream with a coaching business, in which most of the service is delivered via telephone from the comfort of my homes, offices, and backyard deck; when face-to-face meetings are required, everyone travels to me. The temporary vacuum was filled with better business – much more conducive to my good health, sanity and lifestyle preferences.

Detecting this pattern relatively early in the game led to my commitment to a particular process each time I faced an apparent adversity. It goes something like this:

Patterns In Adversity

First, delay response. This allows for analysis when not in the heat of the adverse moment. Because nothing is ever as bad (or as good) as it first appears, it's important not to judge and react too quickly. This is not to be confused with indecisiveness, procrastination or avoidance. I've never dodged confronting difficult situations. It is certainly true that problems rarely reach satisfactory resolution on their own. Nor do they tend to improve with age. However, reacting too quickly usually means reacting wrong.

Second, gather as much useful information as possible as quickly as possible. When confronted with a problem, I go into a massive information-gathering and assimilation mode. It is self-serving to say this, since I am in the information business, but it is my observation that most people respond too quickly to new situations based only on whatever information they already possess. They are, in general, surprisingly lazy and cheap about acquiring new information. Tackling a new-situation with old information is akin to staffing an Indy 500 pit crew with blacksmiths.

Third, be open and alert for new opportunities and benefits. They will certainly evolve from the bad situation. Because I *know* they are there or will develop, I consciously hunt for them and am eager to act on them once identified.

Let me give you an actual, rather recent, example. A few years ago, as a result of failing an insurance physical, I was diagnosed to be diabetic. My blood sugar levels were alarmingly high. I went to several different doctors without getting the kind of assistance I wanted. I went into my massive information-gathering mode. Sorting out this information was extremely frustrating, as there is considerable disagreement and conflict among "experts." After nearly two years of experimentation, I arrived at an eating plan that took off about 25 pounds, and a nutritional supplementation regimen that brought the blood sugar numbers down by about 30%. I also kept searching for assistance. I finally found a doctor (in another state), an M.D., but one involved with "integrative medicine," i.e., natural solutions first, prescription drugs as a last resort. I'm now 45 pounds lighter, have kept the weight off for over a year, have my diabetes thoroughly controlled, qualified for the insurance as "non-diabetic," and do not use any prescription drugs including insulin. The quality of the information provided to diabetics by the medical establishment is so poor, misleading, impractical and negative, that I am busily developing my own web sites, newsletter and information products for diabetics, to teach them, essentially, to make their disease go away and live insulin pill or injection-free. As of this writing, I can't say for certain whether this will develop into a significant business or not. (You can check my progress if you like at www.damnthedoctors.com). But if it does, it will be yet another instance where calamity leads to opportunity. Whether this turns into financial gain or not, it has produced great health benefits. Having been motivated by the diagnosis, I have made myself an alternative health/weight loss expert, sleep better, have more energy, eat a healthier diet, and, overall, am in the best shape and condition I've been in for 20 years.

For many people, a diagnosis of diabetes is one of the greatest setbacks of their lives. Many people suffer acute depression, poorly manage their disease, accept bad advice without question, and let it virtually ruin their lives. For them, doors are closing. For me, new doors were opening. Would I rather not have to deal with it? Absolutely. But I am thoroughly schooled and conditioned in the productive response to adversity, so for me, it became opportunity (whether it liked it or not).

In 2002, my 22-year marriage ended abruptly and, to me, unexpectedly. I consider it the greatest tragedy I have ever experienced. What had been a very clear picture of the rest of my life has been erased and replaced with a blank slate. Certain things will progress and are progressing exactly as planned, but others are now unknown. For the first time in many years, I do not know what I want. I am floundering, mentally and emotionally. The very thought of dating is ludicrous and unpleasant to me. But I am in my massive information-gathering mode. And I am moving from shock and disappointment to optimism, looking for the opportunities that must be coming down the pike. Will this somehow lead to a better life experience for me in the years remaining? When the axe first fell, I'd have said no, of course. But if history repeats itself as historians insist, then my life history guarantees it will.

If there is a certainty about life, it is that a new adversity is lurking just around the next corner, waiting to confront and challenge you. No amount of wealth and success or expertise can immunize you from adversity. It bedevils kings and paupers alike. It would be a very good idea to devise your own *modus operandi* for effectively dealing with it. I hope you do – and may you have an interesting life!

Dan Kennedy is an entrepreneur, author, speaker, consultant and editor of the monthly "No B.S. Marketing Letter," the most popular paid subscription marketing newsletter in America. His books include: *No Rules, The Ultimate Marketing Plan, The Ultimate Sales Letter,* and, with the late Dr. Maxwell Maltz, *The New Psycho-Cybernetics.* He has been a professional speaker for over 20 years. Although semi-retired (at age 49), Dan continues to occasionally accept interesting new consulting assignments and clients, and up to a dozen speaking engagements per year. His information is at *www.dankennedy.com.*

Negotiating the Curves of Life

By Kevin Brown

I thought I was going to die – the broken and twisted frame of my motorcycle crushed the back of my neck with a thousand pounds of pressure like a reaper's scythe. I lay pinned to the ground, deprived of air, my face forced into the dirt at the bottom of an embankment 40 feet from the road. Panic set in. I knew my only hope for survival was to get back to the road above for help, but my arms and legs were immobilized. With each breath out, less came in. I remember praying, "Please God, I'm not expected home for hours. Who's gonna find me? Oh God, please, just let me see the sunrise tomorrow." Taking what I thought was my last breath, I closed my eyes to picture my wife.

Earlier that morning, the Monet sunrise enticed me to set aside my work. I was in the mood for a ride on my bike. There were so many plans for the future that needed thinking through and nothing quieted my mind more than inhaling the cool summer breeze and the feel of rushing wind on my face. I swung my leg over my gold 1987 Suzuki Cavalcade and knocked the kickstand loose; I loved listening to the familiar roar of the 1500cc engine. It still enthralled me as much as from the very first day I rode a motorcycle at the age of four.

As I was driving down the lonely country road in northern Missouri enjoying the spectacular sunrise, I approached an unfamiliar hill with a hazardous left curve at the top. My mind remained occupied with plans for the future, totally oblivious to the danger ahead. My body and bike shot straight ahead, where it should have negotiated the curve to the left. I tumbled over and over down a steep embankment.

Wham! The motorcycle landed on my neck as I came to a stop, chest down in the dirt, head turned to the side.

Laying there, resigned to die alone, I heard the most powerful four words of my life, "What can I do?" I didn't know who said them but I did see leather boots, blue jeans and wrinkled hands from my insect-like perspective.

Suddenly, a 74-year-old superman lifted the motorcycle off my body. Immediately my lungs filled with badly needed air and I hungrily gulped it in. My mind cleared. I watched the boots of my rescuer as they paced back and forth. I listened to him call an ambulance. Then he kneeled beside me to ask again, "What can I do?" I really didn't know. It's interesting, in hindsight, that I wasn't in any real pain - just slight discomfort. We both agreed that I shouldn't move. As we waited for the ambulance to arrive, he asked me my name. He told me his was J.P. Childers. I asked him how he knew to look over the embankment to find me.

He answered, "I was driving along and saw your helmet laying by itself in the middle of the road. So I stopped, frantically searching around, and found you stuck under your bike. As I rushed toward you, I heard you gurgling.

"You lifted a thousand pound motorcycle off me?!!" (This was amazing because being a very athletic 28-year old myself, I always had difficulty lifting it.)

"Yeah, and it wasn't all that heavy either," said Childers. He kept checking his watch and complaining about the length of time the ambulance was taking to reach me. We later found out it had taken a wrong turn and was having trouble finding us.

We continued with small talk to relieve the tension. "I guess you weren't wearing your helmet," said Childers, half-asking, half-assuming.

"I always wear my helmet," I said in defense of my usual safety precautions.

"So, how did it come off your head and get up there on the road?" he asked.

We both paused in disbelief. Childers suddenly noticed that the chinstrap was still fastened to me. It was as if the helmet had been placed on the road as a beacon to bring him to my rescue. To this day, that helmet remains untouched in my study – an important reminder of a higher power beyond man's comprehension.

Somehow, I found the strength to joke with the nervous EMT's who finally arrived on the scene. I had learned long before that laughter can defuse most tense situations and I certainly wanted them calm. While they were ministering and transporting me to the hospital, my thoughts went back in time to more pleasant memories to help calm my mind.

The Meaning of "Quadriplegic."

I listened to the doctor as he told my wife Brenda that I was a quadraplegic. Before the day of the accident, neither Brenda nor I knew the meaning of that word. The doctor explained to her what it meant, "That means you will have to feed, bathe, and take care of his every need for the rest of his life."

I roared back in defiance, "No! I didn't marry a maid or a nurse and I'm not deaf!"

"We can handle it. Don't worry." Brenda said to me softly.

I agonized over what this would now mean. As I watched Brenda continue to talk softly with the doctor, I remembered how we had met. We fell in love in the seventh grade, "going steady" as only kids in junior high-school can. We even shared a first kiss to solidify our relationship. As a token of her affection, Brenda had my name printed on a silver

25

identification bracelet. But just when she was about to present it to me, I started going steady with another girl. Brenda and I rarely spoke after that.

Seven years later, a chance meeting at a party brought us back together. Among a gaggle of giggling girls, I noticed her familiar smile. Brenda's eyes seemed to now show signs of forgiveness. I remembered our first kiss. She was even more beautiful than I had remembered.

Playing it cool; I had headed downstairs to play pool with the guys. Casually, I tested the reactions of my friends with, "Did you guys see Brenda upstairs?"

I was immediately met with well-meaning warnings, trying to protect me from heartbreak. "Don't even think about it. That's Brenda," said Matt. Everyone knew what he meant. Brenda, the homecoming queen. Brenda, the girl who's dating the captain of the football team. *THAT* Brenda. "You are *so* outclassed, she won't even talk to you. Just forget it," added Steve.

I wasn't one to allow the words of others to limit my actions. I not only earned the bracelet back, but a few years later we married. Now our love was about to face the test of a lifetime.

Then the doctor turned and asked me, "Do you have a family?"

"Well yes", I said, thinking that was a foolish question. I reminded him that my mother worked at the hospital.

"No," said the doctor, "I mean a family of your own."

The words stuck in my throat. "No, we actually haven't been married very long. We are not at that part of our life yet. We have talked about it a little bit though."

"Well then, we'll talk to both of you about adoption later. Don't expect to have children of your own." The doctor's words began to thunder in my head as the he rambled on with a jumble of statistics from other men with C-5 spinal cord injuries.

Not a day passed that I didn't cry. Everything looked horribly hopeless. It took a while for me to remember my beliefs about how important laughter is to diffuse a tense situation. I've always believed in it, so why wasn't I using it now? Now, was as about as tense as it gets, so I knew I had better start remembering. From then on, not a day passed that I wasn't able to dry my tears with laughter. I constantly read books that were lighthearted and motivational, watched movies or shows that were funny and built my spirit in every way I could.

Dry Tears with Laughter.

That's why laughter is important, right from the beginning. The only responsive muscles of my body were in my shoulders, so my physique began to take on a new look. When my stomach began to pouch out, Brenda teased, "You look like a little Buddha." I responded without much wisdom, of course, but I knew, even then, that anyone who takes himself too seriously runs the risk of looking ridiculous. So I decided that if I could look in the mirror each morning and laugh, then I knew I was gonna make it.

I've reflected deeply and daily on the Chinese proverb – "One joy shatters a hundred griefs."

It's a fact that some people are dealt a harder hand than others. It doesn't seem fair. Yet, who promised life would be fair? The greater question is not: "Why did this happen to me?" but, ultimately, "What will be my response and how will I deal with it? "

My accident became a crash course, (No pun intended) for coming to grips with my own mortality. Once you come that close to death, you become better equipped to see the miracles of life.

I later found out that my upbeat attitude had stunned the medical team. Six months after the accident, I left Craig Rehab in Colorado and 43 fellow patients with spinal cord injuries. This happened even though I was advised that whatever movement I regained during the first six to 24 months would be the most I could hope for. I was determined to make a step forward each day. I had already regained partial use of my triceps, biceps and chest muscles at that time. Today, although still confined to a wheelchair, I bench press 147 pounds, and am totally self-sufficient. I also cook and clean to boot.

There was one other prediction I was out to defy. Brenda and I decided to have a child of our own. After two weeks we managed to conceive and our miracle child Lauren was born nine months later.

The pregnancy and Lauren acted as a catalyst. I realized that this new member of our family would change my priorities. I had an epiphany: "Life is not about walking, it's about standing tall."

As an ethereal bundle of energy, Lauren is my proudest accomplishment. I never cease to be astounded that I fathered such an incredible child. She knew how to tie her own shoes at age four! But then again she had to be a quick learner out of necessity. Sometimes her daddy is not as fast as she'd like him to be.

As I type this article Lauren leans against the wheel of my chair. She continues to chatter with Brenda as she tries to decide on her day. Every morning I revel in the ordinary. I make my daughter breakfast, take her to gymnastics, and spot her while she does flips on the living room floor. These are the moments I was told I'd never see.

A feeling of happiness warms me. I've been blessed to watch the sunrise fill the sky again and bask in the light of true prosperity. Life is good if you know what to look for and how to respond with laughter.

Kevin E. Brown: Father, Wheelchair Athlete, Professional Speaker & Author. Kevin, CEO of Shae Communications, serves as a mentor and coach to enhance your professional and personal life. Get *GREAT FREE STUFF,* daily inspiration and hire this award-winning speaker today! *www.IamKevinBrown.com* or *866-KevinBrown.*

Inspiration From A Soap Box:
How I Turned $25 Into A $6.6 Million Internet Business

By Corey Rudl

Like most success stories, mine is one of hard work, adaptability, and a lot of trial and error. The problem is, people tend to lose sight of this when I tell them that I turned a $25 investment into a $6.6 million online business that attracts more than 1.8 million unique visitors per month.

The "mom & pop" business opportunists gleefully slide to the edge of their seats, sure that I'm about to reveal (finally!) the secret to overnight success, while the jaded investors of the e-commerce shakedown assume I must be selling more of that hot air that cost them their life savings.

Both groups are, of course, wrong. I offer neither instant wealth nor the Brooklyn Bridge.

But I don't really mind the snap judgments, because my story has become my soap box – it's what allows me to climb up, grab the attention of real people who aren't afraid to get their hands dirty, and inspire them to pursue something "bigger." Sharing the secrets behind my proven successes – and the mistakes behind my most dismal, costly failures – brings the dreamers and the doubters back to reality, but with a new glimmer of excitement in their eyes that still thrills me every time.

It's the same glimmer I'm sure I had when I started my business in my bachelor apartment.

Getting Started

My first venture into online marketing was basically a move of desperation. I had written a book about one of my biggest passions - cars. I'd had it self-published, so I had a garage full of copies. And I'd spent big money (more than I could afford) buying advertising space in some pretty popular car magazines. But all my efforts were going nowhere. I was down to my few last dollars, and no one was buying my book.

Then a friend suggested I try selling my book on the Internet.

So I used my last $25 to cover my first month of Web hosting, and I launched a web site called "Car Secrets Revealed." In that first month, I made $200. That might sound like pocket change, but at that point it was enough to get my attention!

When you experience your first success, even if it's a small one, it's easy to get a little cocky. So after that first $200, I thought I must really know something about marketing. And it's true that I did – after all, I had spent thousands of dollars educating myself, learning from the great masters of direct marketing, like Jay Abraham and Ted Nicolas. The problem, as I was about to discover, was that I didn't yet know anything about Internet marketing.

But neither did anybody else. The Internet was so new as a marketing medium that there were no experts for me to learn from. Now for someone who has always been a voracious learner, this was a little bit of a challenge. I had to find new ways to educate myself - so I dove in head first.

Building A Solid Knowledge Base

If I had to pick one thing that was really critical to my success, the one thing that everything else was built on, I'd have to say it was what I learned through trial and error during the 18- and 20-hour days I spent testing theory after theory.

I quickly learned that although some offline marketing techniques translated beautifully to the Internet, some were dismal failures. And what really surprised me was that it was virtually impossible to predict which would work and which would fail. That's why I'm such an avid proponent of testing everything! I did so many tests in those early years that I could hardly see straight!

No matter what kind of dream you have, testing should be a prominent part of your plan. The great thing about building a business on the Internet is that you can see results incredibly fast. Everything moves at light speed online, so you can start to evaluate the success of any promotion after only 24 hours. In the offline world, it can take months to determine the success of a single advertisement, so it takes a lot longer to compile accurate results.

Every time you test a new theory, you learn a little bit more about what will work for your business. This education is an incredibly valuable asset – and if you do your testing online, it's virtually free.

Turning The Dream Into A Multi-Million Dollar Business

The knowledge base I built in those early years has paid off enormously. That one-man operation in my bachelor apartment has grown into four online businesses that earn $6.6 million a year. I get over 1.8 million visitors to my Web sites every month. But you know what? I'm still learning. And I'm still testing. I don't kid myself – I know I'm nothing special. I don't get millions of visitors to my web sites because I'm some sort of genius. I get those millions of visitors because I consistently test everything! If something stops working, I change it. Even if something seems to be working well, I test new ideas to see if I can make it even better.

I'm just a small-town guy who likes (okay, loves) cars. When I started out, I wasn't privy to any inside information. My customers didn't just start dropping millions of dollars into my lap. I really worked hard (I'm not kidding about the 20-hour days!). I suffered many failures along the way, but I chalked them up to testing, adjusted everything based on what I learned, and eventually I knew enough to create success way beyond anything I'd ever imagined.

Fast-Forwarding Your Success With Today's Resources

Today, of course, starting a business online is a whole lot easier. There are lots of tools and resources to help you get the ball rolling. And you certainly don't need to start from scratch like I did, because you can learn from the trial and error testing that's already been done. Remember that soap box I mentioned back at the beginning? Here's where I get up and shout my most important message:

Take advantage of the lessons that have already been learned!

It's true that I still encourage every business owner to do their own testing, since no one can say exactly what will work best for a specific business marketing to a specific group at a specific time. However, just as there are "rules" for creating successful businesses in the offline world, there are now rules for creating success online. If you don't take advantage of the knowledge base that has already been established, you'll find yourself working your own 20-hour days, and learning some pretty painful lessons along the way.

Final Thoughts

I don't have the magic formula that creates instant wealth. What I do have is an in-depth knowledge of the online world – based not on academic theory, but on my own testing and research.

When I started out in my bachelor apartment, writing about cars, I never had any plans to become an "Internet marketing expert." I just wanted to sell my book. But as more and more people started coming to me, wanting to avoid the years of testing I had already done, I knew my life was headed in a different direction.

I still love cars. But now, instead of writing about them in a tiny apartment, I get to race them! (I don't have to work 20-hour days anymore.) And I'm pursuing another passion: learning through testing and research, staying one step ahead of my competition, and passing everything I discover down to people who are just starting out – the new Internet entrepreneurs who simply don't have the traffic or resources to do the same kind of testing I can now do so quickly.

If a small-town guy like me can build a multi-million-dollar company, armed with nothing more than a $25 investment and a passion for cars, I firmly believe that armed with all the information, resources, and automation technology that exist today, anyone can start a highly profitable

Internet business. Remember: you don't need a lot of money to get started online; you simply need a desire to learn and a commitment to succeed.

⊤

Corey Rudl, founder of MarketingTips.com, is a world-renowned Internet marketing expert. His best-selling course, *Insider Secrets to Marketing Your Business on the Internet,* has helped countless small businesses become hugely profitable. Ask for your free copy of the eBook *How To Create A Fortune On the Internet in 4 Simple Steps* email: *mentors@marketingtips.com*

The Power of Change
One Step At a Time

By Joseph B. Washington II

Over the past ten years I have had the incredible opportunity to speak in front of hundreds of people, encouraging and motivating them to be nothing less than their best. As I write this article, I am preparing for the 2003 Toastmaster International Speaker Contest. The winner will be selected from over 25,000 speakers from all over the world. WOW! Each time I speak I am in awe of the compliments I receive, such as: *"Your speech was simply awesome… Excellent… Powerful and sincere message… Fantastic energy in your speech… Very motivational… Great delivery… The passion was wonderful…"* Of all the compliments I have received, the ones I value the most relate to my passion for speaking.

Why Am I So Passionate About Speaking?

There was a time in my life when speaking was a greater challenge than you could imagine. From the time I spoke my first words until I was about thirteen or fourteen years old, it was apparent that there was something different about me. I stuttered. I tried with everything in me to express my thoughts clearly to others, but it never happened. I can remember times when my older brother, Paul, would gather his friends around me and ask me to speak. He would ask me a series of questions just to hear me stutter. This session became known as "There he goes." I would hear comments like: "Your brother is stupid," or "Is that how he talks?" The part that hurt the most was having my brother participate in the laughter. I'm an adult now, so I know my brother was just caught up in trying to win friends, even at my expense. As you can imagine, I grew up very shy and never wanted to talk around people I did not know. I was so used to the people in my family and neighborhood making fun of me, that after a while I started laughing at myself. I can remember telling my brother in my "There he goes" language that one day I was going to learn how to speak correctly and, when I did, I was never going to shut up.

So I went to my mother who was my biggest fan. She would always tell me that the reason I stuttered was because I was so smart and had so many things going on in my brain at one time, that when my thoughts and my mouth were going at the same time this would cause me to stutter. My mother worked with me. She taught me how to slow my words down, and how to breathe correctly. She would have me use words in a sentence and state their meaning. This was a painful journey both physically and emotionally, and it lasted about five years. There were many days after a session with my mother that I would feel a sense of hopelessness and frustration. I remember feeling like I wanted to cave in, give up and quit. Physically, my jaws ached after many of the sessions. Emotionally, there were times that I cried uncontrollably. My mother made it very clear that success was not going to come overnight.

I could have said, "This is just my lot in life," and settled. However, I believe life is a choice-driven journey. There were many days that I would sit down and ponder over my inability to speak. The pain was always fresh as I replayed the "There he goes" tape in my head. I had to choose whether I wanted to change or not. No one else could make that decision for me. I chose to take action. I didn't realize until years later that this experience would change and shape my destiny.

My decision and commitment to learn to speak correctly has allowed me to travel a road that I would not have otherwise traveled. I speak to many people around the world today because of this decision.

In fact this challenge of stuttering taught me what you must do to bring about *permanent change*.

Commitment:

I had to be committed to learn to speak. I would not give up no matter what. I was committed to reaching my goal of learning to speak correctly.

Habits:

I learned the importance of creating good habits. I developed the habit of slowing down and breathing correctly in order to give my thoughts time to reach my mouth. As a result, I have learned that habits can lead me to great achievements or keep me in the land of mediocrity.

Acknowledgement:

In order to get more out of my life, I had to first acknowledge that I needed and wanted more. I desperately wanted to speak like the other kids. I admitted to myself that if I worked hard, I could one day achieve my goal to speak without a stutter.

33

Necessity:

As my family and friends continued to poke fun at me, I realized that it was necessary that I change. I didn't want to be a laughing stock for the rest of my life. I recognized that I absolutely needed to overcome my "There He Goes" language problem. Someone once said, "Everyone needs to master something. Whatever you do in life, be greater than your calling; choose one profession and master it in all details. Sleep by it, swear by it, and by all means work for it." First, I had to set a priority in order to start the journey towards successful speaking.

Goals:

I set a goal to spend a minimum of 30 minutes each day reading the dictionary. I would then use the words I learned in a sentence. The drive to be successful was spawned by my childhood experiences.

"Goals Are Simply Dreams With a Deadline!"

Dr. Benjamin E. Mays said:

"It must be borne in the mind that the tragedy of life doesn't lie in not reaching your goal. The tragedy lies in having no goal to reach."

Environment:

As I think back, I remember how important it was for to me change my environment. I had to dismiss people who would not accept my stuttering and, instead, surround myself with people who would celebrate what I was attempting to do. I believe that the most important point to consider when you have an opportunity to change is your environment. No change is possible if the proper environment to cultivate that change has not been established.

Nature has taught us that for seeds to grow, the right conditions must exist. It is the same for the seeds of change – the right conditions must exist. The seeds of positive change can only grow when they are cultivated under the six elements: Commitment, Habits, Acknowledgement, Necessity, Goal setting, and Environment. These elements together will produce a harvest of extraordinary results that yield throughout a lifetime.

I have worked hard to get where I am today. I have spent thousands of hours practicing the art of speaking. I have stood in front of the mirror for hours for just one speech. In my quest to become an accomplished speaker, I have read all the "how to speak" books written, joined a professional speaking club, and spent hours studying the video tapes of some of the greatest speakers in the world. I believe that practice does not make *perfect* but it will make *better*. I continue to enhance my speaking ability by using the techniques like forcing myself to slow down and breathe correctly, and motivating myself by listening to my own voice.

Though the journey has been challenging, it has been worth the struggle.

Franklin D. Roosevelt said:

> *"Not everything that we face in life can be changed but nothing in life can be changed until we face it."*

Joseph B. Washington is President of J.W. Enterprises, based in Atlanta, Georgia. Joe Washington has a passion to see people use all of their human potential and find personal success in every area of their life. This drive has led him to develop success strategies on top subjects such as *The Power of Change* and *Remaining Peaceful While Under Pressure.*

A Great Life is Not an Accident!

By Marilyn Joyce, M.A., R.D., Ph.D. ©

It was one of those long, cold and dreary winter days in Toronto. The skies seemed to open up and dump buckets of sloppy wet snow onto the streets. *That particular dismal 1978 day*, however, reset the tone for my entire life. Before that day, life, if one could call it that, was not worth living. Apparently I could neither do nor say anything right. Whatever I touched turned sour, and no one seemed to want me around anyway!

As I sat on the bus going home from work reflecting on the events of the day, tears flooded my eyes cascading down the front of my well-worn excuse for a winter jacket. How had my life become so difficult? What happened to my dreams and aspirations to become a writer and a speaker? To make a difference in people's lives? Emptiness, hopelessness, and debilitating unhappiness permeated my being. I felt useless, out-of-control, and overwhelmed, leading a life devoid of love, joy and fulfillment of any kind.

That fateful day I realized that I had created this barren life out of fear – fear of being alone; fear of what people would think if I did this or that; fear of whether anybody really loved or cared about me; fear of failing; fear of stepping off the fence and taking a stand; fear of not being pretty or thin enough to attract someone who would love me; fear of my mother's wrath and my father's disapproval. I was afraid of living and afraid of dying! I was a 100% people-pleaser, yet I could please no one, including myself! And today's events had proved that my belief was completely true.

The day started out as did every other. Getting out of my bed was a struggle. Depression filled every cell of my body. I forced myself to rise at 5:00 a.m. and move through one hour of intense yogic asanas (exercises). I showered and prepared for work. Then I made breakfast for a man who rarely arrived home before breakfast was served, and for two children who had experienced more mothers in their short lives than most of us have teachers in our entire lifetimes. They seemed to resent the very ground I walked on.

I had married for love but found myself in a loveless union with a man I barely knew. I had simply been a vehicle for entry into a country that otherwise was not accessible to this man and his children. No one had held a gun to my head. I went against my inner knowing, my intuitive sense that something was not right, when I entered into a civil marriage. We all have those moments, when just after we have done something, we realize we have made a big mistake! From day one, nothing I did was good enough for him or his family. Eventually I realized that my choice here was almost an exact repeat of my entire life with my mother's psychological instability and my father's love of the bottle! All of us, before gaining awareness, choose that which we know, that which is, on some ridiculous level, comfortable.

The one reprieve that I thought I had was in my work as an assistant to a podiatrist, a wonderful man who had become my friend. We had agreed that at the start of each day we would share anything bothering us, whether personal or work-related, so that our emotions did not interfere with our work with our patients. Hence, I had openly confided in this man, and trusted him completely. That is why what happened on this particular day was so shocking that it totally reshaped the rest of my life.

A large part of my job was to wash the patients' feet, and relax them by talking to them with compassion, humor and understanding – very easy for a people-pleaser of my caliber. Because of my other work as a yoga teacher, I often discussed the benefits of yoga techniques and good nutrition. On this particular day, I was discussing yoga and nutrition with a patient suffering with Type 2 Diabetes. When the doctor overheard our conversation, he growled at me to meet him in his office immediately. I will never forget his tone of disgust and his level of fury as he screamed at me at the top of his lungs in that tiny office, warning me never to speak about nutrition to any of "his" patients. They were no longer "our" patients. He raged on that I was not qualified to tell people what was healthy or not healthy to eat.

Shriveling to nothing in the corner, I became aware of a deep sense of numbness invading my entire body except for the severe, nauseating pain in the pit of my stomach. What little self-esteem I had was washed down the drain with the water from that patient's foot tub. I was overwhelmed with a sense of uselessness and failure. The doctor and I did not speak another word to each other that day. I got on the bus homeward bound captured by the thought of how to end my painful and degrading life.

My body crumpled into the uncomfortable hard seat two-thirds of the way back on the crammed bus. My tears, held back for the past few hours, burst forth with a vengeance, as I sobbed over my perceived loss of respect from the one person who had believed in me and respected me and my abilities. This was absolutely the lowest moment I had every known. I remember closing my eyes and praying to God with all that I had within me: "Help me find a way out; release me from this endless pain and emptiness."

Out of the corner of my eye, I glimpsed a tattered, muddy book on the floor by my booted feet. Though most of the cover was torn off, I thought I saw the words *Erogenous Zones*. Was it possible that a book by that title had made it to print? Curiosity got the better of me. With great trepidation that someone might see me pick up this unsightly book or glimpse the title, I quickly grabbed it from the floor. Turning away from the other passengers, I sneaked another glance.

I began reading, at first cautiously, and then feverishly! I completely forgot that I was traveling on a bus, as I read one chapter after another, continuously experiencing what we now call "AH-HA" moments. This book was written for me – there was no doubt! Suddenly I felt a hand on my shoulder, and a gentle concerned voice asking if I planned to sleep on the bus. Looking up into warm, though questioning eyes of the driver, I felt disoriented. Completely immersed in this book, *Erogenous Zones* by a relatively new author, Wayne Dyer, I had lost track of time for over six hours, riding to and from the subway station several times with total unawareness!

The next day I called in too sick to work. The doctor knew something was not right. I never missed work. *Never!* A people-pleaser can't let anyone down you know! That day, with feverish excitement, I drove many miles to check out local universities with the best nutrition programs, and to start the process of application. Having been a runaway teenager, I was now applying as a mature student, and just praying that one of the three universities would accept me. My fate was changing. I was accepted by all three!

The doctor, my friend to this day, often says that his behavior that fateful day was the biggest mistake he ever made. In retrospect, his behavior was the best thing that could have happened. That pivotal day launched my career in the field of nutrition and lifestyle management, which in turn has opened up boundless opportunities in every area of my life. I have experienced things I never dreamed possible.

The gratitude that I hold for this doctor, my angel, I express every day through my "chosen" work as a speaker, a writer, and a coach for people struggling with major life-challenging illnesses. I travel the world doing what I love. This doctor was placed in my life to assist me in seeing the truth – that I can dream and that I have the power within me to make my dreams come true. Only I have the capacity to make it happen or can stop it from happening. It is just as easy to find reasons for succeeding as it is to find reasons why you can't achieve your dreams. It is all about your perception, your belief, and your choices.

On that fateful day, I learned that no other person determines our outcomes. Only we can create a different life for ourselves. And life in a pity pot, being a victim to everyone and everything around us, being a people-pleaser to a fault, will never mature into a realized dream! The pity pot holds disappointment and unhappiness. A dream, a vision, holds the promise of something greater, more stimulating, and more fulfilling. Yes, we all have within us the power to create our life any way we want it to be. So what is your dream, your greater vision for your life?

The outward appearance of that book which I found on the bus represented so accurately the outward appearance of my life – tattered, worn, beaten-up, and soiled! The inside of the book was filled with everything necessary to change my life, to shift my perspective. And, as in the book, I held within me everything I needed to step up to a great vision for my own life!

I live as much as possible by Goethe's couplet:

> *Whatever you can do, or dream you can, begin it.*
> *Boldness has genius, power and magic in it.*

Marilyn Joyce, M.A., R.D., Ph.D., International Radio & Television Personality, is one of the world's leading authorities on nutrition and lifestyle for the prevention and overcoming of cancer and other degenerative illnesses. Her lively, information-packed seminars are loaded with powerful, proven strategies for creation of outstanding health and vitality. Check out: *www.marilynjoyce.com* or call *(800) 352-3443*.

Mentors Make The Difference

By Bob Proctor

When I look back at my life, it's almost inconceivable that the person I see in my mind years ago is really me. And I've concluded that if I can win, anybody can!

I grew up in Toronto, Canada, the middle child of an average family. I never enjoyed school, and didn't get particularly good grades. In fact, I dropped out when I was in grade 10. At the time, it seemed like the right thing to do and since many of my friends were joining the Navy, I joined too. I got out of the Navy and moved from one menial job to another. Some jobs only lasted a few hours. It got to the point that whenever I saw anybody in a suit, I was sure they were looking for me so they could fire me. I lived an absolutely miserable life!

To make matters worse and even more frustrating was the fact that every teacher, employer and officer with whom I came in contact knew that I had the potential to succeed, if only I'd change my attitude. Yet not one of them could tell me what "attitude" was – so I continued with my meager existence. It wasn't as if I had deliberately made a decision to do poorly; I just didn't know any better.

Like so many of my generation, I was brought up to believe you had to go to school, get a good education, find a good job with a blue chip company and you'd be secure for life. I've since learned that security is an inside job; if you haven't got it on the inside, you never have it! The thought was: work for 25 or 30 years and retire with a good pension. Well, my hopes of getting an education had gone by the wayside. Because I didn't have any formal education, the idea of getting hired by a decent company never occurred to me. I wandered aimlessly.

Mentors

At the age of 26 my life took a dramatic change for the better. I was desperately broke, unhappy, and unhealthy. I was headed in the wrong direction and picking up speed. However, all of that changed when I met

Raymond Douglas Stanford. I often mention that I've had five mentors in my lifetime. Ray was the first of those mentors. He saw something in me that I couldn't see in myself. Determined to provoke me to think, Ray gave me a copy of Napoleon Hill's book, Think and Grow Rich. He said, "Your way's not working. Why not try mine?"

My life literally spun on a dime. With nowhere to go but up, I decided to try some of the things that Hill was suggesting. Within a short period of time, I began to win. One of the things the book talked about and I took action on was: decide what you want, write it on a card and read the card every day. I've learned that if you tell yourself anything often enough, you'll start to believe it. Seriously! That's the way affirmations work. At first, you have to convince yourself that you possess the quality or character trait you don't think you have, so you pretend. You tell yourself – I'm confident, I'm smart, I'm wealthy, I'm whatever! That's exactly what I did. I wrote on a little card that it was New Year's Day, 1970 and I had $10,000 in my possession! To give you an idea of how confident I was in the idea, it was 1960! I didn't even know of anyone who had that much money! Did I really believe it? No! But I kept reading and re-reading the book. In retrospect, I was literally re-writing the program that was controlling my behavior. Through repetition, I was installing it in the psychic hard-drive of my mind!

Re-writing the Program That Controls Behavior

My income went from $4,000 per year to $175,000 per year and then over $1,000,000 per year. The change I experienced in every area of my life was so dramatic that I wasn't satisfied with the win. I had to know why I had changed. What was so puzzling was I thought I had changed because of the book. So, I went out and bought copies of *Think and Grow Rich* and gave it to my friends and associates. Some didn't even bother to read it, but for those who did, none of them changed! I figured that someone had to know what caused me to change. I decided that I would read every book, listen to every recording and study anything I could find relative to human behavior!

At a time when the personal development movement was just starting, it was difficult to find self-help materials. Unlike today where the market is saturated with all sorts of personal development materials via books, cassettes, CDs, and DVDs, the only thing available to me was records. And they were difficult to come by. In any event, I came across a recording by Earl Nightingale: *The Strangest Secret*. I became obsessed with study and decided to turn my car into a learning center. I went out and bought a portable battery-operated record player and would play Earl's record in my car ... over and over and over again. And every time I listened, I heard something new – it was like I had never heard the recording and was listening to it for the very first time.

In any event, I later worked with Earl Nightingale and Lloyd Conant, two of my five mentors. Through Nightingale-Conant, I met Leland Val Van De Wall, my fourth mentor. Val was a distributor of Earl's material. He was teaching a program in Vancouver and I flew over from Chicago to hear him speak. In retrospect, I would have flown half way around the world to hear this man speak. Val and I spent three days together ... He the teacher, and I the student. As much as I had learned up to that point in my life was dwarfed by what Val was about to teach me. Val's knowledge of the mind and human behavior was astounding. He was able to organize all of the material I had studied and distill it into a simple format that made sense to me and clearly explained why I had changed. Val's explanation of the stickperson concept – a little diagram that explains the workings of the conscious mind, sub-conscious mind, and body – was paramount to turning on a light bulb in a dark room. It's important to note that through Val, I was introduced to Dr. C. Harry Roder, who took the truths behind the "stickperson" to a new level. Dr. Roder became my fifth mentor.

Mentors played an enormous part in my success. They have the unique ability to transfer their higher level of consciousness to you. That is what you require to move forward with your life.

It Doesn't Matter How You Grew Up, or What You've Struggled With in Life – Your Mind is Unscathed by Any Circumstance You've Yet Lived Through. . . And it's Phenomenally Powerful!

By society's standards I should not have won! I had no formal education, I couldn't hold a job. Yet I became quite successful. Why? I have to refer to my mentor, Earl Nightingale, who said, "Success is the progressive realization of a worthy ideal."

Those nine words have served as my life compass. They are a constant checkpoint for me. Have there been any losses? Absolutely... really big ones! But that's where the word progressive comes in. And that's where study comes in.

Our success in life is achieved through understanding and gaining a higher level of awareness of who we are and what we're capable of being.

Many people would be quick to define their success as it relates to an object: a new car, a bigger home, etc. I would suggest you look at those successes as a reflection of your own level of awareness. Success should not be measured by things, but more by the experience and learning gained as a result of moving from one level of awareness to the other. What did it take to get the car, the bigger home? Did it move you out of your comfort zone? Did the goal scare and excite you at the same time? Did you experience and overcome obstacles along the way? If you can answer "yes" to any of those questions – in my opinion – you have been successful. If you can't, then you've merely acquired another thing.

Where There's No Growth, There's No Win.

What is your worthy ideal? What are you trading your time for? We all trade our time for something. The question we should ask ourselves in choosing a goal is not whether or not we're worthy of the goal, it's whether the goal is worthy of us!

Alfred Adler said, "I'm grateful for the idea that has used me."

International best-selling author, business consultant and entrepreneur, Bob Proctor follows in the footsteps of such motivational giants as Napoleon Hill and Earl Nightingale, traveling the globe teaching people how to utilize their infinite potential.
Visit *www.bobproctor.com*

Getting Stuck

By Becky Zerbe

Although I enjoyed my work as a public school teacher, I always looked forward to winter break. After the packages were under the tree and I could take a deep breath, I had two whole weeks to map out the goals for my real passion – work in direct sales and motivational speaking.

I always began my planning in front of the fireplace armed with only with a notepad, pen and cup of tea.

Carefully, I would start constructing the goals I wanted to work on in the coming year. It was so exciting to ponder the prospect of seeing my goals come to fruition. Pictures would even be sketched on the pad to show how it would look if I reached the goal. However, more often than not, the next year when I would take out my journal to start to work on new goals, I would find that few of my last year's goals had become reality.

I Was Always Getting Stuck.

In fact, many times I would find myself simply rewriting the old goals to try again. The problem was getting *stuck in* the goals; not *sticking to* them. Two life experiences revealed to me how I was shooting at the target, but missing the mark.

Twenty-two years ago, I was waiting to deliver an eleven-pound son. It was past the calculated time for the baby to come, and we were *way* beyond ready. In addition to being anxious to be done with the pregnancy, I also had a problem. I wanted my parents to be present for the birth, but they were scheduled to leave on a trip in just a few days. My mother made a plan: we would *walk* that baby out of me.

Immediately we set off for one of our favorite places just a few hours from our home – an Indian monument in the northern part of New Mexico. It was the perfect place to walk on a beautiful August day. After enjoying the scenery and hiking for a bit, we came upon a kiva, a large underground chamber used for centuries by Native Americans in religious ceremonies. Now the only way to get into a kiva is by climbing down a ladder through a small, round hole in the ground. Once in the kiva, the only light source to the chamber is through the entrance opening.

I Had Gone Down That Ladder Many Times Growing Up, and Always Enjoyed the Wonderful, Cozy Feeling of Sitting Inside the Kiva.

Unfortunately, I hadn't considered that a few things had changed since my childhood – namely, the size of my soon-to-have-a-baby abdomen. My husband Bill went down the ladder first. As I descended I noticed that the opening seemed just a bit smaller than I had remembered. I quickly realized, to my horror, I had become a human cork. – Boy, was I stuck! I could no longer keep my feet on the ladder. Quickly, my dad and mom each grabbed an arm and tried to pull me up, with my feet dangling beneath me.

Up Was not Happening.

By that point, my poor husband was standing in total darkness, as I was blocking any source of light. Realizing what was wrong, he tried to grab my flailing legs, and push me out. Seeing the enormous humor of the situation, I began to laugh uncontrollably.

Let me draw you a picture of what happens when one is nine months pregnant and more than just a little tickled. Let's just say that tears of joy aren't the only fluids involved. On this occasion, Bill was definitely in the wrong place at the wrong time. As I was soaking his head, I could hear a very faint, "Stop it!.... Stop it!" I was stuck *in* that hole and I was not going anywhere!

Now, let me take you forward to many years later. I was flying from Albuquerque to Columbus, Ohio to attend a conference. On the plane, I had been visiting with a young boy sitting next to me when the sculptured fingernail on my ring finger became unglued. Luckily, I was prepared for what I *thought* was an emergency. I quickly took out my travel case, and glued my nail back in place. However, at about the same time, my new six-year-old friend announced in an anxious voice, "I have to go to the bathroom!" Now all moms know the "I mean business" voice, so I quickly placed my travel kit on the floor and jumped up to move out of the way. Unfortunately, in my haste, the tail of my denim skirt got caught on the arm of my chair. Off balance, I fell directly onto an older gentleman across the aisle from my seat.

As I apologized profusely, the boy and his mother went around me. Hastily I lifted up to get off the gentleman, when the real emergency became obvious; my finger, still oozing with glue, had firmly adhered to the gentleman's neck!

The first thing out of the man's mouth was, "What the h–?" With my finger dangling, I assured him that if he would just slip over to my side of the aisle, I could explain. "Sir, what I have done is glue my finger to the side of your neck," I sheepishly admitted. "However, if we just wait a minute it will dry and I can twist it loose." What I did not take into consideration was the age of the gentleman. Each time I would twist my finger in an attempt to loosen the nail, his thin, wrinkled skin would twist with me.

His intense aggravation could not be ignored. In an attempt to lighten things up I asked, "Where are you going?" "New York," he muttered angrily.

"Well sir," I explained, "I am going to Columbus. Do you want to go to Columbus with me, or do you want me to go to New York with you?"

After a chuckle, he said, "Lady, I have not had very many come-ons in my life. But, this has been the most original." Realizing my fingernail was not budging, I did the dreaded and called the flight attendant for assistance. Quickly, I went through the entire scenario, and requested a warm washrag or moist towelette. Her first question was "Do you know him?" To which I replied, "Now I do."

She politely left and was very composed until she got to the separation curtain where she almost collapsed in hysterics. Continuing to twist my finger, I finally released it from the gentleman's neck. With sincere apologies, I slipped back to my seat. The attendant returned with a rag and the gentleman spent the next twenty minutes scrubbing the side of his neck to remove the glue.

Now, I was stuck *to* that man, which was different than being stuck *in* that hole. You see, when I was stuck in the hole, I was not going anywhere, and there was no light at the end of the tunnel. However, being stuck to that gentleman gave me options. I could still go places and take him along. I could take action.

Action is the Difference Between Getting Stuck *in* a Goal and Sticking *to* a Goal.

Getting stuck *in* a goal means we have lots of ideas, but do nothing about them. It means dreaming, but not going anywhere. We are stuck in our goals when we find ourselves organizing our desk, using phone time to talk to a friend, or basically not doing anything that directly moves our business forward.

Sticking *to* the goal means you live the dream. You have a plan and consistently stick to that plan until your dream becomes your everyday reality. You spend time wisely by networking, making phone contacts, and booking appointments. You know exactly what you are accomplishing today, and what you need to accomplish tomorrow. You know what it will look like when you get to the end. You are not detoured by interruptions, and are able to separate real work from busy work.

One of the simplest ways I have found to keep on task is through a plan journal. At the end of everyday, I make a quick note about what I did to make each goal happen. If I did nothing I say, "Today I did nothing to further this goal. Tomorrow I will..." This journal lives on my bed pillow so I cannot forget it. Whatever your dreams and aspirations, each one of us must choose daily whether success will stick to us, or we will remain stuck in a place with no wiggle room.Goals, a plan journal and action just might be the glue you need to make your dreams a reality.

A highly acclaimed speaker and trainer, Becky Zerbe uses humor and inspiration to share her expertise in relationships and igniting business growth. She is available to bring her breakthrough strategies to companies and businesses of all sizes at *beckyzerbe@beckyzerbe.com* or *(505)294-1573.*

You Can Succeed

By Tom Hopkins

At age 19, I was working construction. It was hard physical work and paid okay, but the opportunities for advancement weren't great. Someone suggested that I try selling if I wanted to make good money. The seed was planted and that's how I got into sales.

Southern California in the 60's had a booming real estate market, so I decided to get my real estate license. Understand that selling real estate was considered an old man's profession at that time. So the trend was against me, but I was determined. It took more than one try for me to pass that licensing exam, but I did it. Then I started going to real estate agencies on my way home from my construction job every day, asking them to hire me. Needless to say, I didn't make a great first impression, coming in on my motorcycle, dressed for day labor. I didn't even own a suit, which was the standard attire for real estate agents at the time.

I finally convinced someone to give me an opportunity. I was excited, but had to figure out what to wear. I didn't have money to buy a new suit so I decided to wear the closest thing I had, which was my high school band uniform. When I showed up that first morning, the broker was holding a sales meeting. As I walked in, he looked up with surprise and said to the rest of the agents, "If this kid in a band uniform can sell real estate, then the rest of you should make millions."

Selling real estate on a motorcycle wasn't easy. I had to tell the prospective buyers to follow me and hope they didn't get lost on the way to new homes. My first six months in real estate, I averaged $42 a month. For the one sale I made, I was fortunate that the buyers knew how to fill out the paperwork.

I learned it all the hard way, through trial and error. But the key here is that I did learn. I went on to set listing and selling records that still stand today. At age 27, I was one of the most successful real estate agents in the entire country! I achieved my goal of becoming a millionaire by age 30 three years early.

Whether you're in sales now or thinking about going into sales doesn't matter. What matters most is your attitude. What are you willing to do in order to achieve the goals you've set? How many "no's" are you willing to take before getting to the "yes's" that you need? How much are you willing to change what you are today to get what you want tomorrow?

You Begin Succeeding in Sales by Finding Successful People and Surrounding Yourself with Them.

Be with the people whom you'd most like to become. If you want to be average, then stick with average people. If it's your desire to achieve greatness in sales, then learn what the great ones do and do it!

Let me give you a head start on your road to success. I know what the great ones do. I have taught proven-effective selling skills to over four million students during the last 30 years. Selling is my hobby. It's also my passion. Helping others learn better and more professional ways to serve others is what my company is all about.

First, internalize everything you can possibly get your hands on about your product or service. Become a consumer of your product. Use it yourself. Talk with clients who use it and love it. Believe in it! People will say "yes" to you based more on your conviction and enthusiasm for your product that any fact or figure you may quote. If you are new to selling, don't settle for selling just anything. Find a product you can become passionate about. It'll make all the difference.

People Skills

Next, start working on your people skills. There are right and wrong ways to approach people. Your #1 goal when you meet someone new is to have them like you, trust you, and want to listen to you. It may seem elementary, but to have someone like you, you must be likeable. That means you smile. You make eye contact. You introduce yourself. Ask their name. Repeat their name so you know you are pronouncing it correctly. If it's an unusual name, ask for the correct spelling.

Establish common ground. People buy from people who are like them. If you like the same sports team, that's common ground. If you live in the same area, that's common ground. If you're around the same age with kids in close grades in school, that's common ground.

Become an Expert

Develop an attitude of servitude. Let them feel that you're there to help them make a good decision and to serve their needs. People want to have an expert in their corner. Become that expert they call on for advice when the topic of your product or service comes to mind.

In sales, you're not just out to make friends. You want to close sales. After all, it is how you've chosen to make your living. You can't sell something to someone without knowing what they need. So, that's your next step. Determine their needs. I've developed a quick and easy-to-remember method for this. It's called the **NEADS** qualification sequence. Remember that you're trying to determine their "needs" but spell it NEADS to remember what to say.

NEADS

The first letter, "N," stands for Now. Ask them, "What do they have now?" Unless they've won the lottery or inherited millions, few people drastically change what they have now other than to make their lives better. So, knowing what they have now will help you understand where they're coming from.

The next letter, "E," stands for Enjoy. What do they enjoy most about what they have now? They'll want to keep the good stuff in considering any change, so your product or service will need to at least cover what they enjoy.

The "A" stands for Alter. What would they alter (or change) about what they have now? This is where they will tell you what they need. Ask as many questions as you need to get a clear picture of what they're telling you. Repeat your understanding of their needs back to them and get them to agree that "Yes, that's what we're looking for" before going any further. The "D" in NEADS stands for Decision-Maker. This is where you determine how much selling to do with these people. You need to know if they're truly the decision-makers. If they're not, you'll need to find out who else must be consulted and present to all parties who will be involved. Never make a product presentation to a non-decision-maker unless you just need the practice. If they've told you what they need and that they're the decision-makers, then and only then will you move into presenting the benefits of your product or service.

There are many little nuances of presenting products that come into play. You want to have your potential clients sit or stand across from you. That way, you can watch their body language and the unspoken words that fly between them. Don't have them on either side of you where they can communicate silent messages that you miss.

Get them physically involved in the presentation. Hand them things. Have them push buttons, open and close doors, sit in or on furniture, and calculate savings. The more senses you can involve, the more likely they are to take mental ownership of the product. If your product is an intangible, there are subtle ways you can get them mentally seeing themselves after they own it as well.

Since no one wants to feel they're "being sold," expect most potential clients to object about something. It's a natural reflex that few average salespeople understand. The great ones anticipate objections with relish. They know that if a potential client objects, they're feeling moved toward making a positive buying decision. You see, people aren't going to waste their time objecting to something they're not interested in. Makes sense, doesn't it?

The great ones in sales prepare answers to the most common objections for their product or service. The answers are psychologically sound and help the buyers rationalize the decision, if it's truly good for them. Once objections are handled and concerns addressed, when the buyers are ready to take your widget home, there's actually one more thing you must do. Ask for the sale! Few buyers will whip out their checkbooks or credit cards once they agree the product or service is right for them. In fact, a study was done years ago where people were asked why they didn't make a purchase after a product had been demonstrated to them. The most common answer was, "We were never asked!" Don't ever let that be the cause of an average selling career for you! Top salespeople know anywhere from five to 25 ways of asking for the final "yes." Those ways are called "closes." If you're in sales to make money, you'll want to start mastering as many as possible as soon as you can.

You have what it takes to learn to become the best in your field. Just make the commitment and get on with it!

Tom Hopkins is world-renowned as THE BUILDER OF SALES CHAMPIONS. Let him help you improve your skills and make more sales! For more information contact us at *info@tomhopkins.com*. Receive free sales content, tips and closes by subscribing to Tom's selling skills e-newsletter at *www.tomhopkins.com*.

A Firefighter Spirit

Fights For Life

By Rebecca Joy

Photo credit : tigerleephotos.com

Like moths, fire fighters are conditioned to respond to bright lights. Imagine being in a deep REM sleep. All is well in dreamland when suddenly.... The lights come on and you are awakened by a loud blasting tone. The monotonous voice of a dispatcher drones over the loud speaker announcing a brief description of an emergency and the address. Your sleepy body operates on automatic pilot until you are actually on the road responding "Code 3", lights flashing and sirens screaming.

It is with immense gratitude that I have been given the opportunity to provide what I believe is the ultimate service in this lifetime... I am a fire-fighter. I have been a member of the Phoenix Fire Department for 20 years and was promoted to the position of Engineer in 1990. My duties include driving the 38,000 pound fire truck and caring for people. I absolutely love my job.

Every Day Is An Adventure, a Walk Into the Unknown.

My crew and I may be dispatched to a grass fire that within seconds could turn into a house fire with people trapped inside. I am placed in extreme situations daily that are physically, mentally and emotionally challenging. The body, mind and spirit are continually working at their peak, especially when driving the massive fire truck at high speed when responding to an emergency. I always pay attention and use my intuition to every detail – knowing where the other vehicles are, anticipating their next move and always being one step ahead. These are just a few of the finely-tuned skills that I have acquired in the last two decades working in the fire service.

Over the years, many things have changed for me, especially when it comes to responding to intense situations. I remember watching a film of an autopsy in my college EMT (Emergency Medical Technician) class. I was proud that I could handle what I was watching when the instructor in the film extricated the different organs from the dead man's body. He pulled them out one by one, inspecting them as he juggled them in his hands, and then explained the parts to the camera. When he examined the black, ugly lung from the smokers' body, I was thankful I never had taken a drag from a nasty cigarette and still have that picture in my mind!

I was still doing okay when the electric hand saw carved across the forehead in a perfectly straight line. But then I started to feel nausea coming on when the instructor purposefully grabbed the skin of the dead man's face and pulled it down over itself. That's when I lost control. I felt dizzy and began to sweat. I knew I was going into sympathetic shock and managed to make my way outside to breathe in some fresh air and regain my composure. I remember thinking at the time that it was definitely time for self-evaluation. "What the heck am I doing? I can't help people if I respond like that to watching a simple film!"

This experience happened to me over 20 years ago. Since then I have never come close to having the same reaction. What I learned is that there is a mental shift which takes over the whole body. The body has incredible response mechanisms when one has a focus or a task, such as in "putting a body back together"or fighting a fire. You are no longer the observer; you are the doer. The body goes into hyper-awareness. Intuition kicks in full force. You don't have time to stop and ponder about the angulated femur fracture sticking out of the thigh.You just do what needs to be done.

Firefighters are Definitely Adrenaline Junkies.

Without having a second thought, we risk our precious bodies by putting ourselves in potentially hazardous and contagious situations. More often than not, there are no clues as to what awaits us on the other end of the call. Many calls are routine: a stove fire, a child having an asthma attack, a man with chest pain or – the opposite extreme – the tragedy that waits amid twisted sheet metal on the freeway.

Some emergencies to which a firefighter responds can trigger an internal response that is extremely personal. Certain experiences can create life-changing behaviors and attitudes. I had such an experience back in 1993. I was assigned to work with a Battalion Chief as a F.I.T. (Field Incident Technician). Our job, among many, was to respond in a Suburban vehicle to major incidents where there were multiple fire trucks. Our job was to "take command" and supervise the scene.

Late one September night on the streets of South Phoenix, there was a three-car accident. One vehicle had rolled over, with reports of multiple people ejected. The road was a narrow two-way street and very dark without street lights. We were the last unit to arrive behind a long trail of fire trucks and ambulances. There wasn't much room off the side of the road because of an irrigation ditch. We parked as the other trucks did, half on the dirt and half on the street, with our warning lights flashing. I had decided to go to the back of the Suburban and open the door to retrieve a camera so I could take pictures of the scene.

As I reached for the camera, I heard a voice in my head gently say, "Put the equipment away; you won't be needing it." I listened. It was too dark to take pictures anyway, so I returned the camera to the vehicle. A split second after I stepped to the side of the Suburban, I heard a loud crash. A white, half-ton pickup truck had just slammed into the back of our Suburban! My pelvis would have been crushed on impact had I been still standing there! A drunk driver had been hypnotically mesmerized by our emergency lights.

At the time, I didn't realize how lucky I was to be alive. However, six months later, my brush with death hit home very clearly. We tragically lost a firefighter in a similar accident. Once again, a drunk driver ran into the rear of an ambulance as Firefighter Tim Hale was unloading a gurney from his ambulance. Tim died from massive internal crushing injuries. He left behind a wife and two young children.

Only a few people know of my brush with death. I know I am extremely fortunate to be alive today and it has changed my perspective on what I do daily. Dear reader, please understand... In the blink of an eye, your life, as you know it, may be over. We hear this every day, but I know this to be true. I know this to be true because I witness it happening to others almost every day. At the time this incident happened, I was married and had two young boys, ages one and two, who were waiting for Mommy to come home the next morning. I thank God I did!

I live in a world where as a firefighter I can and do make a positive difference in other peoples' lives. It is an honor to have the opportunity to provide this ultimate service. Because I do what I love, I feel a sense of purpose and full of life.

What a Wonderful Opportunity to Shine My Light!

Expressing and showing gratitude is extremely important to me. Every night I thank God for everything, everyone and all experiences. I do the same thing before I start my day, giving a simple prayer of thanks. Throughout my day, I pay attention, listen to the subtle voice of wisdom, and appreciate the beauty of the Earth. What an incredible world we live in!

Across the street from my fire station is an old, rundown house. In front of this abandoned dwelling is a shrine left behind by the former occupants. In it is a statue of beautiful Mother Mary. Every third day, as I finish my shift, I drive by this magnificent statue. I am humbled with a deep sense of gratitude to God that once again, I return home safe and sound. I am reminded to give thanks for the divine opportunity to be of service, and to touch the hearts of many on this Earth.

Rebecca Joy is a 20-year veteran of the Phoenix Fire Department. At 5'6", she loves driving her 38,000 pound fire truck and being of service to the community. Rebecca resides with her two young sons in Tempe, AZ. Her first book, *Tales from the Firehouse*, will be published in 2003. Please visit Rebecca's Web site: *www.phxfirespirit.com*

Go For The Gold:

Seven Steps to Becoming a
C.H.A.M.P.I.O.N.

By Dan Kuschell

Inside each of us is the seed of unlimited potential with the knack to win. Those who are prepared to pay the price and take action have the ability to tap their inner potential and live as the Champion they were born to be.

Step One: What's Your Dream?

Your past doesn't matter and neither does your present. The only thing that matters is where you want to go. As long as you have a dream, you have the ability to create your life.

I grew up at the main crosstreets of Vernor and Pitt in the inner city of Southwest Detroit. My dad worked in the auto industry and struggled to provide for our family. After five lengthy lay-offs and two failed businesses, he was forced into bankruptcy. I experienced the embarrassment of living on welfare and the humiliation of having to accept food drives, church donations, and family support just to survive.

I learned one of the most valuable lessons as I watched my dad struggle to make ends meet even though he was employed by one of the largest companies in the world. True security is not the name on the building, not the guaranteed income, and not the benefits we receive; rather, it's the skills and the attitude we learn to apply. In fact, you attain true security when you develop those rare qualities people want, namely a positive attitude, the ability to negotiate communicate, network and lead.

Step Two: Live With Purpose

What do you love and live to do? Answer this question and you have your purpose.

I thought that sports would be my way out of the city. My dream was to play pro-baseball. By my junior year of high school, all the dedication, work, and commitment appeared to be paying off, as numerous colleges and major league teams were contacting me. My dream was becoming my reality, until one cold Spring afternoon.

Step Three: Learn how to Handle Adversity

When one door closes, another opens. What adversity have you been facing that could be a springboard to bigger and better things?

That Spring afternoon, 15-20 scouts armed with stopwatches, charts and radar guns lined the fence at our high school. In an instant my future completely changed. A simple play that I had done hundreds of times before changed my destiny. In one moment, I went from being a so-called "Blue-Chip Prospect" to a "Cow-Chip Suspect."

I held onto my dream and attempted to play through my damaged rotator cuff. Little did I know, however, that I was also preparing for my future, planting the seeds of character, persistence, and commitment. Four shoulder injuries, a shattered wrist, and two elbow injuries over the next few years left me hanging by a thread as I struggled through massive rehab and conditioning to get back to 100%. But inevitably, the thread broke.

All the hard work, dedication, and commitment certainly created many highlights that I'll never forget. After I got through the years of "what if's" I realized that I gave it all I had, and today have no regrets.

When you look at your decisions, consider this question: Knowing what you know, would you do it the same way? In my mind, I went out on top because I left it all on the field. Pursuing the dream was certainly the springboard to bigger things to come.

Step Four: Seek Words of Wisdom

"If you make the same commitment to your life and career that you do to baseball, you'll be a major success, no matter what you do." My dad shared those words with me as I struggled through my third injury. I had no idea how this simple concept would mean so much to my future.

I was left wondering, "Could I find something else that gave me the fulfillment to live with purpose and seize the day?" After college, I learned about sales and personal growth. In 1992 I decided to start my own business. A year later my business partner embezzled all the money from the bank account, leaving me penniless. As a result, I was on the verge of losing my home and my car. My credit cards were maxed out. I thought bankruptcy was my only way out. I gave up.

I went to work at a local health club selling memberships. I had lost my purpose and got depressed, started partying four to five days per week and smoking heavily. It was all I could do to try to forget my business failure.

Step Five: Find a Mentor

In early 1994, one of my friends who knew I was desperately looking for a change introduced me to a business opportunity. "Michael Jordan has a coach. Barry Bonds has a coach. Who's your coach?" The words rang as the speaker shared the words that would change my destiny. I could learn from people who had been where I wanted to go and ultimately save time and money. It became my passion, as I sought out the best of the best. I attended over 100 different seminars, read dozens of books, and must have listened to over 1000 different tape programs searching for the "missing link" to go from mediocrity to significance. The more I learned, the more I wanted to learn. Lifelong learning became the mantra that has taken most of the great leaders in life from student to teacher.

Step Six: Recognize the Defining Moments

What challenges are you facing right now that could be opportunities in disguise? For the next five years I went through a transformation, learning skills such as negotiation, communication, leadership, goal setting, persuasion, and business building. Although I was applying my new skills to my career, my bank account was still empty.

I was becoming a master at sales... selling my dinette set, my bed, my living room set, my furniture, my TV, my car, and other things to make ends meet. I thought that attending more training would give me the secret I needed to succeed. I was obsessed with cracking the code to find the missing link.

Step Seven: Find the Acres of Diamonds In Your Own Backyard

After five years, I finally had enough. I was ready to quit. I was sick and tired of missing out and figured that I simply didn't have the talent and wasn't good enough. I made my decision and drove to Louisville, Kentucky to tell my mentor face-to-face.

What was originally going to be a day of resolve ended up a day of destiny. My mentor changed my focus, got me to raise the bar and live up to a higher accountability. She told me that if we worked together we would have the number one producing office in the country. Until that day, I never saw myself as a top producer. Even though I had attended numerous trainings, I was missing inner belief.

At that moment I threw all of my materialistic, financial goals out the window and changed my focus. I took the information I had learned and developed a simple journal system that would transform my life. I created the program around three questions and affirmations:

- What am I grateful for?
- What am I happy about?
- What have I done well today?

I answered those three questions daily and did the affirmations twice per day. And though I thought I was the same person doing the same presentations as before, something miraculous happened. I accomplished more in the next two months than I had in the previous eleven. My business grew, my income skyrocketed, and my opportunities exploded. I started attracting the right type of people in my life, including the woman of my dreams.

I taught these principles to others, duplicated the process, and watched their lives transform right before my eyes. Soon I had built an organization of thousands and we cumulatively grew the business to millions of dollars in product sales. I began teaching the message to hundreds and thousands of people nationwide. Little did I know I was building the foundation for a future book, seminars, keynotes and workshops.

Even though the company we represented ultimately shut down and we lost the business, I didn't skip a beat. I continued to consult with companies and individuals to explode their income and improve their performance and results.

The moral: You'll find acres of diamonds in your heart when you commit to living your life as a C.H.A.M.P.I.O.N. That is:

C = Committed to...
H = Great HEALTH
A = Take ACTION
M = Find MENTORS
P = Live with PURPOSE
I = INVEST in self
O = OPPORTUNITY seeker
N = NEVER quit on my dream

Remember that you were born to win. Stand up and accept your Gold Medal as an award-winning Champion in the Making.

Dan Kuschell is a direct-marketing expert and author. He offers innovative keynotes, trainings, and coaching in sales mastery, writing copy, and peak performance. Contact Dan at *dan@achampionvision.com* or call *1-800-211-4580* USA and *623-907-4750* (Outside USA).

www.achampionvision.com

"THE Obnoxious Marketing Genius"

By Joe Polish

I have been called a lot of things throughout my life, but the one that had kind of stuck is "*An Obnoxious Marketing Genius Who Knows How To Make His Clients Lots Of Money Real Fast.*" I don't know if I particularly like the "obnoxious" part, but if there's one thing I've done consistently and will continue to do, it's help a lot of others make more money, in easier ways, while working less.

It wasn't always this way. My mother died of cancer when I was four years old, and my dad was devastated by the loss. That began a nomad-like childhood where we moved every couple years. I was a real shy, wimpy kid, so moving around forced me to learn to make friends quickly, which has helped me a lot in my life. I think most people don't realize how much they can handle. I learned through those early struggles that people are very adaptive.

I was a good student and a good kid until high school, when I went beyond the typical teenage rebelling. I was pretty crazy. I went from the shy kid to a "maniac" with dyed-yellow hair shaved on the sides. I was the personification of '80's punk. And I partied hard.

After graduating from high school, I attended New Mexico State University and worked odd jobs. I didn't have much money, but I had all kinds of energy. I also had an entrepreneurial spirit although, I didn't know what to do with it.

My business experience began, as so many stories do, with frustration and failure. At the age of 23, I was barely making a living as a carpet cleaner, living from job to job, and relying on credit cards to keep me afloat. I was tired of it and wondered what else I could do. I happened to meet a very successful businessman and asked his advice on which different field to switch to. The guy let me have it. He asked me tough questions and told me about the size and potential of my present field. He suggested that if I switched businesses, I would carry with me the same attitudes and behaviors that were holding me back where I was.

So I Decided to Stick with What I Was Doing.

I followed the examples of advertising I saw used by other carpet cleaners. I wasted a bunch of money on an ad agency, and was struggling to create a steady flow of new customers. Finally I discovered direct-response marketing. I found excellent materials from a direct-response guru named Gary Halbert. Gary's writings opened my eyes to an entirely different way of thinking about advertising. I immersed myself in all the marketing books, tapes and seminars I possibly could. My thirst for information was unquenchable. I found other marketing giants like Dan Kennedy and I discovered million-dollar secrets. Armed with this new knowledge, I developed entirely new strategies that revolutionized my business. At a rapid pace, I was able to create an entirely new marketing approach never before seen in the industry.

Before long, other carpet cleaners began asking me how I was doing so well. They made feeble attempts to copy some of my advertising. I decided to put everything I was using so successfully into a "kit" that I sold to others in the industry. Since that time I have continued to develop many more strategies and successful marketing concepts, that people from all over the world continue to buy and use the materials available through my company, Piranha Marketing ("Eat Your Competition Alive!"™). Currently over 3,700 Piranha Marketing Members from around the world use my marketing programs to transform their businesses into money machines.

Now my focus has expanded. I consult with giants in various other industries in addition to the carpet cleaning industry. I also have my "Genius Network," a monthly series of audio programs featuring exclusive interviews with famous authors and speakers, business leaders, and top experts in fields ranging from time management to selling. I'm sometimes asked, "How do you get such a remarkable, ever-expanding list of celebrities and hugely successful entrepreneurs to be interviewed for your Genius Network???" My response is *"I ask them."*

A Classic Success Principle: Ask for What You Want.

Here is a partial list of my interviews in the Genius Network library: Robert Kiyosaki, author, *Rich Dad, Poor Dad;* Michael Gerber, author, *E-Myth;* Mark Victor Hansen, co-author, *Chicken Soup for the Soul;* Joe Sugarman, inventor of Blu-Blockers sunglasses; Brian Tracy, famous speaker/author, and the list goes on. (For a complete list visit: *www.thegeniusnetwork.com*.)

I love interviewing top experts and asking them the questions to which I personally want to know the answers. After doing more than 80 interviews,

I've learned a *lot*. In fact, I've probably benefited from the interviews even more than the hundreds of monthly Genius Network subscribers.

Speaking of interviews, I've been interviewed myself quite a bit, and I'm constantly asked to share a "Success Secret" or two. One of my most common recommendations is…

"What Others Say About You Is Infinitely More Believable Than What You Say About You… So Let Others Say It."

Testimonials are so underutilized in today's business, it's pathetic. Think about it! You probably have many clients who love you, who think your product or service is awesome – and they are more than willing to give you compelling testimonials – and yet you may not be taking advantage of this amazing opportunity!

Testimonials have helped me go from being perceived as a "young, brash, obnoxious, inexperienced guy" to making over $7,000,000 from carpet cleaners in the last several years.

To illustrate how compelling testimonials can be, here are just two of the thousands of testimonials I have received over the years.

"About three years ago I was near bankruptcy. My house had to be foreclosed on, and I was going through a tough divorce. In the settlement, my ex-wife had taken the most profitable part of my business…Then I heard about your marketing ideas in a trade journal. I decided to give it a try because of your incredible guarantee. I was so broke that I had to use your payment plan on my VISA…Since becoming a Piranha Member, I have been able to enjoy the good life. In the first six months of being a Piranha Member, my girlfriend and I took our first vacation to La Jolla, California. Hey, it was not much, but it was all I could afford at the time. The following year, we went to Paris and London. …Did I mention that I've only used about five of your ideas of the hundreds you have to offer, and that I suffer from a severe negative personality trait? You see, I procrastinate. Thank you!"
– John Stewart, Healthy Choice Carpet Cleaners.

"Joe has been such an amazingly consistent, results-producing consultant, I continually go back for more. I've worked with him in one capacity or another over the past eight years, ever since the days when my brother Bill hired him as his marketing consultant for EAS and his book, 'Body for Life.' He is one of the best kept secrets in today's marketing world, and I'm just happy that I "discovered" him early on. As long as I am in business, I will look to Joe for more and more marketing brilliance. (I'm) an extremely happy client."
– Shawn Phillips (fitness expert and author of *ABSOLUTIONS*).

I'm sharing these testimonials with you to illustrate how powerful it is to have others say positive things about you. Claims are more believable when you are not making them yourself. It turns your happy clients into a powerful sales force! And after reading testimonials like this, I go from being an "obnoxious guy" to someone people are eager to listen to. The power of testimonials is incredible!

Testimonials add credibility. They make your company seem more believable. They remove the "fear" out of doing business with you.

How Many Testimonials Should You Use? *Use Them All!*

(Would you like to discover the best and easiest ways to get awesome testimonials from your best clients? I've prepared a FREE REPORT just for you. Go to *www.thegeniusnetwork.com*, click on the "affiliates" tab and request your copy today.)

Use testimonials in all your marketing efforts – direct mail (letters, postcards, newsletter columns, inserts), email, etc. You can even use photo testimonials (custom postcards and Web site photos), audio testimonials, tapes and CD's, etc. These have a lot of impact.

Testimonials... I Love Them!

To wrap this up... 12 years ago I was the least likely person to become what some people call a "legendary success coach." Imagine a once broke, unsuccessful carpet cleaner being paid well over $7 million by members of his own industry for his advice! Unlikely? Certainly. But by transforming obstacles into opportunities, having a constant thirst for improvement, and a passion for marketing, and the praise and support from happy clients, it's now an ongoing reality.

I invite you to visit my website, *www.thegeniusnetwork.com* to obtain more information about my Genius Network Interview series. I'd love to share these monthly "success breakthroughs" with you.

Joe Polish is President of Piranha Marketing and conducts an Interview of the Month Series called *The Genius Network*. To find out more about Joe Polish and Piranha Marketing, please visit his website at *www.thegeniusnetwork.com* or *www.joepolish.com*

Learning to Build

By David Baulieu

I often wondered what made successful people successful. Through my own experience, I have found it to be the culmination of not one particular trait or action, but many. Along my life's journey, there have been numerous ups and downs. During the challenging times, my very deep-rooted beliefs emerged from my soul so I could continue forward towards the outcome I desired.

As I was growing up, many events took place in my life. As with most people, I had no idea what these events were doing to form my inner beliefs. Looking back at them now, I can see how they significantly established the path to where I am today.

Forming My Inner Beliefs

Growing up, I was a competitive swimmer. I swam year round from age seven to twenty. While I was competing, I had no idea why I was doing as well as I was. I seemed to win a great many races with what seemed very little effort. At age 16 my times were fast enough to come very close to making the Olympic trials. But something happened at that time. I started not to swim as well. Now when I look back, it is obvious to me why this was happening. When I first started swimming, I always practiced with people better than I was. I am a very competitive person. That made me want to be right there with those older and better swimmers. As I grew older and my friends starting going to college, I became the oldest and best swimmer on the team. That had some benefits, like meeting the woman I married, but it also started a process of no growth. You see, without having people around me to inspire me to be better, I just didn't go any further. My goal was not to be a great swimmer, but to have fun with my friends, be like them, and be as good as them. When they moved on, my swimming days were over.

A few years later, while observing beautiful corporate jet airplanes flying out of an airport close to where I grew up, I saw my next dream as clearly as I saw those planes. I was going to fly on board those airplanes. I had no idea how, but I was going to get there. My Mom and Dad couldn't afford to send me to school, so I had to find a way on my own and I did. At many schools, it takes two to three years to obtain an Airframe and Powerplant license, which is what you need to be able to sign off on work done on airplanes. That was not fast enough for me. I believe that when you make a decision to do something, you do it with great zeal. I went to school forty hours a week for an entire year. Within fifteen months I had my license.

The airport I grew up near had one of the largest concentrations of corporate aircraft in the world. I sent my resume out to every company there. Three months later I received an offer to work with the American Express Company flying on board their plane as a flight mechanic. Thus, I achieved my goal in less than eighteen months. Corporations have flight mechanics on board so if the airplane breaks down while in transit, it can be fixed right at that airport. The biggest thing I had not anticipated was the pleasure I had in meeting all the corporate officers of American Express as well as many other corporations. I also was privileged to meet a past U.S. president, a Secretary of State, and many heads of state. I traveled all over the world on their planes, a direct result of that decision I made a couple of years earlier. Here are a couple of more nuggets I learned from this: make a goal so big and so emotional that the "how" doesn't matter. It also taught me the importance of making a decision. (Prior to making the decision to enter the field of aviation, I made some really poor decisions, but this was a great one.) As Tony Robbins says, "It is in that moment of decision that your destiny is formed."

I worked with American Express for five years and then went to General Electric for one year. It was during this year that my life changed completely. While traveling, I came across a publication called *Success Magazine*. I had never read anything like it before. I always had a lot of time to kill sitting at airports, so I read it cover to cover. Inside one edition was an ad for the most interesting book I could imagine – Napoleon Hill's *Law of Success*. In my travels with American Express, I had admired those with whom I was traveling. But I learned that these high-powered, very wealthy people were people just like me in many respects. What I couldn't figure out was what made them different. Napoleon Hill taught me the difference. He became my mentor, and for the first time I realized why I was where I was. It was in that moment that I made another major life-changing decision.

I Decided to Become an Entrepreneur.

Exactly what I was going to do was the hard part to figure out, but I knew I was headed towards something totally different! I had been in the corporate world, as was my wife, Jill, and her parents. For all of them the only good job was a big corporate one. So when I decided to leave the corporate world, I knew it would pretty much send all my relatives, including my wife, into a tailspin! I figured the easy way out would be if I were to get laid off, and I did! Since Jill and I needed a new home, I decided I was going into my new profession of building homes

63

In May of 1986 I started building my first house in Patterson, New York. Through research, I decided I would build an all steel frame house. I recruited my dad to help me because he built the house I grew up in and knew a lot more than I did. It was a fantastic experience and taught me the real value of having someone with me who had the experience I didn't. After finishing that house, I spent almost the next three years "trying" to sell land specifically for development. I was devoted to this career. I really loved it; in fact, I loved it too much. When October, 1987 came along, and Black Monday with it, the New York area really was hit hard. My land sales career went straight down with the stock market. Being young and enthusiastic, I stayed with the career for more than a year and a half after that. Finally it hit me in May of 1989 to move south where the real estate market was very robust.

Arriving in Charlotte, NC in September, 1989, I decided I should work for either a builder or a developer first so I could gain local experience prior to setting out on my own. Although I didn't realize it at the time, I was about to make the biggest mistake of my life. I had a choice to either work for the most well-respected developer in the area, or with a friend who worked for a small local builder. I chose my friend. Even though I made some great contacts and gained some good experience, the builder went bankrupt. I lost valuable investment cash.

As Difficult as Those Days Were, Those Events Did Start Me on the Course that has Led Me to Today.

I love building homes so I was intent on staying the course. It was during those days that I met my future partner and mentor. Steve had the experience, and I had the goals. So we set off in a whirlwind and built large custom homes during the next three years. We participated in home shows, won awards, and received a great deal of public attention. The best thing I did during this period of time was to partner with one of the top real estate agents in our area. She guided us to the right plans to build and was willing to help finance us. Of course she then had an interest in selling the houses we built. It worked out tremendously well for all of us and gave me a world of experience. Even though I had a wonderful relationship with my building partner, in 1995 I decided to go out on my own.

Up to this point the most homes I had built per year was nine. For many years, in the back of mind, I had dreamed of building seventy-five homes a year. Now I was going to do it. I made the commitment to myself and put it on paper and stated it in public. In June of 1996, I set out on the journey and by the end of 2000 my company built and closed eighty homes. In 1997 I teamed up with Dale Huffman, whom I had met years earlier while working with that bankrupt builder. He has many talents that I don't possess, and he is totally committed to our mutual benefit. The value you gain by having someone like Dale around is priceless. In the company of this type of person, you will be unstoppable. Today we gross between $8.5 and $11 million a year and are now setting up for our next growth curve.

I Have a Belief, One I Adopted from the Great Zig Ziglar.

It is simply this: "Once a task begun, leave it not until it's done, and be it great or small, do it well or not at all." Although along my road there were many bumps, curves, hills, valleys and seemingly impassable roadblocks, I stayed the course. I believe in persistence – not foolish persistence, but believing so strongly in what you want that failure is not an option.

I believe "Whatever you dream, you can achieve." I set a goal, a big one, one that many wouldn't touch and certainly one that many doubted I could ever achieve. During this process, I also attended numerous self-improvement and business seminars. Most people I told about them couldn't understand why I spent my time like this. What they didn't understand was the very straightforward but extremely important principle I had used since I was child – that is that you achieve an unequaled advantage by having strong mentors.

Many might say you must have the self-determination to conquer without outside influence, but that is not my opinion. Nor is it how I achieved success in my life. I believe that you must always have a mentor: someone you admire, someone who can show you an easier path, someone who will help pull you up the ladder in times of need, someone who is willing to share, and someone who is bigger than life to you. Talk with any successful person, or read the biographies of such, and they will tell you they had a mentor in the beginning. They will also tell you they *still* have mentors. Growth is critical to success; you can grow at warp speed with a mentor.

Have huge goals, ones that scare you so much that you have no idea how to attain them, and you know you cannot achieve them on your own. Create a great team that sees the vision, have a mentor, and then hold on! You are in for the ride of your life!

David Baulieu is CEO and owner of Merritt Homes located in North Carolina. As well as building homes, he provides easy step-by-step seminars to those who wish to build their own homes and also to homebuilders wishing to enhance their business. Call David anytime at *704-948-4663*. He would love to talk with you. Or you can use email: *david@merritthomes.com*.

From the Shadow of Elvis to Solutionary Dynamics

Triumph Over Adversity

By David E. Stanley

I have found that adversity comes in many different ways and wears many different faces. My boot camp in adversity and what ultimately became my training ground for learning how to turn tragedy into fuel for motivation began when my Mom and Dad went through a divorce when I was a young boy. My dad, William J. Stanley, a World War II combat veteran was fighting a losing battle with alcohol. He had been part of the first wave to hit Omaha Beach on June 6, 1944. The depiction of D-Day in Steven Spielberg's "Saving Private Ryan" offers just a glimpse of the carnage and horror my father experienced not just on D-Day but throughout Northern France and in the Battle of the Bulge. Alcohol had become the antidote for Dad's emotional baggage and bled into his personal and professional life.

My First Taste of Adversity

My mother decided she couldn't live with the situation. She thought it would be better if my two older brothers, Billy and Ricky, and I were out of the picture while she initiated divorce proceedings. We were placed in a boarding home in Newport News, Virginia. It was a defining moment for me. I'll never forget the experience – it was my first taste of adversity. The boarding home was old, dark, dirty and dingy. Other kids saw their families every weekend but no one came to see us. I also suffered from having to wear uncomfortable braces on both legs. Born with a clubfoot, I had undergone multiple painful operations to correct the problem. Confused and hurting, I used to lie in my crib and cry myself to sleep at night. I couldn't understand where my parents were. My brother, Ricky, would hear me crying and come to my crib and say, "David, don't cry; someday things will get better." But I still felt abandoned and alone.

In 1960, my mother finally came back. With our belongings packed, my brothers ran to the car while an aide carried me. We looked for Dad, but instead there was someone else. Mom had managed to get a divorce and remarried in 1960. She introduced us saying, "Boys, this is your new father, Vernon Presley. This is Elvis Presley's father." Just like that, I had become part of Rock and Roll's first family. We took the car from Virginia to Memphis, Tennessee, the home of our new stepbrother, Elvis Presley. As we entered the gates of the Graceland Mansion, I pressed my four-year-old face against the glass looking at the home where I would spend the next 17 years of my life. My brother, Rick, nudged me and said, "David, I told you someday things were going to get better."

Elvis's Kindness and Generosity

As we entered the house, there stood a young man who was 25 years old. Elvis Presley had just returned from his Army stint in Germany. Even at that early age, I recognized Elvis's kindness and generosity. He understood I was a victim of divorce and confused about how I ended up moving into his home. As we stood there in the foyer, Elvis walked over to me, bent down, gave me a hug, and welcomed me into his family. After my experiences in the boarding home, Elvis's hug made me feel extraordinary.

I spent the next seventeen years of my life growing up with my world-famous stepbrother. Although it was exciting to be part of some of the music industry's most historic moments, our family's lifestyle of the rich and famous was also very surrealistic. When I started school, I began to realize just how hard it was going to be to live up to the image of being Elvis Presley's little brother. I had an identity problem. I didn't know who liked me because I was David Stanley or who liked me because I lived at Graceland. This had a profound affect on me. At a young, impressionable age when I needed the acceptance of friends, I couldn't find any. This situation planted the seeds of rebellion, making me vulnerable to peer pressure and instilling in me an insatiable need for acceptance. Frustrated and unable to get along with my classmates, I dropped out of school in 1972 at the age of 16 and went to work for Elvis as a personal aide and bodyguard.

Life in the Fast Lane

From 1972 to 1977 I lived life in the fast lane. Sex, drugs and rock and roll were the themes of the day. I was making poor choices that were quickly leading to self-destruction. I found myself modeling the actions of my mentor, Elvis Presley. By 1974, his use of prescription drugs had begun to turn into abuse. By the summer of 1977, he was totally addicted. In three short years, Elvis had gone from the lean 168-pound powerhouse the world saw in his Aloha Hawaii concert to a figure who weighed 255 pounds. He was living dangerously close to the edge. On August 16, 1977, 17 years after I moved into Graceland, I walked into Elvis's bathroom and found him dead. His death was a direct consequence of his inability or refusal to make positive decisions and implement a plan to take control of the problems in his life. Instead, he allowed his problems to control him.

At My Lowest

When Elvis died, I was left with great memories, a substance abuse problem, and a 9th-grade education. Elvis left his entire estate to his daughter, Lisa. My stepfather, Vernon, fired me and then accused me of killing the man who had been my brother, friend and father figure. I hit the streets with nothing and certainly no idea of how to go about living a "normal" life. I was at my lowest.

By 1980 I was teetering on the edge of self-destruction. I was living the "I, me, mine" fast-paced, quick fix, disposable lifestyle. Haunted by the memory of Elvis's lifeless body cradled in my arms on that fateful day, I realized my life was following a similar path. I realized that I had to change. I made a decision, took action and implemented a plan that helped me take the first steps toward overcoming the adversity of my surrealistic upbringing. I eliminated my abuses, took my GED test, earned a degree in Communications and worked to establish myself as a speaker.

Starting with very limited finances, I often spoke to crowds of just 15 people and slept in hotels where the roaches seemed bigger than I was. I spoke 48 weekends out of the year to any audience that would have me. I put a little food on the table and paid for my college education.

The Hard Lessons I Learned

The hard lessons I learned from my life with Elvis, his tragic death and the years that followed formed the backbone of my keynote address "From The Shadows Of The King" and later became the formula for my *Solutionary Dynamics – Solutions For Success* keynotes and seminars. As Elvis's stepbrother and bodyguard, I saw his satisfaction come from the joy he gave to audiences through the gift of his music. My satisfaction as a speaker comes from seeing people with talents and dreams and knowing I have the ability to deliver the tools to help them achieve those dreams. Nothing is more exciting than to see a person break out of their bonds and take flight – to use their God-given gifts to make their lives extraordinary. The seeds of the power of encouragement were planted in me the day Elvis picked me up and made me feel I was special.

Most Valuable Lessons

While I learned some positive lessons from Elvis, my most valuable lessons came from his self-destructive demise. Elvis was the classic example

of the person who wakes up and suddenly discovers he has everything –
and it's not enough. Unfortunately, Elvis missed out on life's most
important lessons. That cost him more than his dreams – it cost him his life.

You Better Have Substance

Elvis often said to me, "David, once you hit the stage you better have
substance." As a motivator, I teach people to think at the level of the
solution instead of the level of the problem. I have learned and truly believe
that within each and every one of us lies the unlimited capacity to reach and
maintain new levels of excellence in our personal and professional lives.

As a result, I have been able to make lasting positive changes in my life
and have condensed those lessons into a powerful yet simple formula -
Quest Definition + Decision - Fear + Action + Focus + Quest Management =
Success. This formula is the essence of my program *Solutionary Dynamics*.
When unlocked, it can empower each of us to turn adversity into personal
triumph, identify what we really want out of life, turn the ordinary into the
extraordinary, maintain motivation and creativity, and strategically position
our lives for success.

David E. Stanley is an internationally renowned motivational speaker, best
selling author and creator of *Solutionary Dynamics*™. His powerful programs
empower audiences, companies and individuals to reach
and maintain new levels of excellence in their personal
and professional lives.

For more information about David E. Stanley visit
www.solutionarydynamics.com

C'est l'Eclaircie

By Carol Young

The word "*l'eclaircie*" is a French idiom for the appearance of light after a long, difficult time of darkness. It can simply mean the rising light of dawn, the spray of light down through the clouds after a storm, or, symbolically the release of universal joy and the sense of new beginnings at the end of a war. L'eclaircie finally became a part of me after a long difficult journey.

I never believed that I would be one of those to someday be homeless. After I lost all I held dear, the painful test for me was the development of humility. I found a strengthened courage to shed all worldly burdens and let my spirit flourish. The lessons of providence lifted me away from the allure of all meaningless diversions and compelled me to choose only that which is most cogent to my life's purpose. I came to a perfect trust in the movement of a Spirit of light. Hope was my last and most precious possession and I learned to be free from negative influences in my life.

The word "disaster" comes from the ancient Greeks who believed the stars to have divine influence. "Dis-aster" means to be disconnected from the stars – the sense you have when you experience the great "Alone". The Chinese symbol for crisis means "danger plus opportunity." When you are choosing not to do what your inner Spirit is calling you to do, nothing ever seems to work well. We are most inspired to change when disaster or crisis motivates us toward a higher way of life.

My time of change came when my marriage of 12 years ended. I had lived a life of complacency... surrounded by an abundance of material possessions. Some would have considered my life prosperous. It was not. When it became necessary to divorce, my husband – a successful attorney – put me through five years of destructive divorce proceedings. I was put into the position of having to choose between my integrity or just doing anything it took to protect myself and my children from violence. The situation became clear at the outset... I would be losing all things material. The possibility included the loss of my life, if I allowed it to happen.

I had tried to endure after my divorce and persevered mightily to recover from the financial impacts. Yet, over the next ten years, an increasingly debilitating illness and financial difficulties eventually brought me to homelessness. I still had so much to learn!

The homeless world I eventually came to live in was one wrought with pain and loss of hope for the souls residing in it. I found the challenge encountered for homeless people is to transform fear and shame into courage and dignity through the humility of their state. The condition of homelessness for many in their mind is sudden and cataclysmic. Most don't realize that they arrived at this dismal state because of a series of past choices. The seed of a bad choice can appear subtle and benign at the outset, but will grow over time to produce the weed planted. Rarely is it planned or chosen, but if not rooted out when it becomes apparent, will grow to choke life. One will then have to be urged by the will to live and fight back what is destructive, or lay back and die. When, with hope, courage is chosen, it is here a Spirit of light blossoms. Out of an agonizing test of pain comes an intensity of powerful creativity not normally found out of the mundane comforts of everyday complacency. After coming to this determination by watching my fellow homeless friends, I painfully began to see how I came to be where I was. My choices, no matter how innocently made in the past, brought me to this place.

I eventually came to realize that destructive people are a blessing in a way that will reliably impel us out of the immutable trap we abide with them. I had to make decisions toward choices for survival that I would never have otherwise made. Unfortunate as it seemed, I had to release my desire for all things material in life and allow what was truly important to fill me. To release was to be filled with peace. To be filled with peace moved me toward true prosperity.

There were eight ethnically diverse children living with their families in the shelter. The beautiful essence of the natural joy of life still in their souls will forever be part of my memory. By them I was reminded that every child has a chance if they can but realize the beautiful gift of spirit they have within and have a mentor to guide them.

I always wanted to write, and this seemed like the perfect time to start, so I involved the children in my new project. To make the time fun as well as productive for all of us, I decided to loosely adapt an early American folk tale, "Bear Coat," for the framework. Its message would deal with the suffering as well as the hope of these children. The children named all the peripheral characters, but L'Eclaircie was the name I chose for one of the two main characters.

As our story formed, it began to address the children's fears, concerns, hopes, and dreams through archetypal symbolism, and the laughing colors of their imagination. The end result of this story-building process was that the children learned to use a computer, dictionary and thesaurus. They learned the meaning of the words "onomatopoeia" and "alliteration", some French and the joy of creating something good in their lives. A possibility evolved in their minds that choices made with their own power and integrity and spirit could even change their lives for the better. The concepts in our extempore project gave them a new way of thinking beyond their experience, and hopefully, into their futures.

Although I understood at this time that I still had some learning to do in order to wholly perceive the rising light of dawn, in hindsight, I realize this moment was but the beginning after a long difficult time of darkness for me - *c'est L'Eclaircie*, it is the new light.

The way to my present life of peace and prosperity was long and difficult. This was only achieved by a continuous chain of choices, all linked by pain and joy, sorrow and hope, loss and more loss, down to the true core of what my soul is in this life revealed. Then and only then, the unending abundant gifts of what real wealth is began to flow forth. Most of these riches came in the form of people. All people in my life become teachers. The most difficult ones were often the more potent, bringing essential lessons to be learned and blocking my path until I either learned them or took a circular detour. That only brought me back to my same place again. I eventually learned to refute a tenacious cycle of destructive actions in my life by moving past them and saying, "No more!!!!" When good choices become a habit of mind and heart, its measure is shown by the type of people we choose to allow into our lives, and the people who are drawn to us.

I have now continued on my journey as a writer. This was always something I had wanted to be but fear and lack of belief in my abilities held me back. After I took the first step, new people came into my life who held the greatest of Spirit within them. Situations evolved in such a way that still fills me with awe. Right thinking and action propelled me onward toward true prosperity. Every day I am shown the way to my own great awakening. I know without a doubt this is the path that I was meant to be on. It is this spiritual awakening that has brought success into my life and is now manifesting in a quiet and sacred process.

A Lakota medicine woman, Ti Manua - *Life of the Prairie*, has since asked me to write her story and I can think of no greater honor. I know I am blessed with a greatness of purpose beyond my own human dreams. A beautiful humility has finally filled my heart and the joys of life have manifested. *C'est L'Eclaircie!!!*

Staying in Love

When the Marriage

is Over

By Janet Attwood and Chris Attwood

Are you expanded or are you contracted? If you want the essence of the wisdom of this chapter, that is it. Divorce happens because two people contract to the point that they want nothing more than to dissolve a commitment and a relationship into which they had blissfully entered. And does this only happen when we divorce? Of course not. Our business relationships, our friendships, and even the very best marriages all go through cycles of expansion and contraction. It's the nature of life. To remain contracted (separated or alienated) from another is only the result of confusion – thinking anyone outside of us is responsible for our experience of life.

The secret to staying in love in any relationship is to find the way back to expansion. This chapter will share some ways of doing that. The most important one is simply realizing when we contract and having the desire to once again open our hearts and minds.

In the Bible it is said, "Ask and it will be given unto you." Be aware when you contract, and then ask to open again. It may not happen right away. Sometimes you need some time to heal, but that is OK.

A Model of Staying in Love

We were once married. We are no longer. Yet we continue to enjoy an incredible relationship as best friends and business partners. We have both entered into other relationships, and have even introduced each other to other people. While our connection no longer is a romantic, physical one, we continue to have a deeply loving, emotionally fulfilling relationship.

How can this be? A better question is, how could it be otherwise? We married because we felt a deep love for each other. What could cause that to change? The answer is it never did change. But layered on top of our love was a great deal of hurt. We have been able to return to the love in our

relationship, even as the outer expression of our love has changed, only because we came to realize the hurt we felt had nothing to do with the other person. It had only to do with ourselves. We hope our story, as told in our upcoming book, *Staying in Love When the Marriage is Over: The Gifts That Are Possible When The Heart Stays Open,* will provide lessons for many, whether married or divorced (www.stayinginlove.com).

Feeling Expanded – Falling in Love

Think about how you feel when you're feeling expanded. Remember the time when you were head over heels in love? Didn't it feel wonderful? Does it get any better? How did you treat the object of your affection? Did you notice:

- Giving comes naturally.
- Being considerate and thoughtful is a joy.
- Seeing the best in the other is effortless.
- Doing things for the other is a treat.
- Listening is fun.
- Just the thought of the other brings delight.
- Gratitude for even small gestures is spontaneous.
- Thinking of the other's needs is automatic.

Is there anything more wonderful than "being in love?" And yet how many marriages have begun on this heavenly ground, only to be torn apart by acrimony and divorce a few months or years later?

Ultimately, the love we feel for others is just the love we feel for ourselves. The anger, hurt, or distress we feel toward others is just those feelings we have about ourselves. The mistake our intellect makes is to think that what we feel has anything to do with anyone else. The reality is our world is as we are. When we feel pain, hurt, anger, or upset toward someone else, these feelings are the signal to us there is something in us that needs to be healed.

Our emotional body functions in a way that is very similar to our physical body. What do you do when you feel pain in some part of your body? If you break your arm, do you tell your arm, "You shouldn't hurt me. You're being unkind to me. You should stop making me feel this pain." Of course not.

When we feel pain in our physical body, it's because there is something needing attention. When we feel pain in our emotional body, it's for the same reason. We can blame someone else for our pain, and feel separated and suffer, or we can realize this pain is a gift to help us heal and step up to another level of loving.

Does this mean we should grin and bear it when we hurt? No. Sometimes we need to take some time to ourselves and allow the pain to diminish, so we can open our hearts and minds to the healing.

We need to take responsibility for ourselves. To think there is anyone else but us who is responsible for our hurt, unhappiness, and suffering, is to live in delusion. We are the responsible party. And the good news is that entering back into love depends on no one but us.

The message of *Staying in Love* is this: life is bliss when we are able to love unconditionally. And the opportunity to live a life of unconditional love is wholly our choice.

Practical Steps – From Contraction to Expansion

So, what can we do when we feel contracted?

1) *Notice.* Become aware that when you get angry, feel frustrated, are disappointed, depressed, anxious or tense. These are signals from your emotional body that some emotional wound needs to be healed. When you notice contraction, have the desire to return to expansion and ask for help.

2) *Take time to feel.* When we contract, we've been trained to try to find some way to stop the pain. We want to fix it and make it go away. The truth is the best thing we can do is take some time to allow the emotions to flow. Be kind to yourself. Take some time by yourself. Allow yourself to feel the emotional pain and notice where in the body it is lodged. Often we will sob and sob as we locate that area of hurt. When we allow ourselves to feel that area of hurt, and allow it expression – not directed **at** anyone, but just released – an amazing peacefulness comes over us. Now we are ready to step back into expansion.

3) *Investigate.* No one "makes" us feel contracted. We do that to ourselves. When our thoughts conflict with reality, we contract. We investigate the truth of those thoughts and we naturally and effortlessly return to an expanded state. The Work of Byron Katie (*www.thework.org*) has been of great value for us in investigating the truth of our beliefs. Katie's four simple questions and the turnaround are incredibly profound. As we investigate our false beliefs and discover the truth, the world opens up to us. As Katie says, "When we argue with reality, we always lose, and only 100% of the time."

4) *Breathing.* When we are faced with some danger, we gasp for breath and stop breathing. When we recognize that we are contracting, we must consciously take deeper breaths which help to settle the body and allow us to return to an expanded state.

Lastly, don't wait until you've contracted. Begin to live your life so that expansion is your natural state. For us, this has meant:

- **Transcendental Meditation – (TM).** TM is simple, effortless and can be practiced anywhere (*www.tm.org*). TM allows the mind to experience the inner state of expansion and then to begin to live that in our daily lives. For us, the effects of this simple practice have been profound. It has been the foundation for the effectiveness of everything else we've done.

- **Diet.** Ever notice how your moods swing when you eat certain kinds of foods? Our minds and bodies are intimately connected, so to live an expanded state of life requires a balanced diet, with good organic, wholesome, nutritional foods.

- **Rest.** "What do you mean I'm cranky!!?" Some say that one hour of sleep between 9 PM and midnight is worth two hours after midnight. We know that when we shortchange our sleep, staying expanded just doesn't happen much.

- **Exercise.** Don't we love those endorphins? Those wonderful chemicals are produced when we exercise and contribute in a big way to feeling expanded. Take time every day to exercise for 20-30 minutes and you'll notice that you're feeling expanded more often.

- **Inspirational Reading.** When we are awake to it, we discover that we live in a world that is always expanding, that is always filled with love. It is only our beliefs, our habits, that make us think it is any different. Reading and absorbing material that helps us to see the world through those loving eyes is one of the ways we can keep ourselves grounded in a life of love. That which is true stands the test. Some of the oldest writings about the nature of life inspire us with the vision of life lived in love.

In the fall of 2001, Janet Attwood and Chris Attwood partnered with #1 bestselling authors Mark Victor Hansen (*Chicken Soup for the Soul*) and Robert G. Allen (*Nothing Down, Creating Wealth*) to create *The Enlightened Millionaire Program*. This innovative program combined principles of creating wealth with a massive commitment to philanthropy.
In 2003 Janet and Chris are telling the remarkable story of their marriage, divorce and the incredible relationship that they now share in *Staying in Love When the Marriage is Over*. Readers who would like to receive advance chapters of the book can go to *www.stayinginlove.com*.

My Failures on the Road to Success

By Luigi Peccenini

I Was Not Born to be a Businessman…
But it Was My Destiny.

Setting the Stage for Entrepreneurial Success

Like many others, I was not born wealthy. I am the only child of a modest Italian family. By age 16 I was spending my summer holidays as a factory worker.

At 18, I began asking myself three questions: "Who am I?" "What is the meaning of life?" and "What am I supposed to do on this earth?" Today these questions are still present in my mind. I've always thought that life is a wonderful gift, and that anything I would do and anybody I would meet along the way would help me to find the answers.

At 19 I went to work as a sales person, because even though I was often the top student in my high school class, my parents could not afford to send me to university.

By age 24, I had become a highly paid head of sales in a company in Milan. But I gave up that job to become a door-to-door encyclopedia and self-study language course sales agent, without salary, on a commission basis only. Why? To wake up each morning and be free to decide what I wanted to do for the rest of the day. *I wanted to take risks and invent my life.* I was willing to pay any price for my freedom.

In my life as an entrepreneur, I have experienced both highs and lows. Early on, I made a poor choice regarding business partners, and lost everything as a result. But however unfortunate that might have seemed, it provided me with invaluable lessons. Throughout this article I will reveal six of the lessons that I have learned that I wish to share with you. The first of these – one that I learned from this experience – is:

Lesson 1: *Good partners are rare. If you choose the wrong ones, it's your responsibility alone.*

After six months of working in someone else's business to help get me back on my financial feet, I was able to create my first company in the

www.mentorsmagazine.com

language teaching industry, and became successful selling other company's products. All of this was setting the stage for what was yet to come...

In January 1968 I founded Computex. It was a pioneering venture; the first in Italy to offer computer training to private individuals, at a time when the 1BM 360 was as big as a cupboard and the computer industry was in its infancy. Four years later I sold Computex to a Swiss company for nearly $1 Million. At 32, I had tasted the kind of success that I wanted to have in all my ventures.

I have always believed in the value of education. So while spending an average 12 hours a day managing Computex, I attended university from 1969 to 1973, studying nights and Sundays. At 33 I earned my degree in foreign languages and literature.

Discovering My Niche: Language Training

In June 1972, I decided to enter the English language training business, and founded the company that was destined to be my life's work: Wall Street Institute. I was excited about the possibility of applying the student-centered teaching approach I had created in Computex to helping others learn languages. I developed a program that combined self-directed and teacher-assisted learning methodologies. The program integrated advanced multi-media tools with human interaction. It was self-paced, highly flexible, and extremely convenient for the learner.

When I started Wall Street Institute, with no experience in the language training business, virtually no resources, and the necessity of competing with Berlitz and other giants in the industry, "professional advisors" said it couldn't and wouldn't work. But *I* knew that those companies were using the same methods that they had been using for as many as 50 years, and that people needed a new way to study and learn a foreign language. By 1978, Wall Street Institute had 25 learning centers in Italy; by 1980 that number had doubled thanks to the magic of franchising.

Lesson 2: *Listen to all advice, but then make your own decisions.*

I am obsessed with excellence. As early as 1972 I had first dreamed of creating my own teaching and training materials to ensure that Wall Street Institute was offering its clients the very best tools possible. In 1980 we began production of English On-line (EOL), a state-of-the-art multi-media language instructional program. Completed in 1983 – 11 years after I had first imagined it – EOL offers Wall Street Institute the opportunity to provide its students the best English learning method available in the world.

Lesson 3: *Believe in your dreams.*

In order to develop English On-line, the company invested all its available cash and borrowed from banks and private investors, planning to face heavy financial exposure through high sales. But it didn't work. In 1985, with 50 franchises in Italy and one in Paris, the company had to close its doors. I lost everything, including my physical health.

But I didn't lose my desire or let go of my vision. In January 1986 I used my last $2,000 to place an ad in Lugano, Switzerland, looking for a partner able to invest $150,000. By April I had the money I needed, and set up Wall Street Institute Lugano. By 1990 the company had established 15 franchisees in Switzerland and regained control of its Italian operations. Between 1988 and 1995 Wall Street Institute successfully entered Spain, Portugal, Germany, Chile, Mexico and Venezuela.

Solid, well organized, international and highly profitable, Wall Street Institute was ready to be passed to the hands of a multinational company with the financial power to develop it further. In January 1997 I sold the company to Sylvan Learning Systems for $26 million.

Lesson 4 (Three in One): *Never give up. Learn from failures. The bigger the problem, the bigger the opportunity.*

Probably my most prominent characteristic is that I never give up. I've always considered my failures as stepping stones on the road to success. I never blamed anybody and took full responsibility for my mistakes. I learned from them. Even from my very serious illness I discovered how to stay healthy, young and more energetic than ever.

Serving People. My Foundation: The Tao Te Ching

I may now have my answer to my third question "What am I supposed to do on this earth?" I have dedicated over thirty years of my existence to education. This may be my modest contribution to human beings.

With my passion for education, and convinced that life is body, mind and spirit, I set up a foundation to promote a healthy life-style: nutritional education, illness prevention, psychological well-being and a more human approach to management.

I also would like to extend the teachings of the *Tao Te Ching* (the ancient book of Chinese wisdom attributed to the great master Lao-tzu, whose principles have been guiding my life for over twenty-five years) to create a better understanding and solidarity amongst people.

"I have just three things to teach: simplicity, patience, compassion. These three are your greatest treasures. Simple in actions and in thoughts, you return to the source of being. Patient with both friends and enemies, you accord with the way things are. Compassionate toward yourself, you reconcile all beings in the world." (Tao Te Ching–verse 67).

Lesson 5: *The best way to be happy is to create happiness around you.*

The Challenge Continues

Following two years of "digesting my past and exploring my future" after the sale of Wall Street Institute to Sylvan, in 1999 I resolved to be in "the country of the future" – one which will shape our planet in the next three decades. I decided to "launch the China Adventure," founding Wall Street Institute China and opening our offices in the World Trade Center in Beijing. It took the company just two short years to become the market leader, and today there are four Centers in Beijing and three in Shanghai, serving 10,000 students and generating yearly revenues over $20 million. Beginning in 2004 WSI China will start expanding to the major cities of China.

I personally love this country, its people and its more than five millennia of history and culture. With my long-term educational projects, I expect to live in China for many years to come.

So we have come to what for me, at my age, is the most gratifying lesson...

Lesson 6: *Abolish the word "retirement" from your vocabulary. Stay young. Challenge yourself, and enjoy life!*

Luigi T. Peccenini began his career in sales and marketing management. He is the founder of several companies, including Computex, the Wall Street Institute, the Wall Street Institute China, and Unileader (*www.unileader.com*). He can be reached by contacting Paola Gay at +34 932 701 656 or via email at *pgay@unileader.com*.

Angels At Our Door

By Dottie Walters, CSP

There are many kinds of mentors in our lives, I have learned. Some we watch and learn from because they set a brilliant example. One of these, for example, is a former State Senator of Arizona, Somers White. He is a talented professional speaker, international consultant and executive who always has time to be interested in, and care about, his friends. When we find someone like that in our lives, I believe we should think of them as a teacher, someone to emulate. They set an example for us to follow.

Then there are family members who are mentors to us. And there are all the wise people who await us so patiently in the books at the library – the people of accomplishments and ideas from the past.

Family Mentors

Perhaps your greatest mentor was your grandmother or grandfather. My Grandmother told me that angels bring opportunity to knock at the door of our heart; then they call us, and ring the bell, and even kick the door! But many people just sit inside and never open the door. They think opportunity has passed them by. I asked my grandmother if I could open the door if an angel came to our house. She said, "Yes, but the angel will give you a message, and then have to hurry on as angels have many messages to deliver every day. Besides," she explained, "angels always leave the same message."

I was so excited! I visualized the angel with the big mailbag over her wing. "What is the angel's message?" I asked. She had me write it down: *Arise and go forth!*

Arise and go forth means you are to get up and get going – no matter what! The solutions to your problems may well be the opportunities to create new business, to write, to use whatever gifts you have been given. Don't wait. Use your energy and creativity.

My grandpa came to the Untied States from Scotland on a sailing ship. I remember him singing to me about Loch Lomond where our ancestors lived. One day I fell down and skinned my knee. Grandpa picked me up and sat me on his lap. What he told me has helped me in many hurtful situations. He told me to put my right hand fingers around my left wrist, below my thumb, and to be quiet. When I felt the beat in my wrist from my heart, Grampa explained that it was the Scottish drums beating! He told me they would always be there, every day of my life.

Then he sang to me *Scotland the Brave!* And told me that sometimes in life we had to lie down and "bleed a wee bit." He told me that was all right, but then my responsibility was to get up and fight the good fight again. "Listen for the bagpipes and the Scottish drums! They are always close, Lassie."

It was when my husband, Bob, returned from 4 years in the Marine Corps in the terrible battles of the South Pacific in World War II that I remembered my grandfather's story. We had bought a small dry cleaning franchise and a little tract GI home for our family of two children, but then a big recession hit the United States. No one was having any dry cleaning done.When I saw my husband put his head down in his hands, I knew it was time to get up and fight the good fight – to listen for the bagpipes and feel the beat of the drums. I asked Bob to give me two weeks to find a source of income for our little family.

Focus Your Intelligence on Solutions!

In high school I had been Advertising Manager and Feature Editor of our Alhambra High newspaper. One of my ideas was a "Shoppers Column" – paragraphs about the local shops. Each shop paid for their story. My idea was to do such a column in our little town for the weekly *Bulletin* newspaper. But I did not have a car, nor a typewriter, or even any typing paper. At that moment another mentor stepped forward to help me. I have always loved to read biographies. One of my favorites is Albert Einstein. I remembered some advice I had read from him. He said, "Dottie, stop fussing with lack and failure. Focus your intelligence on solutions!"

So I asked my good neighbor to loan me her typewriter, and she gave me a whole ream of typing paper! Soon I had a sample Shoppers Column ready to show the publisher of the Baldwin Park *Bulletin*. However, when I got the baby stroller out of the garage, I realized that my two babies had grown and would not fit into it!

Then I heard Mr. Einstein telling me again to "focus on solutions." The moment you do, the solution pictures flash into your mind! I ran to the bedroom, took the pillows off the bed, grabbed my clothes line rope, and devised a second seat behind the first one on the baby stroller.I slipped my typed sample Shoppers Column into my shoulder bag and off we went.

Before we had gone very far, the wheel came off the stroller! This time I thought of another of my friends of the mind, Amelia Earhart. When my friends were leaving for college some years before and I realized there was no way I could go, I had read about her. Here are the words she gave me in that book. "Some of us have great runways already built for us. If you have one, *take off!* But if you do not have one – then understand that it is your responsibility to grab a shovel! You must build a runway for yourself and for all those who will surely follow you!" I took off my shoe and hit that wheel back on with my heel every time it fell off.

When I got to the newspaper office there was a sign on the front door. It said, "NO HELP WANTED." My heart sank. Then my good friend of the mind, newspaperman Ben Franklin spoke to me. Ben said, "Dottie, they have no money to hire anyone. So do not go in and ask for a job. Go in and offer to buy space for your Shoppers Column every week at their wholesale price. Your column will be an interesting new feature for the newspaper. You will sell the paragraphs to the merchants at the retail-advertising rate. The difference will be your profit. If you will do this, I promise you the profits will pay your house payment in four weeks!" Ben was right.

Shoppers Column

One of my advertisers for the Shoppers Column was a rather gruff furniture store owner. After I sold him a paragraph in my first Shoppers Column, I went into his shop to ask him to advertise again. He had his feet up on the desk and a cigar hanging out of his mouth. He was angry.

"Why did you put my ad half way down your column?" He yelled.

I gasped, "Oh, did you want a special place? Where would you like your ad to be placed? "

"At the very top, of course!" He replied. "And you are not going to move me out of it. How much extra is the top spot?"

Ohh! I had not thought of charging extra for that placement, but I quickly replied, "Does double price sound fair?"

"Yes," he said, "but I want a contract in writing that says that I get that spot every week!" He threw a calendar and 2 sheets of blank paper at me, and a sheet of carbon paper. "Count how many weeks until the end of the year," he ordered. "This will make a copy for each of us." We both signed it. Then he pulled out his checkbook and gave me a check for a double priced Shoppers Column ad in top place for the rest of the year!

Bob bought me a very nice 2-door model A Ford. I retired the baby stroller, bought a new pair of flat shoes and threw away my old shoes stuffed with cardboard.

I have often wondered if my furniture store owner knew that he was teaching me how to sell placement and long term contracts. There are mentors and teachers all around us. Are you listening? Are you reading? Are you thinking?

Business Turnaround

Then one day, four merchants told me they had decided not to advertise in my column. They told me the Rexal Drug storeowner was not advertising with me and they all liked him very much, so if he did not use my column, they would not do so either! I drove to his store, as I had several times before, but could never find him in. This time I saw him standing in the prescription department in his white jacket. I ran back and asked him to look at my advertising column because the other merchants wanted to know his opinion of it. He made his mouth go into an upside down "U" without saying a word. All the energy fled out of me, and I thought "I can't make it to my little car." So I sat down at the soda fountain. The young man working the counter came up to me and asked what I wanted. I only had 10 cents, so I ordered the smallest Coca Cola.

Just then two ladies came up and sat on the stools to my left. I was almost in tears. One of the ladies turned to me and said "What in the world is the matter with you?" I showed her my Shoppers Column and explained that I didn't know where to turn because Mr. Ahlman would not look at it and give me a comment. I told her I would lose our home, because the money for the ads I was to have picked up that day would have made the house payment. She took the *Bulletin* out of my hand and read every word. Then she spun around and called the owner to come up front. She was his wife! She asked me who the four other merchants were who had decided not to advertise in my Shoppers Column that day. Then she told her husband to sit down and write a check for a Shoppers Column ad for their drug store for a year, to give me the ad copy. Then she told me that she was going back to the phone to call my four other ad prospects.

I learned later that her husband was the kindest of men and so generous that she had decided to take over all of the advertising decisions. I had been talking to the wrong person! She soon came back and told me my four advertisers were waiting for me with checks in hand.

We became dear friends with this wonderful couple. When they took the soda fountain out of their drug store, my husband bought it. He and our son installed it in our den. Many speakers who have visited us here in Glendora, CA, have sat on those very stools where my business – and my world – turned around.

Next I decided to put together a short talk called, "What Does Your Customer Really Want?" I called the service clubs in town and asked if they would like a free luncheon speaker on Customer Service. They all said "yes!" I put a copy of the *Bulletin*, turned to my column, at every place at the table. I told them that what customers like me wanted from them was their interest. I passed around a little basket and asked them each to put their business card into it, writing the time and day they would like to talk to me about advertising in my column on the back. I took along a little prize for the drawing of one card. Then something amazing happened!

Advertising Business

By the end of that year, when those annual contracts would soon have to be renewed, a group of the merchants came to our little home. They asked me to start my own advertising business and all offered to become my first advertisers. I asked them why they wanted me to do it. What they told me was a very important lesson.

1. Because you keep your word.

2. Because you have good ideas in your column that have helped each of us.

3. Because we know you are reliable.

The business they wanted me to start and run was a welcoming service for new area residents. We called it *Hospitality Hostess*.

Hospitality Hostess

The merchants each gave me a check for the first three months of the new advertising service they wanted. Many of these clients needed special printing for us to distribute to the families we welcomed. So my husband set up a printing business and did very well with it.

When the merchants who advertised with me opened new branches in other cities, they asked me to keep expanding the *Hospitality Hostess* service. I used the method of speaking free to local Service Clubs to promote this new advertising business. Within two years we had 4,000 annual advertising accounts, four offices and 285 employees.

In the meantime, business people who heard me speak asked me to speak for a *fee* to their employees and other organizations they belonged to.

Soon those speaking clients asked me to find other speakers for them, and our *Walters International Speakers Bureau* was born.

Sharing Ideas

Today we publish *Sharing Ideas*. The largest independent magazine (yes we feature lots of ads!) for professional speakers. My daughter and I have written many books on the subjects of business and speaking, and with our grandson, Michael MacFarlane, our Speakers Bureau sends paid speakers all over the world.

While college was never a possibility for me, I am so grateful to my friends and clients, both those who are alive now, and those who have spoken to me from the pages of the books they wrote. One day a lady in my speaking audience said it was ridiculous for me to think they had all written books for me. I asked her, "Who did they write them for?" and got a standing ovation.

Dottie and her daughter Lilly are the authors of many books and other products on paid professional speaking. Michael MacFarlane, Dottie's grandson, is active in the *Speak & Grow Rich* seminars Dottie conducts. Together they own *Walters International Speakers Bureau.* To reach Dottie Walters see her Web site at *www.walters-intl.com* Phone *(626) 335-8069* Fax *626-335-6127* Mail address: P.O. Box 398 Glendora, CA 91740.

How You Think

© 2003 Kim Muslusky

Determines Your Life

To Succeed In Business,
Change The Way You Think

By Bradley J. Sugars

If you really want to succeed in business, you need to come to grips with the fact that the most important challenge facing you lies not in the boardroom, on the factory floor, or even out there in the marketplace. It's in your head.

You see, whether you're able to realize all your business dreams or not is nothing more than a product of your imagination.

Get your head around this and you're well on your way to succeeding in business. That's right – you need to change your mindset.

Here are Four Powerful Ways to Do This:

1. Be objective. When you're running a company, it's very difficult to get an objective and honest answer to a problem from yourself. You've invariably got vested interests that color your thinking. Pet likes and dislikes can ruin the most well intended business plans.

So how do you do this? Simple. Make sure you work *on* your business and not *in* it. You see, business owners these days tend to spend far too much time working *in* their businesses rather than *on* them. It's probably always been that way. However, to succeed, this has to change. It's the single biggest impediment to success that I've come across in all the thousands of companies I've worked with. Yet it's understandable. You see, when the vast majority of business owners first dreamed the dream of "going it alone," they ventured out into the world of business by sticking to their field of expertise. A hairdresser opened a hairdressing salon, a motor mechanic opened a mechanical workshop, and so on. Sounds logical enough, but all they achieved was buying themselves another job. They ended up working *in* the job instead of *on* the business.

It would have been far more sensible had that aspiring business person opened a business in which they had no previous experience or expertise.

They would then have had no option but to work *on* the business, relying instead on the expertise of team members who would actually *do* the work.

2. Be accountable. This is such an important concept because it is fundamental to achieving success, not only in your business life, but in your private life as well.

You might be surprised to learn that 95% of people don't accept responsibility for their lives. They just bumble along blaming others for their lot in life, and living their life in denial. If you want to succeed, you've got to make a quantum leap in your belief patterns. This may also require you to challenge the way you view life. But do whatever it takes. Take control of your life. Assume responsibility, and you'll be amazed at how you suddenly you start making progress towards achieving your dreams.

3. Allow yourself to fail every now and then. If it's not OK to fail or make mistakes, you won't try new things. The willingness to fail is the sign of a true leader.

Remember, perfectionism leads to pain. Strive for excellence instead. This, of course, is something for which we are all ill-equipped, as it is something that's not even touched on in schools or universities.

4. Become a *generalist*. Our current education system is geared towards producing *specialists.* But to succeed in business, you need to be the opposite. Let me explain ...

Henry Ford knew one of the common sense secrets to entrepreneurial success. It is the opposite of everything we're taught as a specialist employee. "When I need to know about finance, I call in my finance manager and ask him all the questions I need to have answered. The same goes for any other subject," Ford said.

In Other Words, the Most Effective Leaders in the World Are Generalists Who Employ Specialists Who are Smarter Than They Are.

A specialist (often known as an employee) is easily replaceable. A specialist is taught to follow. A specialist ends up working for a living, rather than living a life.

The generalist, the person I refer to as the entrepreneur, works today to make money for the long-term. He/she works to build wealth rather than make income. He thinks for himself. He takes on the risks and reaps the rewards and, more importantly, collects long-term income from the work he does today and every other day.

In the business world, employees are taught to acquire higher and higher levels of education, to specialize, to work hard and to make enough income to pay taxes, the mortgage, and then to exist until retirement.

In the truest sense of the word, generalists are leaders. They live by the principle that it's better to have 1% of one hundred people's efforts than 100% of their own. Becoming a generalist is the first major task facing anyone considering venturing into business for himself or herself. It's the single biggest mindset change all employees who want to start their own businesses must make. Being the best at your trade, your profession or your job in no way means that you'll succeed in the world of entrepreneurial business. In fact, this is often the biggest hindrance to the success of most businesses.

How Do You Achieve All This? There Are Only Two Ways: the Hard Way or the Easy Way.

Let me tell you about the easy way. It's all about emulating what other successful businesspeople have done – those who have played the game and won. You see, business is just like a game, and you need to play by the rules if you want to succeed.

Everyone knows, and accepts, that sporting stars need coaches. Without them they simply wouldn't succeed. So what is it about business people? Why don't they, as a matter of course, have Business Coaches?

The case for a Business Coach has become unassailable, at least to those serious about success. More and more businesspeople are realizing that in today's fast-paced business environment, there's no way they can stay abreast of developments, let alone ahead of them. And it's no shame to have to accept the critique of an outside business expert – people in business have been listening to the advice of others for ages. The trouble is, they have usually been listening to the wrong people! Family, friends and colleagues have all featured prominently as "confidants," but at what cost?

The fact of the matter is that if you model your business on someone else's, chances are you'll reap the same results they did. Let's put it this way: If you want to bake a different cake, you need to use a different recipe. It's no good using someone else's success secrets or tips, and then expect to get different results from those which they achieved. If you want to model yourself on someone – many do, and it's a sound philosophy – at least choose a winner! Why model your business on a mediocre one?

Sound too simple? Then read on. It's all about stepping back, taking a good hard look at your business, then setting some very definite personal and business goals, and appointing a coach to help get you there.

Understand this: the coach is the only person who can see the forest for the trees. It's the coach who'll ensure you stay focused on the game, who'll make you run more laps than you thought you could (or should), and who'll tell it like it is. The coach is also the only person you can hire who'll act like your marketing manager, sales director, training co-ordinator, partner, confidant, mentor and best friend – all rolled into one.

Does having a coach guarantee you'll achieve success? The answer is *no,* and for a very good reason. You see, although the coach will be there to guide you every step along the way, it's still you who will have to take to the field and play the game. It's your business, after all. You've got to actually do the work, because you're the only one who can be truly accountable. And when you get there, your success will be all the sweeter for it.

Making this mindset change isn't easy – it involves radically altering the very way you think and perceive. Yet it must be done. And it must be maintained when attempted. Like quitting smoking, you can do it on your own, but it's very, very difficult. It is much better to do so with professional help. Business is no different. You can go it alone, or you can do it so much quicker and with more certainty with a Business Coach. The choice is yours.

Entrepreneur, author and investor Brad Sugars financially retired at the tender age of 26 and is the International Chairman of *Action International Business Consultants and Trainers*. If you would like to learn how to realize the dreams you have for your business visit *www.actioncoaching.com.*

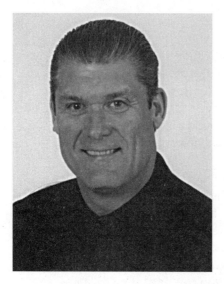

Can You Believe It?

By Vic Johnson

"Belief is the basis of all action, and this being so, the belief that dominates the hearts or mind is shown in the life."
– James Allen (*Above Life's Turmoil*)

William James, the great psychologist and writer of the early twentieth century, said, "Belief at the beginning of a doubtful undertaking is the one thing that will guarantee the success of any venture." You will rarely attempt something you don't believe possible and you will *never* give 100% of your ability to something you don't believe in.

One of the best known stories about the power of belief is about Roger Bannister, the first person to run a mile in under four minutes. Before his accomplishment, it was generally believed that the human body was incapable of such a feat. Bannister, a medical student, held another belief. "Fueled by my faith in my training, I will overcome all obstacles. I am brave! I am not afraid to face anyone on the track. I believe this is not a dream. It is my reality."

As soon as he broke the barrier, belief about the feat changed and his record only lasted 46 days. Within two years more than fifty people also ran a sub-four-minute mile. Thousands have done so since. Today it's not uncommon for it to be done by a talented high-schooler. What happened in 1954 that hadn't happened in the previous 6,000 years of humankind that allowed Bannister to achieve this? It was not the human body which changed; the human belief system did!

Perhaps my favorite story about belief was written by Cynthia Kersey. In *Unstoppable* she told about a college student, George Dantzig who always studied late into the night. He overslept one morning, arriving 20 minutes late for class. He saw two math problems on the board and quickly copied them down, assuming they were the homework assignment. It took him several days to work through the two problems. Finally he had a breakthrough and dropped the homework on the professor's desk.

Later, George was awakened at 6 a.m. by his excited professor. Since George had been late for class, he hadn't heard the professor announce that the two unsolvable equations on the board were mathematical mind teasers that even Einstein had not been able to answer. But George Dantzig, *believing* that he was working on just ordinary homework problems, had solved not one, but two problems that had stumped mathematicians for thousands of years.

How Many Great Things Could You Achieve If You Just "Believed" They Were Doable?

Some years ago I was listening to a friend speaking to a business audience. She quoted a teaching by David Schwartz from *The Magic of Thinking Big* that rocked my life. She said, "The size of your success is determined by the size of your belief." Now that was the first personal development book I ever read and I've read it at least 20 times since. I'm sure that I had heard that concept many times before that night. But it impacted me so much that I wrote it down and must have looked at it a hundred times or more in the thirty days after that.

I spent the next few months focused on strengthening my belief in myself and in what I wanted to do. I took to heart what Wayne Dyer wrote in *You'll See It When You Believe It:* "Work each day on your thoughts rather than concentrating on your behavior. It is your thinking that creates the feelings that you have and ultimately your actions as well." So I worked each day on my beliefs by constantly affirming myself using written and verbal affirmations. The years since have been an incredible rocket ride.

Lest you think it's that easy, you should know that *I worked hard* on my "belief thinking." The work dominated my life at that time because I was determined to change my beliefs. It is a lot like physical exercise: the more you do the stronger you become. I love what Emmet Fox wrote: "If you will change your mind concerning anything and absolutely keep it changed, that thing must and will change too. It is the keeping up of the change in thought that is difficult. It calls for vigilance and determination."

Quite frankly, that's where most people miss the boat. They either half-heartedly try to change their belief systems or they don't stick with it long enough. Wallace D. Wattles wrote "There is no labor from which most people shrink as they do from that of sustained and consecutive thought; it is the hardest work in the world." And yet it is the "sustained and consecutive thought" that is the first and primary labor of achievement.

Nightingale-Conant says Napoleon Hill is considered to have influenced more people into success than any other person in history. And his most quoted line from *Think and Grow Rich* describes the power of belief, "Whatever your mind can conceive and believe, it can achieve." Just believing that statement, truly believing it deep down inside, is a bold step toward living your dreams.

Lisa Jimenez, in her great book *Conquer Fear!* writes, "Change your beliefs and you change your behaviors. Change your behaviors and you change your results. Change your results and you change your life."

So How Do You Change Your Belief System?

1. **Prepare to win.** Nothing will strengthen your belief system more than knowing you're prepared. His pre-race training was the key to Bannister's belief that he could achieve his goal. Remember his words, "Fueled by my faith in my training, I will overcome all obstacles."

2. **Take control of your thoughts.** It's your choice what you think about. Think success and that's what you get. Think failure and that's what you attract. To help in controlling your thoughts, make it a habit to affirm yourself. I had a box of business cards with an old address that I was going to discard. Instead, I flipped them over to the blank side and wrote affirmations on them. I had two identical sets, one for my car and one for my office. Throughout the day I would read my "flash cards" aloud. (If you're in your car, only read while you're stopped for a traffic light :-)

3. **Re-evaluate your situation.** One of my mentors, Bob Proctor, teaches that "our belief system is based on our evaluation of something. Frequently when we re-evaluate a situation, our belief about that situation will change." And when you re-evaluate, spend more time looking at the positive side of your circumstances. In *Why Some Positive Thinkers Get Positive Results,* Dr. Norman Vincent Peale says, "Never build a case against yourself."

4. **Don't worry about "how-to-do-it."** One of my early mistakes was trying to figure out *how* I was going to do something before I'd believe I *could* do it. Dr. Schwartz, again in *The Magic of Thinking Big,* writes, "Belief, strong belief, triggers the mind to figuring ways and means and how-to... those who believe they can move mountains, do. Those who believe they can't, cannot. Belief triggers the power to do."

   Interestingly, Dr. Schwartz wrote in 1959, "Currently, there is some talk of building a tunnel under the English Channel to connect England with the Continent. Whether this tunnel is ever built depends on whether responsible people believe it can be built." Even though they had no idea of "how-to-do-it" at the time, enough "responsible people" maintained a belief in this project and we have the famous Chunnel today.

5. **Finally, you must act.** The New Testament writer said, "Faith without works is dead." Until you act, you're not committed and belief is not cemented. As W.H. Murray wrote, "Until one is committed, there is hesitancy, the chance to draw back, always ineffectiveness." Your action and commitment will be greatly rewarded, for as he goes on to say, "Concerning all acts of initiative (and creation), there is one elementary truth, the ignorance of which kills countless ideas and splendid plans: that the moment one definitely commits oneself, then providence moves too. All sorts of things occur to help one that would never otherwise have occurred."

What great challenge lies in your path today? Do you sincerely want to overcome or accomplish it? If the answer is yes, then *Can you believe it?* Can you believe the magic is really in *you!*

Recently I was dramatically impressed by a passage in *The Message of a Master* by John McDonald. It sums up the reason why most of us don't have the belief to succeed: "The cause of the confusion prevailing in your mind that weakens your thoughts is the false belief that there is a power or powers outside you greater than the power within you."

And that's worth thinking about.

Vic Johnson (*vic@asamanthinketh.net*) is an accomplished author, speaker and founder of four of the hottest personal development sites on the Internet, including *www.AsAManThinketh.net*, where he has given away almost 200,000 e-Book copies of James Allen's classic book.

Unstoppable Belief!

By Cynthia Kersey

You've identified your purpose and set goals that you're passionate about. Now you're ready to make it happen. Eagerly, you share your idea with a friend over morning coffee. Before you can get out two sentences, your friend cautions you that what you want to do has been tried before – *unsuccessfully*, mind you – and perhaps this isn't the right time for you to throw caution to the wind. After considering your friend's comments, you can't help but wonder: *"Maybe this is going to be a little more difficult than I had planned."*

If you reach the end of the day without claiming temporary insanity for conceiving such a ridiculous idea in the first place, consider it a victory. Without a doubt, your dream is most vulnerable immediately after its inception.

The most important step you can take to keep your dream alive is to pursue activities that will strengthen your belief system and minimize your vulnerabilities. Just as our body's immune system can be bolstered by proper diet, exercise, and relaxation techniques, our belief system can be nurtured and strengthened as well. Fortunately, we can take specific actions to achieve this goal.

Five Steps to Developing an Unstoppable Belief System

Step 1: Take Immediate Action

You might wonder what taking action has to do with strengthening your belief system. Your actions reflect your beliefs, and it is *what you do* that demonstrates what you believe. By taking even the smallest steps, you are communicating to yourself and to the world that you believe in yourself and your dream.

In the beginning, you may not *feel* very brave and confident, much less unstoppable. However, by taking consistent action, you will generate the feeling until eventually you are confident, down to the bottom of your soul. Every action you take raises your self-esteem and confidence. You're no longer sitting around waiting and hoping for something magical to happen. You're the creator of that "magic." With your growing self-esteem, you realize your dream is possible.

Step 2: Watch Your Internal Language!

Are you plagued by negative thoughts? The "yeah, buts?" It is *critical* that you cut those thoughts off as soon as they start. You may have heard the expression "thoughts are things." Whatever you think about constantly, you will achieve. If you're continually focusing on how difficult your goal is, you will never achieve it. List some of the negative self-talk in which you routinely engage. Think of how you could modify that dialog to have a positive effect on your thinking and on the results. For example, instead of asking yourself, *Why me?* or *Why can't I?* Ask yourself, *What can I do to make things better, to turn my life around, to improve the situation, to achieve what I long for?* These questions instantly change your focus and empower you.

Step 3: Neutralize Fear and Risk

Fear is a natural reaction to change. It's probably the number one reason people hesitate to start anything new and opt instead for the way things are – safe, comfortable, and familiar. It's important to realize that *everyone* experiences fear when venturing into unknown territory. Fear is a natural and physiological response designed to alert us to the fact that we need to prepare to cope or we need to escape. However, the difference between successful and unsuccessful people is their response to fear. Successful people acknowledge fear and manage it by confronting the cause and determining how they can *prepare* for the challenge ahead. They decide on certain actions that will enable them to feel as competent and confident as possible.

Identify one fear that is stopping you from achieving your goals. Neutralize it by deciding what you can do to prepare yourself for the challenge. Then make the commitment to do so. If the outcome isn't what you planned, congratulate yourself for your courage and consider what you've learned from the experience. Modify your plan and take action again

Step 4: Find Others to Believe with You

It's hard enough staying positive during challenging times even when you are supported by positive people. Associating with negative people can mean the certain death of your dream.

Unfortunately, it may be difficult to eliminate all the negative people from your life. Your mother or father, a business associate, a best friend, or even your spouse might be a negative influence. And since many of these people have known you for years, they probably think of you in terms of your past experiences and not in terms of who you are today or the person you can become.

97

Take an inventory of the people in your life. List the ten people who are most involved in your life. Then rate them from one to ten. Ten would go to someone who builds you up and is totally supportive. A one rating is for someone who robs you of your dream, tears you down, and is a negative influence. Add up your score and divide by the number of names. If you have an average score of seven or less, you need to eliminate or minimize the involvement you have with the energy drainers, and find others who can support you.

Sometimes it's easier to find support from a complete stranger. A stranger doesn't carry preconceived ideas about what you can or cannot do. In chapter 6 of *Unstoppable,* I discuss how you can meet supportive people to build your team. The message at this point is everyone needs someone to believe in him or her; those who are closest to you may not be the best people to fill that role. The key is to find someone who does.

Step 5: Dealing with Critics and Rejection

It is said that "everybody's a critic," and that never seems more true than when you're pursuing a dream and trying to enlist support. There will always be well-meaning people who want to "protect" you from your "unrealistic fantasies." Critics tried to discourage many of the people in *Unstoppable.* They were told a variety of untruths such as: they were unqualified; their ideas wouldn't work; there was no market for their products; they were too short, too young, too early, or too late. They ignored the negative input and achieved their goals. Here are just a few examples;

- Prior to accepting Paramount's offer to host a late-night talk show, Arsenio Hall was told by everyone: *"It's too hard to crack into the late-night ratings. Television isn't ready for a black talk show host. This is America, and you can forget it."*

- Not understanding his desire to become Mr. Universe, Arnold Schwarzenegger's family pleaded with him, saying: *"How long will you go on training all day in a gymnasium and living in a dream world?"*

- In response to Muriel Siebert's application to be the first woman to buy a seat on the New York Stock Exchange, officials responded: *"The language on the floor is too rough and there's no ladies' room."* She bought a seat anyway and remained the only woman there for nine years.

- Responding to his desire to become a recording artist, Ray Charles' teachers said: *"You can't play the piano, and God knows you can't sing. You'd better learn how to weave chairs so you can support yourself."*

- When auditioning for a part in a high school musical, a teacher rejected Diana Ross, saying: *"You have a nice voice, but it's nothing special."*

- Trying to convince her she didn't have the right look, fashion photographer Richard Avedon told Cher: *"You will never make the cover of* Vogue *because you don't have blond hair or blue eyes."* When she did grace the cover, *Vogue* sales set a record.

- Commenting on the first manuscript of an unpublished author, a New York Publisher told James Michener: *"You're a good editor with a promising future in the business. Why would you want to throw it all away to try to be a writer? I read your book. Frankly, it's not really that good."* Michener's first book, *Tales of the South Pacific,* later won a Pulitzer Prize and was adapted for stage and screen as *South Pacific.*

- When hearing his plans to launch Perrier in the United States, several consulting firms advised Gustave Leven: *"You're foolish to try to sell sparkling water in the land of Coca-Cola drinkers."*

The only opinion about your dream that really counts is yours. The negative comments of others merely reflect *their* limitations – *not yours*. There is nothing unrealistic about a dream that aligns with your purpose, ignites your passion, and inspires you to plan and persevere until you attain it. On the contrary, it's unrealistic to expect a person with such drive and commitment *not* to succeed.

Do your homework. The most effective way to counter negativity is to learn all you can about what you want to accomplish. Identify the primary challenges you will face while pursuing your goal. Formulate strategies for overcoming each one. Armed with knowledge and a plan, you will be in a much stronger position and more confident when your critics offer unwanted advice.

Believe in yourself and there will come a day when others will have no choice but to believe with you.

Cynthia Kersey is a nationally-known speaker, columnist and author of the best-selling, *Unstoppable* and the upcoming *Unstoppable Women.* A former top sales executive for Sprint Communications, Cynthia captivates audiences by delivering keynote presentations on how to be unstoppable in their business and life pursuits. You can order her books, programs or bring her to your next meeting by contacting her at *888-867-8677* or *cynthia@unstoppable.net.* Join "The Unstoppable Challenge" by visiting Cynthia's Web site at *www.unstoppable.net.*

Psychological Keys to Wealth

By Van K. Tharp, Ph.D.

People are always looking outside themselves for the "next best thing" to lead them on the road to riches. What if all you need is already inside of you? What does it take to become so wealthy that you can basically have and do whatever you want?

There are key elements that come up repeatedly. These are key psychological elements, not strategies or methods to become wealthy. When you understand and overcome these obstacles, you can choose the better path and allow strategies for wealth to appear.

1. Commitment

Imagine that you are driving across country to an important meeting. You become hungry and stop for a meal. You order a hamburger and it turns out to be the worst hamburger you have ever had. It's very burnt and the sauce is terrible. What would you do? You'd probably complain, but the owner tells you to get lost. You're in a hurry and need to get to your meeting – your prior commitment is much more important.

Now imagine that you have no particular place to go. You stop in the same hamburger stand and get the same terrible hamburger. You complain, and the owner tells you to get lost. Do you move on this time? Probably not. You have nothing to do and this seems to be a health hazard. You threaten the owner that you'll report him. This makes him madder and he threatens you back. You complain to other customers, who agree with you. You organize opposition to the poor service and food. You spend two weeks in the town, because of a poor hamburger.

What is the difference between these two situations? In the first situation, you have a commitment. In the second situation, you are just drifting. When you have a purpose, it's much easier to bounce off things. When you are drifting, it's easy to get sidetracked by whatever gets your attention.

However, there is even a higher level of commitment. It's the commitment that comes when you find your purpose in life. It means that even if you have accomplished all your goals in that area, you'll still keep at it. Why? Because it is you! It gives you immense pleasure! It seems to be what you are supposed to be doing! When you have that kind of commitment, most people usually find incredible wealth as a result.

2. Taking Responsibility for What Happens to You

I frequently play a marble game in some of our workshops. In the game, each person starts with a kitty of $100,000 and must place a minimum bet of $10.00 on each draw. There are different colored marbles placed into a bag. 60% of the marbles are winners and 40% are losers. With some marbles you will double your bet (risk) or you can win 10 times the amount that you risk. Conversely you can lose the amount that you have risked or even lose five times that amount. It is all based on the color of the marble that is drawn out. Marbles are replaced after every draw, so the odds are always the same. For people who understand "expectancy," the bag of marbles represents a pretty good positive expectancy system.

If you control yourself and practice sound bet sizing (i.e. being aware of how much you are betting), you'll have a good chance to make money in the game.

During a 50-trial game of this nature, we usually experience a long losing streak of perhaps five or six losses. Some people in the seminar pull out the marbles. When someone pulls out a losing marble, they repeat the process until they get a winner. As a result, whenever a long streak happens, it seems to be associated with the person pulling the marble out of the bag (person X).

When we play a game like this, at least 30% of the audience will lose money. In fact, some will lose everything and go bankrupt. When the game is over, I ask people "How many of you think you lost money because of Person X drawing those losing marbles?" Several people will raise their hands, indicating they've learned nothing from the game. They've assigned blame to someone else. As a result, they do not realize that *they* made a mistake through their own bet sizing. In situations like that, you can always find someone to blame and never learn from your mistakes – not until you take responsibility for the results you get.

When you first learn about this topic, it is perhaps the hardest concept in the world to comprehend. How could I be responsible for all of the bad things that happened to me? Gradually, as you accept it, you can look at various events and begin to perceive your role. When you finally begin to really understand your role in everything that happens, you get a tremendous surge of exhilaration. Knowing that you are responsible for what happens to you means that you are in control of what happens to you for the rest of your life.

3. Application of the Golden Rule

The Golden Rule as stated in the New Testament is "Do unto others as you would have them do unto you." The same rule might be restated as the "Whatever you give away, you get back many times over." This applies to emotions, to thoughts, and to physical things.

Think about someone who makes you angry. Notice the phrase in our language "makes you." Now send out anger toward that person as you think about what they've done. As you do that, notice what happens to you. You probably get more and more angry. Your anger grows stronger inside of you.

Now think of the same person (if you'd like to do transformation) or someone else who needs help. Picture that person in your mind and send them love. See them surrounded with a golden light or feel them surrounded by an intense love. Notice what happens to you as you do this. You feel love growing inside. This is a simple application of the Golden Rule – whatever you give out, you get back.

This same principle also applies to the realm of ideas and things. If you concentrate on enriching someone, you usually come up with a solution that enriches you.

When I think about the most successful people in the trading industry, they become most successful because they enrich other people. The typical path is to become good at the markets and then enrich others by managing their money. Ironically, the more you enrich others through managing their money, the more wealthy you become.

4. Clearing Out Psychological Blocks

What stops most people from applying the first three points are psychological blocks. We all have such blocks and they can be insidious. The first step is to be aware of them. Look at your blocks honestly and work on those that are limiting you and placing you in a position where you are repeating patterns of negative behavior. In fact, my finding is that many people don't find their purpose or their commitment until they've done a lot of psychological clearing.

For example, the first key point was commitment. When you are committed and you've found your purpose, you won't be sidetracked by poorly made hamburgers.

The second point was taking responsibility for what happens to you. Most people can admit to taking *some* responsibility for what happens to them. However, most of us also carry around wounds and personal scars associated with other people or events. Despite our best efforts at taking responsibility, it's always much easier to see the role that others play.

In my consulting work, people will say, "That person really crossed the line this time. I can never forgive them." Frequently the story is one side of the issue and may not even be true. I've seen many examples of people making up issues and turning them into "reality." Nevertheless, when it comes to issues of this nature, the last thing most people are willing to do is admit responsibility, at least not until they clear out whatever issue was behind the problem. In fact, some people remain bitter at people who are no longer in their lives. Who is this hurting? Certainly not the person who is no longer there.

Finally, the third point was the application of the Golden Rule – you get back what you give out. It sounds simple to say "give out wealth and enrichment" and you'll get it back. However, knowing the principle and applying it are two different things. Time and again people hear this age-old adage but make up reasons why they are not in a position to do it. Stop now! Spend one week giving of yourself – your smile, good deeds, charity, your time – and see what comes back to you.

In the unique arena of professional trading coaches and consultants, Dr. Tharp is a world-renowned leader. His mission is helping others reach peak performance and becoming the best trader or investor. For more information on products and courses, visit *www.iitm.com* or call *1 800 385 4486.*

Have You Met Yourself Yet?

By Dawn M. Holman

There is no greater reflection of who you are than the state of your most intimate relationships. There is no greater teacher of who you can become than the self-truths revealed by a life examined.

When you were little, you responded to the world with uncensored clarity. Gems fell from your mouth – so full of truth that sometimes your parents roared with laughter or squirmed in silent embarrassment. Where did that perceptiveness vanish, after you became so-called "older and wiser?"

Do you remember how exciting it was to be asked, "So, what do you want to be when you grow up?" Are you still that exuberant about who you've become... and the life you dreamed you would live?

Lost in Crowded Places

Could it be that we were taught to work *too* hard at growing up? If the key to our life's greatest expression is evident by the age of seven, how did we manage to turn away from ourselves?

Countless conversations with people from diverse socio-economic and cultural backgrounds have taught me one very profound and universal truth – the greatest single cause of struggle is not taking the time to figure out *who* we really are.

Echoed by many, this is what a 63-year-old family counselor with lung cancer said: "How do you admit that you don't even know yourself? Explain to your children that they can't possibly know their father because he doesn't really know who he is himself? I used to scratch my head at some of my wife's friends when they'd get into these mediation groups and ritual-like things. But I have to admit, she grew steadily more peaceful with her life than I ever did. How can we possibly think that we know what we want, when we never take the time to find out? When we just buy into the way everyone else lives, no questions asked?"

Forgetting to Know Me

This one oversight of "forgetting to know me" in preparation for life has, in turn, been amplified into a pandemic of uncertainty called "not enough." It goes like this: I'm not smart enough? I'm not good (*worthy*) enough? I don't have enough money?...

Then, we swallow the next unexamined lie and convince ourselves that we're broken and need to be "fixed." No wonder so many of us get caught in the trap of trying to build ourselves up on the outside, to make ourselves feel good on the inside. We never realized, all the while, that we always were "enough." That strength grows from the inside out. That life is like a continuous construction project, one day's work at a time.

Fortunately, I've also witnessed the "power of the unsinkable soul" as producer of an international series to help people face death… and life, for those given a second chance. The privilege of being invited into the "real life" journeys of thousands at such an intimate level revealed masterful insights. Timeless truths which I have since powered into "doable" strategies and "workable" wisdom to help catapult people forward into a life of heightened success and meaning… so fewer will look back with regrets.

I'd like to share two of the biggest regrets from a global collection of revelations – a subtly hilarious and poignant wellspring of life's deeper meanings:

Goals You Don't Want to Score Along the Game Plan of Life

1. Too Much Armor… Not Enough Amour

As one middle-aged man elaborated: "It took being stopped in my tracks to realize how much my family meant to me all these years. *I knew* that I loved them, but *they* didn't really know. I learned too late that I needed to be more aware of what makes the people in my life feel loved. God, I never thought to ask! Now I see that some of the things I took for granted were *their* expressions of love. I missed some very important signals. Now, I lie here questioning whether I loved well enough, and whether I was ever truly loved in return."

A young mother lamented: "Deep down inside, I've always felt that I didn't really deserve to be loved, so I never opened up to the idea of accepting myself, warts and all. I created a marriage and a family with my emotional defenses up. And, reacted badly to anything that triggered those feelings of not being good enough. I feel so sad for not letting them in the way I could have. Please tell them that these tears are real."

2. Living Like a Chicken Instead of Flying Like an Eagle

A father of three said: "I wish that someone had asked me when I was younger, 'What's so important to you that if it were taken away, it would make your life feel diminished?' Then, I might have persisted and set my sites higher. I barely peeked at that place inside me that knows what makes life worth living. Do you know what it's like to die knowing that you didn't do the things that mattered most? That you didn't make a difference… because you weren't really here?"

A newly-retired female executive said: "You know, somewhere along the way we're duped into thinking that if somehow we can bank enough money, we'll have all the time in the world to enjoy our dreams. But I finally realized there's only one promise we'll ever have to keep – the promise to ourselves.

"I lived my life, doing what most people normally do, in order to get what I wanted. Now I realize it wasn't the way to get what I wanted after all. I regret having 'played it safe'. From where I sit, a few failures along the way seem a small entrance fee to the learning curve of a bigger life.

"That's why I told my daughter that there's something special that she is meant to do, and to take the time to figure it out. And if *it* seemed scary, that's just the small part of herself trying to protect her from something that will bring her more happiness than she could ever imagine."

The Mask Is Off

In short, either we make the time to examine our lives, or time takes us. There are only two choices – yes or no. Everything else is just a stage of indecision in between.

You may find it valuable to imagine what it would be like to smoothly evolve into your life's work – with no line of distinction between work and play. To expand within a love life where the balance between the male and female aspects of being allows perfect spiritual love to grow between two people. This is being re-connected to your center.

Our brand of "socialization" has created the only species on earth plagued by chronic stress disorders. I wonder if you could imagine letting go of your "to do" list and merging into an awareness of how you direct your energy, rather than spend your time? One might, you know, become less stressed *and* more productive, even lead a more meaningful life – at work *and* at home.

How would it feel if you reclaimed authorship of your life? To help you imagine this, see yourself rewriting the parts that no longer serve you. Delete those nasty balloon-popping people and places that have misdirected your internal compass of authenticity. Scour the corners for the gremlins that cause you to doubt that you deserve to realize your dreams – that assault your sense of worth, hiding just to dupe you into sleep walking through life.

Maybe you'll dream tonight of new ways to untangle yourself from the editorial board of your mind. Maybe you'll wake up and see clearly that you've had it right all along, from the moment you arrived. That you've suffered only a temporary blindness and just forgot that you already knew.

Don't wake up too quickly. Maybe you'll see why people suffer in the first place. Maybe you'll come to understand that sometimes when the answer goes over your head, you have to look above for it. Or maybe you'll continue to resist the epiphany of thousands before you – that suffering is all part of a plan, a plan much larger that any of us can see. That maybe we go through the pain to make it a greater journey home.

As an expert witness of what it truly means to be human, I will leave you with the one thing I do know for sure – that the ultimate goal in life is to finally be at home with yourself. Because when you're truly who you're meant to be, there is no more struggle. Just as a butterfly no longer struggles within the confines of its cocoon. It's the ultimate freedom for which you have yearned.

Maybe you'll direct some time to answer the immortal question: "If not now, when? If not you, who?"

Maybe then... you'll commit to being the fullest expression of who you are.

You now have permission to play your grandest story, as if no one is watching. So be it.

© *Dawn M. Holman 2003*

Dawn has touched the lives of millions as producer of an international award-winning audio series on cancer, as author of *There is No THEM* and the forthcoming book *It Takes Two*, and as the co-author of *Fighting Love*. An international keynote speaker and master storyteller, she is also a popular media guest and talk radio host of *For Love & Money*. Dawn invites your contact: *dawn@dawnholman.com* or *619.709.1637*

Walk Your Talk With
Praxis

By Bob Proctor

Goals, tenacity, courage and faith have been and always will be personal qualities required to enjoy any degree of success in your life. The universe operates in perfect harmony! You are living and working in a dynamic global marketplace that leaves little room for error. In future, only those individuals whose beliefs are sound, in harmony with the laws of the universe and integrated with their behavior, will emerge as real winners.

Praxis Power

Praxis is a word that, until now, could be found in the vocabulary of very few people. What the airplane was to travel, what email is to communication, likewise Praxis will become to human development. Praxis has the potential to cause wonderful things to happen in many areas of your life

Praxis is the integration of belief with behavior. When you take time to digest its meaning, you'll realize you're working with a huge idea. Praxis describes the mental-physical state a person is in which causes them to get the results they are getting. A deep understanding of this word will put you in the position to achieve any result you choose.

Are possibility, power and profit within your reach? Absolutely! The position you find yourself in today is without precedent. All of the preceding generations put together never experienced the changes you have already seen in your short lifetime.

Dr. Christopher Hegarty, an international authority on how to adapt to the tremendous changes taking place, tells us, "You can no longer look to the past in an attempt to predict your future. A large part of the present is obsolete and, for most people, much of the future is beyond comprehension." He also mentions that this is the most exciting time in all of human history to be alive, if you have the proper information.

Today, success has become a subject – one that can be studied, understood and enjoyed by anyone. In the past, success was perceived by many as something that was inherited – a lifestyle a very select minority enjoyed. Successful people were generally viewed as being lucky. The beautiful truth is that successful people are not now, nor have they ever been, lucky. This is an orderly universe of which you and I are a part. That order, which is an expression of "Divine Law," leaves no room for luck.

The late Dr. Wernher Von Braun stated, "The laws of this universe are so precise that we have no difficulty building a spaceship, sending people to the moon, and timing the landing with the precision of a fraction of a second." For you to enjoy a successful, well-balanced life in our fast moving world, you must align your mind and body with those laws.

Today, the most advanced educational programs are introducing disciplines that have always been practiced by enlightened individuals, to create this mind-body alignment. The idea is not new. On the contrary, it's ancient. Unfortunately, for many years, these disciplines had become like a lost language. However, clearly understood and properly utilized, the concept of praxis will produce results that will amaze and delight you. Praxis is a mind-body discipline that anyone can learn.

Praxis

Take a moment and mentally play with this word. Praxis means *"the integration of belief with behavior."* When you first run that definition across the screen of your mind, you might be inclined to think that everyone's beliefs are integrated with their behavior. But, that's not correct. And, more often than not, when a person's beliefs *are* integrated with their behavior, those beliefs are false, causing the results to range from bad to disastrous. Then there are many other situations where a person believes something that is sound, but they fail to integrate that belief with behavior. The behavior becomes a physical contradiction to those beliefs. Again, the results are unwanted.

The First Big Lie

There are two ideas that, for the past few decades, have received broad acceptance by a very large segment of the world's population. These two ideas should have been more carefully scrutinized, because they were not true. Many of the people who believed these ideas and integrated them with their behavior lost... and the losses were devastating. Some may never recover.

The first big lie that most people heard early on in life, and accepted as a part of their belief system, has to do with education. We are raised to virtually deify an educational degree. Go to school, earn a degree and you'll get a good job. There are literally thousands of people walking the streets with a degree in hand, and no job. What happened? *Praxis.* These poor souls integrated their belief with their behavior. Unfortunately, they believed a lie. They believed that getting an education was getting a degree. That's not true.

Education comes from the Latin word "Educo," meaning to educe, to develop or draw out from within. Education is about developing your God-given powers. This is demonstrated by what you *do,* not what you *know.* We have been recognizing and rewarding people for what they *know,* not what they *do.* Unfortunately, one lie generally leads to another.

The Second Big Lie

The second big lie that many people believed and integrated with their behavior deals with our work. For decades, corporations worldwide have preached, "You give us loyalty and we will give you security." Like sheep, millions of individuals blindly followed, not thinking, never analyzing the offer being presented. Had a person carefully studied the promise, they would have realized that no company in the world could give a person security, regardless of service or loyalty. Security, real security, comes from within. If you haven't got it there, you haven't got it. When a person gives up freedom for security, they generally end up with neither.

If a person believes there's security in a job and loses that job, he or she is demoralized – feeling everything is lost. Interview any one of the thousands of competent people who are victims of layoffs, down-sizing, right-sizing or re-engineering. They were loyal. They thought they were secure in any one of a thousand large corporations. Ask the people whose severance pay is all gone. See how they feel. Find out how secure they are with the belief they had. Many of these people are resentful, blaming the company. In most cases, the company did the only thing they could in an attempt to stay alive.

Blame is always inappropriate, regardless of how justified you may feel. We are all responsible for where we are and the results we are experiencing. If your results are not to your liking, you should examine your beliefs. Check to see if your beliefs are integrated with your behavior.

The promise corporations made was not viable. Nowadays, companies are still making promises, but the promise has changed. Now they're saying, "You give us performance and we will give you opportunity for growth and development." That is a sound idea. It is in harmony with the laws of the universe. Integrate that belief with your behavior and you *must* win.

What Do You Believe?

Courageously begin to analyze your beliefs, one at a time. Ask yourself if you have sound reasons for each of your beliefs. As you do this, you will find that many of your strongest convictions have absolutely no foundation, and that some of your beliefs are totally absurd. For the most part, many of your beliefs are inherited – you didn't even develop them yourself.

Developing and reviewing your own personal belief system is the most important mental responsibility you have been given. You would be wise to make a written list of your beliefs. Then, step back and look at your list as if it belonged to a stranger. Hopefully you have a good sense of humor because some of what you are going to see will probably be quite comical – at least, that is the conclusion reached by most people who complete this exercise honestly.

The Beautiful Truth

It is well established and clearly documented that you've believed an over abundance of lies with respect to who you are and what you are capable of doing. It's high time that you begin to tap into the beautiful truth that, if you can see it in your head, you can hold it in your hand.

You are a spiritual being and, as such, have potential without limitation. You can improve every aspect of your life until your entire life is an open and obvious expression of your own inner beauty and limitless potential. Happiness, health and prosperity are normal and natural states for you to experience. There should be no room for lack or limitation in your world. The only thing that stands between you and all the good that life can offer is a sound belief system that is in harmony with the laws of the universe. Combine that with the effective use and application of Praxis and you've got a winning combination.

International best-selling author, business consultant and entrepreneur, Bob Proctor follows in the footsteps of such motivational giants as Napoleon Hill and Earl Nightingale, traveling the globe teaching people how to utilize their infinite potential.
Visit *www.bobproctor.com*

Small Steps,

Big Results

By Susan L. Gilbert

Remember the story of the tortoise and the hare? When challenged to a race, the hare was faster, thought he would win, and lost sight of his goal. In the end, it was the tortoise who reached the finish line first with his small and consistent steps.

Whether you are an entrepreneur who "does it all," an employee working specifically in sales, management, marketing, customer service, etc, or a larger company with separate departments and staff for each necessary business function – remember that small steps, done continuously with focus, will pave your golden road to success.

If you could use a more powerful lens through which to see your life, would you use it?

There are stars that have been in existence since the beginning of time, but we have only been able to see them recently through a new and more powerful lens. You can choose to use the powerful lens of focus in your work and in your life to see paths and opportunities you might otherwise miss.

We make choices every day. We can zip around and appear busy, expending a lot of energy like the hare; or, we can map out a course with a navigating tool that will bring more ROI – return on investment – for your time and energy. Knowing how to create goals and follow through on them is placing focus on the outcome and then working backwards. 80% of the things you do account for only 20% of your results. And vise versa.

What is Focus?

Focus is where you place your attention. It is awareness. It is clarity of purpose. When action follows this focus, we create our desired results.

In fact, you are always focusing on something, whether you are aware of it or not. If I spent some time with you, I could tell you what you are focusing on. How? By looking at the results you are getting in your life. The results you get are always the result of your focus.

The problem is this focus is usually not *conscious* focus. It's automatic focus. We unconsciously focus on something we don't want, and then when we get it, we feel like a victim and don't even stop to think that we created it in the first place. What is more, we don't realize we could choose to create something completely different if we could only get out of the cycle of unconsciously focusing on something other than what we want.

Focusing on what you do *not* want, ironically, makes it happen. Focusing on not being poor makes you poor. Focusing on not making mistakes causes you to make mistakes. Focusing on not having a bad relationship creates bad relationships. Focusing on not being depressed makes you depressed. Focusing on not smoking makes you want to smoke. And so on. I think you get the idea.

The only thing you have total and complete control over is your own mind, your own thoughts and the way you communicate these thoughts. The words you use when you are communicating is a dead giveaway for what you are really thinking.

Luckily, This One Thing — Your Mind That You Do Have Control Over Gives You Tremendous Power.

Remember, *The Land of I Can* states, "The Power is in the knowing." Know that you have the power to focus your attention and your thoughts and therefore achieve the results you desire.

Athletes understand focus. They imagine the shot, feel the movement, and focus on the results *before* they act. They *know* this works. We as individuals, business people, or employees can do this, too.

On November 15, 1993, Dr. Tom Amberry made 2,750 consecutive free throws and stopped without a miss. He was seventy-two years old at the time and had only been practicing for a year and a half. Dr. Amberry wasn't a trained athlete, nor did he want to become one. He did this to demonstrate the power of focus and concentration. Most of the time, for most people, all the focusing and thinking is going by at warp speed, on automatic, without much, if any, conscious intention. Your job is to learn how to direct this power by consciously directing your focus to the *outcomes* you want. If Dr. Amberry can do this, you can, too.

When faced with a particular action or decision, it is ideal to learn to narrow focus for that one desired outcome and widen focus in-between. By practicing in one minute increments, you are re-training the way your mind auto-focuses.

Let's use a typical dilemma some of you who are employees might face: If you want the day off, and your boss thinks you need to be in the office, staying focused on the outcome and creating a win/win solution is the only way you will create the desired results. Desired results that have you both feeling like winners.

You know your boss will want you to work that day, and from his perspective, you understand why. He's on a deadline. You also know that you would love to spend a day with a high school friend you haven't seen in twenty years and who is in town just this one day. Bartering with why your needs are more important than those of your boss is not focusing on the thoughts, the words, the action needed to create your desired outcome.

Focus on creating a solution that will work – a way to create a win/win, acknowledging each party's needs. Go into the discussion understanding that the other person involved in the decision has a valid reason for his or her position. Remove emotions from past interactions. Stay away from concern or fears about the outcome. Focus on resolution. Stay present on a common goal that serves both of you. Could you stay late the night before and come in early to complete the project? Could you complete the work at home and deliver it to the office first thing before picking up your friend at the airport? Focus on achieving a solution that serves both of you. Focus not for an entire 24 hours, but for 60 seconds – one minute – when it really counts.

Apply Focus to Any Endeavor.

If you work in customer service, focus on your desired results – customer satisfaction. This is your focus, not just "taking the call." Choose your desired outcome and work backwards to determine the steps you can take to create a satisfied customer. Then focus.

Focus also diminishes procrastination. Our tendency to put off important steps falls away when we are focused on their importance in reaching our goal. In fact, procrastination loses its negative connotation when we learn to procrastinate the less important steps in order to focus on the critical 20%.

Procrastination becomes essential to your success when you learn to procrastinate the "time thieves."

Awareness is Really the Partner of Focusing.

Imagine when you are focusing that you are wearing blinders. As you begin your project or enter into a critical conversation, narrow your blinders to focus only on your desired outcome. The blinders should shut out both internal and external distractions. Afterward, widen the blinders to sustain energy. Repeat this over and over for the duration of your day. As you practice concentrating on those outcomes that you desire in small increments, you are re-training yourself to think differently. You are intentionally choosing your thoughts. This is the power of intention magnified by focus. The result you desire will unfold. Trust this.

Practice Focus. One Minute at a Time.

You are taking small steps to improve your focus and you will reap big results.

Susan L. Gilbert, Copyright 2003

Susan L. Gilbert is a Focus Expert. She teaches a new edge on basic business principles using imagination and focus to create more opportunities and make wiser business decisions. Author of the award-winning book *The Land of I Can*, Susan is a widely quoted expert in the business world. Her keynotes are motivating yet results-oriented and her mentoring is available to both individuals and companies.
www.susangilbert.com

A Powerful Path

to
Success and Fulfillment

By Jay Aaron

Four Key Qualities:
Purpose. Mission. Passion. Vision.

Do you want to do something great? Do you want to make a difference? Here is what you need:

1. A sense of purpose about who you are and what you do.
2. A clear vision of the future you intend to create.
3. An unstoppable sense of mission.
4. A passion in your life, your words, and your actions.

Purpose is the *foundation* from which actions and results flow. Mission is the *fuel*. Passion is the *energy* – the *thrust* that propels actions toward the attainment of the *desired future* – the Vision.

Ghandi embodied all of these qualities. His purpose was definite – to free India from outside rule and return self-government and freedom to the people of his beloved country. He had a clear vision of the India that "could be," and communicated his vision so that anyone could understand it. Ghandi was clearly on a mission to bring this vision into reality through non-violent means during his own lifetime. His total dedication to achieving this vision – his passion – was so strong that it inspired a nation of people to make a symbolic march to the sea which ultimately changed the fate of the Indian people.

Purpose

Purpose is "the reason for which something exists." It is the heart of the matter. Purpose is what we are here for, the foundation upon which an organization, business or project rests.

The Burnham Rosen Group states that a clear purpose answers the question – "What will make [me/us] proud?" and therefore represents the "best values" of an individual or group. "A purpose serves to imbue life and work with meaning." You can use it to "identify priorities, resolve conflicts, and create momentum."

One friend's purpose is "to create music that touches people's hearts and souls." Another says that his purpose is, simply, "to love and be loved."

Habitat for Humanity's organizational purpose is "to bring families and communities in need together with volunteers and resources to build decent, affordable housing." British Columbia's *New Society Books'* business purpose is "to publish books that contribute in fundamental ways to building an ecologically sustainable and just society."

Mission

Mission is a task or aim that you believe you are honor-bound to carry out. Out of this sense of duty, you attach special importance to a mission, and devote special care to its fulfillment. Mission implies a sense of urgency.

When you or an organization is on a mission, an uncompromising sense of dedication expresses itself as zeal. Being on a mission is very attractive, because it energizes and focuses us, and every achievement is an opportunity for celebration.

In the movie *The Blues Brothers*, Jake and Elwood are "on a mission" to save their childhood school. My neighbor is often on a mission to find the freshest foods for her next meal. Nothing will stop her from visiting every farmer's market and organic grocery for miles around when she is intent on getting exactly the right ingredients.

Mark Victor Hansen and Robert Allen are currently on a mission to create "enlightened millionaires." About.com is on a mission to provide "the most human online experience" to people seeking information on the Internet.

Passion

Passion is the coupling of an "intense emotion" with "a keen interest." Sometimes this emotion might be *joy*, in relationship to something you *love* to do. However, passion can also arise from other emotions. *Intense grief* over their children's deaths coupled with a *burning desire* to help others launched the founders of Mothers Against Drunk Driving on their mission.

I am passionate about entrepreneurship, and helping entrepreneurs, businesses, and organizations to think big, to think "outside the box," and to develop multiple, residual income streams. I am passionate about nature and wild places, and the need for their preservation. I am passionate about making the world a better place for those who follow.

The staff, volunteers and members of the non-profit organization *Trust for Public Land* are passionate about "preserving land for people." The people who own and work for the online for-profit company eBay are passionate about helping buyers and sellers worldwide get together for each other's mutual benefit.

Vision

Vision is an *anticipation* of future events and experiences. Your vision describes the world (through all the senses) as it will be when your desired outcome is fully achieved.

Clear visions use expressed timeframes as reference. Companies, organizations, and projects sometimes have visions as short as weeks, months or years. Some Asian companies have 100-year visions. Certain Native American peoples envision the world in even longer periods, asking themselves how their actions today will impact the seventh unborn generation.

Having a vision has several significant benefits. A compelling vision galvanizes the whole – the whole person, organization, project, company, nation, or even the world. When President John F. Kennedy declared his vision that America would put someone on the moon within a decade, the whole nation became cheerleaders or participants in this cause.

Without a vision you are often like a ship without a destination – undirected, at the mercy of the prevailing winds. The media and popular culture – and all of the negativity and cynicism they project – can cause you to feel troubled and out of control. The universal "law of attraction" states that whatever you put your attention on, you experience more of. So having a clear, powerful, positive vision is an antidote to negativity. It gives you hope, compels you to move forward, and makes it easy to dispel energies and obstacles that stand in the way.

To paraphrase Stephen Covey: "Begin with the end in mind." Goethe wrote: "Whatever you can do, or dream, begin it. Boldness has genius, power and magic in it." Having a powerful vision is often all that is needed for the ways and means to reveal themselves to you.

The vision is not a goal. Vision is the "master goal." Vision is about the whole, the total achievement. Many people or groups may work on related tasks and focus on achieving many smaller goals which together result in the vision being realized.

Alignment

Purpose, Mission and Vision are qualities that individuals, organizations and projects can display. Passion, however, is a uniquely human quality. Individuals and groups can bring the passion that is necessary to drive organizations and projects to turn their visions into reality.

A start-up commercial airline, for instance, might have as its purpose "to provide enjoyment to travelers while flying them safely." This company may be on a mission "to become – and remain – the most highly rated customer-service airline in the U.S." The company's vision might be "to become, within five years, the airline against which all others are judged." With these working in harmony, all of their choices and actions will reflect their desires and be designed to attain their vision most easily.

Still, no matter how clear these are, it takes the dedication of people fueled by their passion – their belief that their participation is valued and is contributing to a purpose, mission and vision with which they agree – to bring it all to fruition. A great deal of power springs from aligning passionate people with organizations or projects that reflect their purposes, missions and visions. The synergy that is generated by such alignment (where $1 + 1 = 11$, instead of just 2) results in faster, greater achievements.

The alignment of people and the projects in which they are engaged also leads to much joy for employees and participants. Marsha Sinetar's directive, "Do what you love, the money will follow," is about the enormous power you generate when you bring your passions, mission, purpose, and vision to your own business or project.

Purpose, Mission, and Vision "Statements"

Purpose, mission or vision "statements" are quite popular, yet often misunderstood.

An individual's or company's "mission statement" may instead be simply a compilation of desired goals, with no true mission stated clearly. Or a "vision statement" may instead refer to a sense of purpose, but say nothing about a desired future.

This is not criticism of the value of existing statements. Instead, it is a call to greater awareness about how all of these qualities are essential to each other and to the whole. The most successful and fulfilled individuals, organizations and projects equally embrace purpose, mission and vision. They use them in harmony and are propelled by the passion of the individuals involved.

Use this article as a guide to review and edit – or create – a document that includes your unique individual, company, or organizational purpose, mission and vision. Then set out on a passionate course to bring these into reality. You, others, and the world at large will be better for it.

Jay Aaron, M.A. is an author, speaker, consultant and coach. He is C.E.O. of Aaron Enterprises, dedicated to helping individuals, companies, and organizations achieve powerful and fulfilling results.
Web site/"New Thoughts" e-zine: *www.jayaaron.com*
email: *mentorsmag@jayaaron.com*
(Article © 2003, Aaron Enterprises)

How to Make Improvements in Any and Every Area of Your Life:

The Continuous Improvement (Kaizen) Approach

By Joanne Mansell, Kaizen Coaching

Let me ask you something... If you could have, do or be anything – what would it be? What areas of your life do you want to improve? For most of us these fall into a handful of categories:

- Family/Relationship
- Health and Fitness
- Business/Career
- Financial
- Social
- Spiritual and Mental Growth

Before you answer, consider how much your life and your future mean to you – this is your *life* we are talking about! Really think. What do you *want*? To put it another way, "What is success to you?" Bob Proctor uses Earl Nightingale's definition "Success is the progressive realization of a worthy ideal."

Dream big. Paint a huge image in full color and detail of what you would have if time, money and other perceived obstacles ceased to exist. Hear it in full surround-sound stereo! Allow yourself to feel it within you – is it joy, satisfaction, love, energy, enthusiasm? What are the feelings outside yourself? If you want a house by the beach be sure to add the feel (and smell) of salty air on your skin to the pictures and sounds of beach living.

People call me the "Kaizen Coach" because I am so passionate about Kaizen – the Japanese philosophy of Continuous Improvement. In *Building an Extraordinary Business,* I explained Kaizen as one of the best ways to build success:

A useful analogy can be found in constructing a house. You build a house on solid foundations, one brick at a time, improving the structure until you have created the house you want.

This Concept of Kaizen Relates to Your Life in Two Main Ways:

1. *Your habits.* Each step taken toward your goal matters. Each time you do something to help achieve your objective, it improves your "fitness" and moves you closer to what you want. The progress may appear

insignificant, yet each part is necessary to create the whole. Enough small steps will cover even the greatest distance. You will find that, over many years, what you achieve will be awe-inspiring.

2. *Effect over time.* What appears to be a small or even insignificant shift in the beginning can yield large results over time. A one-degree shift in direction doesn't matter much from here to the doorway, but from a harbor or airport, one degree over thousands of miles dramatically changes where you end up. The same principle applies to your goals. If you make a small shift or change in the beginning, the results may take time to become visible, whether you are talking about your body or your business.

How to Implement Kaizen

I believe that commitment is the only barrier. For you to *really* implement Kaizen you must *want* to change your life now I will give you a few ideas on implementing Kaizen. Keep it simple and keep doing it consistently! Some examples:

Family/Relationship

- Get home early enough one night a week to read a bedtime story to the children.
- Take the time to say good-bye to your spouse with meaningful eye contact and a hug, instead of running out the door and calling "Bye. See you tonight."
- Have a date once a week or once a month where you spend quality time together.
- Sit together each night and discuss your day. Better yet, talk on a walk around the block so you get some fresh air and exercise as well.

Health and Fitness

- It can be overwhelming and feel impossible to "cut out" something for "the rest of your life." Instead, work on small improvements that will create enough difference in how you feel to keep the momentum going. Allow yourself a day a week off your diet or exercise program so you are less likely to have binges or give up on the program.
- Since we know we "should" be drinking 8-10 glasses of water a day but find it very hard, start with one extra glass.
- Eat an extra piece of fruit or serving of vegetables. Introduce a meal or two of raw fruit and vegetables into your diet each week.
- Drink less alcohol.
- If you don't want to join a gym, go for a walk around the block each day. Take your spouse or a friend with you!
- Introduce "incidental exercise" by taking the stairs rather than the elevator, getting off the bus a stop earlier, or choosing a parking space further from the shops.

Business/Career

- Read journals or magazines to keep you current in your field.
- Spend time with a mentor to "learn the ropes."
- Invest time to plan your day so you work smarter not harder.
- Make one extra sales call a day, or write some extra prospecting letters each week.
- Do some research about launching a new career, business or a change in focus.

Financial

- Create a savings plan. As it says in *Richest Man in Babylon* "Pay yourself first."
- Create an abundance mentality by making regular contributions to a charity.
- Enlist experts to help clarify your financial goals.

Social

- Go to social events weekly or fortnightly such as movies or dinner with friends.
- Join a club or take classes to pursue an interest you have always had such as photography or writing.
- Join a gym – you will meet great people and get fit as well!
- Find a buddy to exercise with you. Having someone waiting for you to walk or cycle keeps you moving towards your goals.

Spiritual and Mental Growth

- Take a few minutes each week (or day) to relax and meditate.
- Read your goals at least once a day.
- Set aside time to read books that will help you grow and enrich your life.
- Strive to learn new things each day.
- Spend time feeling grateful for the things you enjoy in your life.

What else will help? Support, strategies and motivation. Often these three come from one or more coaches or mentors.

Support: Find someone to help you through rough patches. Find a coach, mentor, spouse or friend who will "be there for you" and believe in you.

Strategies: Find someone who has "been there." "Modeling" is a great strategy. Copy the techniques, thoughts and approach of someone who is a master at the skill, and adapt them to suit you and your circumstances.

Motivation: Remember to connect with your goals in terms of all your senses: what it looks, sounds, and feels like. What else can you do to stay motivated? What rewards can you give yourself? What motivation tools can you use?

Another of my favorite concepts comes from Anthony Robbins. He talks about taking "Massive Action." In *Awaken the Giant Within* he also talks about Kaizen which complements his ideas. He calls it CANI (constant and never ending improvement) and says, "Small improvements are believable and therefore achievable." To change, if you feel overwhelmed by the idea of Massive Action, perhaps you can break up the tasks into more manageable pieces and then move to take a few actions, consistently. These approaches fit together very well and are fundamental to achieving outstanding results.

Imagine someone who is overweight and wants to change, starting right now. Massive action would be to go through the house and dispose of all the high fat, high sugar "junk" foods. Kaizen would be to make sure that the food bought in the future has high water, low fat, and low sugar content, providing energy and vitality. Massive action might be to go for a long walk. This needs to be backed up by the sustainable actions of Kaizen – to keep walking or exercising consistently.

A friend of mine is an executive coach. He explains Kaizen as "a just – noticeable difference." Maybe that term works better for you. Whether you choose to call it Kaizen, CANI or "a just noticeable difference," make sure you do it! The kaizen approach is to start with one thing today that will make a difference to your life. Then add another thing tomorrow or next week – be faithful about adding small and consistent steps that lead you in the direction you want to go. Make this an unconscious as well as a conscious habit.

Why Your Success Depends on Implementing This Approach

If you improve 5% per month, that is 80% in a year or 220% in two years! It compounds because the improvement becomes part of the new target and builds on itself. Albert Einstein said the greatest mathematical principle was "compound interest." This shows that the most powerful principle for personal development is to apply Kaizen.

If you make a 1% increase or improvement in something every day of the year, at the end of the year you have a 3740% increase. This improvement is 37 times your starting point. Now that is truly massive action!

So, pick the term that works best for you – Kaizen, CANI or "a just – noticeable difference." It does not matter what you call it – only that you implement it! In the end, the difference is you.

Joanne Mansell, Kaizen Coaching... Mind, Body, Life Fitness®
Co-author *Building an Extraordinary Business*™
Life Coaching, Business Coaching, Sportsmind®
Phone +61 0416 181 654 Fax +61 2 9412 3109
Email: *Joanne@kaizencoaching.com.au* to book your complimentary session!
For more articles see *www.kaizencoaching.com.au*.

Pay Attention to

Traffic Lights

By Louise Griffith

The time is now to let your light shine. Our world needs what you have to offer. When you honor the wisdom within you and step into your personal power, you appear in the world as the authentic and courageous person you are. Others will be drawn to you because of your vibrancy and passion for life. Are you ready to be all that you can be?

Can you remember learning to drive a car? Do you still recall the day you slipped behind the wheel, having passed the exam? Perhaps you felt both fear and excitement. The day had come. You had done it! You were in charge. With keys in hand and gas in the tank, you triumphantly turned on the ignition. As you drove off on your own for the first time, you may have heard some final words of advice, "Keep your hands on the wheel, don't drive too fast, and pay attention to traffic lights."

Letting your light shine is somewhat like driving a car for the first time. You conquer your fears, empower yourself, and move forward to greet life. This feeling of success propels you into the next moment. What would your world be like if you experienced this feeling of exhilaration on a daily basis? Consider the positive impact in your relationships with others and with yourself as you view life through this lens.

In the Metaphoric World of Traffic Lights, You Know "Red" Means "Stop."

As you think back, what stopped you from pursuing your dreams? Was it choosing to be mediocre instead of successful, complacent rather than proactive, or was it a fear of failure? Fear is a powerful negative force that can keep you from becoming all that you can be.

Each person lives with fears unique to his or her life experience. Some people fear not being good enough, while others fear being too powerful. Some people fear not doing it right, while others fear being too successful. The list can go on with extremes going in negative or positive directions. How you think determines your life. These thoughts can connect you to your inner wisdom or they can disconnect you from your personal power. Train yourself to listen to your wisdom rather than your fears. Don't go through life on cruise control. Navigate with intention. Conquer fear with a plan of action. You hold the keys to transformation.

Change begins with awareness. A successful plan combines the knowledge of what is no longer serving you with a vision of what you would like to create in your life. Sometimes, you ask people you trust to support you in ways that will be helpful. Other times, you step out in faith believing that even though you don't know all the details, things will work out, perhaps better than you may have imagined. Faith is a type of knowing and trusting that brings you peace and courage when you need it.

Pay Attention to the Traffic Lights in Life.

You can do this by listening to your internal dialogue, commonly known as "self-talk." These messages impact the way you see yourself and interact with others. Choose to live your life consciously, learning when to stop destructive thought patterns and relationships that diminish who you are. Be proud of who you are and what you know.

There are many warning signs along the road in life, which can help us navigate the path ahead. Sometimes when the light turns yellow, we speed up. Other times, we slow down. Good drivers execute caution and pay attention.

What signals in your life are you looking at and which ones are you choosing to ignore? Many people have issues involving self-worth, elements of stress, or confusion regarding one's life purpose. Pausing allows you moments for quiet reflection. When you consider the quality of your life, the relationships you hold sacred, and your passions for living, you consider options to move you forward. Remember that you are in the driver's seat. You are the one who chooses to use the gas pedal or the brakes.

Many people are living with internal scripts that were written for them by others. Who told you what you could or could not do? Was it a family member, a teacher, or a peer? Perhaps you heard messages that impacted you in a powerful but negative way, such as: " Can't you ever do anything right?" "Don't get a big head." " You'll never amount to anything." Those messages were a reflection of the person speaking them and not about you. However, many believed the messages. They incorporated them into their life script and have been living life as though those messages were true.

Today cars rely on the efficiency of computers to run more smoothly. You can figuratively apply the editing features of a computer to your life's script. "Cut, paste and delete " are just a few of the tools we have all become familiar with in our technological world. Use them in the real world of authoring and editing your life. You can accept the script you were given or change it. You decide. You can rewrite your own script and value yourself as the shining light you are.

An elementary teacher told Einstein that he wasn't bright, he wasn't good at math, and he wouldn't amount to anything. Can you imagine our world without the contributions Einstein made? Elvis Presley was told in high school he was not a good singer and should not try to pursue his goal of singing on stage. Whether or not you believe he was a gifted musician, you probably agree that he made an impact that changed the world of music forever. Oprah Winfrey was pulled off her job as a co-anchor for the evening news at WJZ-TV in Baltimore because she didn't fit the profile others had created for success. She didn't let that stop her. She believed in herself. Oprah continues to be a bright, shining light in the world. All three people recognized the traffic lights and acknowledged them. They decided to trust their internal sensors and not be stopped by other's opinions.

When you edit your script, refuse to be negatively impacted by what you have experienced. Discover the courage to create a life you love. Understand that this new way of living will present you with many choices. Become aware of opportunities as they arise. Live life by choice and not chance.

Circumstances in Life Can Put Us in the Pause Mode.

Perhaps you are in one now. Consider your options. Is it best to stay in idle or shift into gear? Remember you are in the driver's seat. You can also choose the time to move. Only you can make it happen.

Take time each day to be grateful for the blessings you already have. Gratitude is an excellent habit to form and one that will serve you well. It's important to acknowledge the circumstances in your life, be they discouraging or uplifting. By doing so, you stay connected to the present moment. Gratitude can connect you to joy.

A "Green" Light Means "Go!"

It's time to honor the person you really are. It's time to stop pretending that you are less of a person than you are. You are more than enough. You have the resources inside you to be all you want to be. You can pursue your dreams. You can take courageous risks, embracing challenges along the way. Decide you are worth it. Begin living from this truth. You can create your life story and fill it with joy, wisdom and love. Be conscious of your choices. Move forward with intention.

Since you have the power and opportunity to choose your path in life, create some excitement and enjoyment. Although you cannot predict or choose the traffic lights you will encounter in life, you can choose creative responses.

These keys will take you where you want to go:
- Take time for reflection
- Write your own life script
- Conquer your fears with a plan of action
- Replace negative self-talk with positive self-talk
- Practice gratitude
- Celebrate who you are

Of Course You'll Hit Some Stoplights Along the Way.

You may even take a detour once in a while. However, you are still behind the wheel and in control. The time is now to let your light shine. Be confident and authentic. The world waits for you and the gifts and strengths you bring. Deal with the stops that hold you back, pause often, and accelerate ahead into the life you have created. Above all, enjoy the drive!

International speaker, success coach and licensed psychologist Louise Griffith helps people ignite their passions into action. She can be reached through her web site: *www.OneShiningLight.com*, by email at *Louise@OneShiningLight.com*, or by calling *952-435-5656*.

20/20 Foresight from 20/20 Hindsight:

If Only I would have known...

By Wendy Robbins

Who else wants to be a millionaire? I've made millions. As it turned out, misplaced trust in a deceptive associate disguised as a "mentor" became my greatest treasure.

Who are you when confronted with someone wanting what you have and willing to do anything to take it away from you? Who are you when you're lied to, betrayed, and must confront greed? Do you hate, resent, blame, judge, defend, and/or shut down? Where does your faith take you?

Those are choices usually made in reaction to circumstance. It's easy to make sense of shutting down, especially when a "friend" betrays trust. It's a stretch to be compassionate when you feel destroyed. We're told, "It's just business. That's typical." I think that's garbage. How we do anything is how we do everything.

Rape Isn't Sex

For over a year I blamed my associate and chose the victim role. How grateful I am to have come full circle. It's not the size of the problem – it's the size of me. I'm now bigger then my problems. Painful lessons, tests, and challenges are profound when a dark teacher tests your ability to trust, forgive and learn about discernment. I now feel compassion for this lonely liar.

For a long time I angrily asked, "Why did he betray us?" "Why did he lie?" Then standing before a mirror, I reflected on the reverse. I asked better questions. Where do I betray myself and others? Why do I believe in scarcity instead of abundance? Why am I so afraid that I don't trust? When do I lie to get what I want and justify it as though that makes it right? Why is this disgusting person in my life as my teacher and my reflection? Why even now do I judge him?

For a while, I told myself "He's bad; not me, I didn't do anything. I've been wronged." Then after holding on to the hate and separation, I finally "got it" that we are one. If you haven't experienced that fully, then the concept will be just an idea. When you come to experience everyone as your teacher, guide, mirror, a part of yourself... when you identify with "your enemy's" pain, fear, loneliness, shyness, lack of self-esteem, neurosis, anger, hurt, as yours. Then you will know compassion. You will change dramatically with this one understanding.

The truth is that we are stories, and fragrance upon bones. We're dancing molecules made up of every story ever told. Scientifically and spiritually, we are made up of the same stuff as the ones we call our enemy. How can I make war with myself? Yet we do. We rationalize and accept it. We don't love what is. We fight what is. We commit to suffering, pain, and separation as though these things are a healthy state of being.

We are Born Pure, Passionate, Loving, and Compassionate

So when did we stop acknowledging our magnificence and allow our inner flame to sputter and deaden the light in our eyes? Why do we now hide that child-like wonder of the one inside that loves because it doesn't know any other way?

When did we start believing that contraction of self was better than expansion of self? Why have we shriveled into little, tight, fearful places rather than claim what is rightfully ours? We are nothing and we are everything. We are the sculptors of matter, instant manifestors, and naked creators all abundant and pure. Yet, when did we forget?

When did we start defending our small, small, small selves and say "This is enough" in monotone voices? "This is all I deserve." "Who am I to..?" When did "I'm not worthy" become words worth believing?

When did Childhood Dreams Disappear?

When did innocence grow up and wear lipstick or a tie? What has it cost us? Why do we forget who we truly are and buy into the story that makes us feel less than we are and defend wearing a face of resignation, defeat or cynicism? We medicate and pretend all is well, despite the pandemic of prescription drugs in America for depression and anxiety!

Sure, lots of us are "successful, wealthy, admired." We put on a believable show terrified at times of being found out. "I'm literally worth millions, so why don't I fully feel worthy?"

Where are our inner children – the ones before the painful stories took hold and choked our joy, leaving us with tell-tale lives as a victim. We are not victims. We are not entitled to be victims. We are powerful, masterful, passionate, kind, giving, trusting people. Those words are the costumes that my bones choose to wear. It's all a masquerade, an illusion, a dream, this life of ours. I like the silky, velvety skin called passion – masterful, powerful, kind, giving, and trusting – touching and seducing potential into my life.

When you take your last breath, will you care about the money? How much you have worked? How clever you were? Who betrayed you? Or, will you focus on how much you gave? How much you served? How much you loved? Did you make a difference? Is the world a better place because you were in it?

Are you an angel on earth or just another human – surviving, telling bitter, sad stories, playing the victim because it's so easy to judge and blame? It's more difficult to take responsibility, isn't it? Or is it? This life, this dream is full of stories. Are they inspiring, uplifting, motivating and full of life, gratitude, and laughter? Or are you pretending? Looking good? Caring about what others think? Defending? Making excuses? Judging? Are you authentic? How many masks do you wear? Are the layers so thick you can't distinguish who you really are and who is lying?

When did Someone's Distorted Story About You Become Your Truth?

When did you allow it to make you feel inferior, unworthy, powerless or passionless? Like me, you may not remember the circumstance, name or face of half the people who hurt you so long ago. So why trust them more than your own beloved self? This miserable stuck state is not the way the game must be played. If you think it is, that's laughable in a heartbreaking, way. If misery is your truth, then why bother defending it?

Do you write yourself love letters? Where is the spark? Where is the Martin Luther King, Mother Teresa, Buddha, and Christ within us all? Why do we forget?

If this is all just a play of consciousness then we write the words, invent the circumstances, stories, and soundtrack. How predictable is the tale we are creating? Or how evolved, exciting, memorable is your life?

If you had six months to live, what would you do with your life? What if you had a week? A day? This day? An hour? A minute? This minute? You can choose to skim over the words, or really take them into self-inquiry.

Quiet your mind. Close your eyes. Ask the questions. Listen to the answers. Write them down.

It's Just a Shift, Friends. Direction vs. Misdirection

You are not the ghost of the dead. You are one word away from shifting consciousness. You are…You are…What is the word you are looking for? You are alive.You are perfect. You are aware. Here's the truth: if you don't believe it, you won't be. If you do, you will. Simple. Surrender. Live.

Some of us believe the lies. It is merely a test to see the truth. Everything around us is a miracle! Why worry about your next breath, or wonder if you truly deserve to take one more? It's all a game. A test! Who will remember who they truly are and who will live as a faded streak – a blur, a blob – one who doesn't matter? Who will take? Who will give? Who will care? Wake up. If you complain, become cynical, resigned or negative, what can you possibly contribute to others? What hurt your heart so much that you've shut down your ability to give and to receive?

We're Here For a Short Time

We're here for a short time. It will be over and all that you'll care about in your last breaths is how much you loved and were loved - it's not a mystery. Why wait till you are gasping? Take the breaths now, and be new with each one. We are the love that passes all understanding. Love and be loved. Your legacy is to Be the bestower of bliss. Angels on earth all of us: remember. Wake up. You are a chemist in the laboratory of the Infinite. What will you create?

Wendy Robbins and Jorli McLain created a multi-million dollar business selling "The Tingler®"– their patented head massager distributed in 3,500 stores and top catalogs world-wide. *Everythingforlove.com* receives 1.4 million hits a month and attracts major media attention. Within 14 months they will become a $10,000,000 company committed to people's wealth. they are the creators of *"DON'T MESS WITH ME – THIS AIN'T MY FIRST RODEO"* Club (a subscription-based service, best of 20/20 foresight from 20/20 hindsight) and they speak nationwide to "Tingle the World!" Contact them through: *thetingler@earthlink.net* or *310 288 1519* or email *wendy@everythingforlove.com*.

The Last Mile:
How to Create an Unlimited Life and Ignite Your Own Economic Boom!
By David Adlard

When most people think of the term "last mile," one of two scenarios usually comes to mind. In athletics, marathon runners face the challenge of running 20-, 30-, or even 50 mile stretches. As a high school and college wrestler, I remember the five- and ten- mile runs that were a part of my daily routine. I reflect back to the beginning of every season during what I call the "weeding out" process. For many, the first five-mile run was just too much to endure and the thought of repeating the process daily was unimaginable. Even for some of those who were in relatively good shape, the last mile had to be walked. I remember with vivid detail the muscle aches, the shortness of breath, and the beads of sweat running down my brow. That last mile was something.

If you're not an athlete or you can't relate to that definition, maybe you're more familiar with technological terms. I remember three or four years ago when I was trying to get a high-speed Internet connection installed at my office. I kept being told that I was too far from the "the hub." The "last mile" refers to the space between your computer and the closest main on-ramp to the Internet (or hub). If you live in a small residential or rural area, chances are you still can't get high-speed access unless you use some sort of wireless connection. In this current "information age," trying to do business or reap the full benefit from the Internet with a dial-up connection is like trying to harvest acres of wheat with a set of cutting shears instead of a combine.

No matter what definition you use, the "last mile" is almost always the difference between mediocrity and greatness. Inside each and every one of us (and within each and every organization) there are inevitable "stopping points." Personally, we face different stopping points in various aspects of our lives – marriages that are just "OK" instead of exquisite, relationships with family that are fair instead of joy-full, and financial situations that demonstrate lack instead of abundance. No matter what the situation, we all either consciously or unconsciously reach these last mile markers in our lives and fail to claim the prize that is our birthright.

Now I know what most people will be thinking at this point. Their minds, maybe even yours, are already starting to exhibit the number one symptom of failure's disease ... excuses. I call it the "Yeah-but syndrome." "Yeah, but my wife and I are too different," or "Yeah, but my boss doesn't understand or appreciate me," or maybe, "Yeah, but I don't have the money to start my own business." Or this one is always popular, "Yeah, but I don't have the time." Yeah but, yeah but, yeah but. Yeah, but what about the top two percent? What about the people that *do* have the great relationships? What about those folks that are living abundant lives on every level? What makes them different? The simple answer is that they have learned how to run their last mile. They are doing it every day... and so can you.

The first thing that you must understand is that most folks are programmed for failure. It doesn't happen quickly. It starts when we are kids and happens slowly over time. Everything your parents taught you about money and financial independence is probably wrong. If they are living abundant lives and are financially independent, then there is a chance I am wrong. But, for 98 percent of you, I will be right on the money (excuse the pun).

I Love the Discovery Channel.

You can learn a lot about life, especially about programming from the various creatures our Creator has put on this earth. There's a little desert-dwelling animal called a sand wasp that has an interesting habit. The sand wasp is programmed to always check out its burrow before it enters and to look around inside the burrow for anything dangerous. After finding nothing, the cautious wasp brings the food inside the burrow and begins to eat.

Now, let's suppose we add a human being to the equation. Let's say this human is a few yards away, hiding behind a cactus or a rock. As soon as the sand wasp enters the burrow, our human races over and moves the food a few feet away from the entrance to the burrow, then runs back to his hiding place. The sand wasp comes up and sees the food has been moved. It now pulls the food back over to the edge of the hole and goes back down to double check for danger. The human again runs over and pulls the food away from the hole and returns to his hiding place.

The wasp comes up and sees the food has been moved again. Now the wasp must repeat the laborious task of pulling the food back over to the edge of the hole and going back down to check if there is anything dangerous there. The human again goes over and repositions the food. The wasp again pulls it back to its original position and goes down to check for danger. How long do you think this would continue?

The sad thing is that you can actually do this experiment until the wasp dies. It will repeat the same process over and over and over again until it drops dead from starvation. The sand wasp is a victim of its programs. The human on the other hand is not. He could have quit the little game at anytime. Unfortunately, most people are more like sand wasps than scientists. Many of us just don't use our God-given gift of choice to change our programming. Instead we defend it. We justify and rationalize with words like, "That's just the way I am," or "I'm no good at that," or any number of other excuses.

It's Time to Stop!

We've got to start utilizing what I call "last mile thinking." Choose now to run your last mile and be a   human and not a sand wasp. Let's use our billion dollar brains and let's get them programmed properly. Let's develop an abundance mentality instead of one of scarcity. Let's think *from* our goals and not *about* our goals. We need to focus on solving underlying issues instead of just trying to overcome obstacles. *Focus on the roots, not the fruits.* Then and only then can we break the barriers that hold us back from running the race we were born to run.

Yes, each and every one of you is destined for greatness. Within you lies a blueprint for success that will bring happiness and prosperity beyond your wildest dreams if you will but decide to participate. You see, the last mile is also the first. You must choose to start and you need to start now. Not tomorrow, not next week, not next year. Surround yourself with successful people and let's get started running this thing together!

David Adlard has been a successful entrepreneur for 20+ years. He has owned, operated, bought and sold multiple companies. David is a powerful speaker and a massive marketer as well as the author of *Evolution of the American Dream.* He can be contacted at *816-356-3304* or by email: *info@davidadlard.com* or visit David's Web site at *www.davidadlard.com.*

Uncovering The Hidden
Secret To Success

By Debbie Friedman, C.Ht.

Have you ever arrived somewhere and didn't remember how you got there? Or you missed your exit on the freeway? These occurrences indicate you are operating in a trance-like state where your conscious mind has escaped and your subconscious has taken over. In "highway hypnosis" the conscious mind is overloaded and the subconscious mind takes control of your thoughts and actions.

As a Clinical Hypnotherapist, I've discovered this can hold you back from success. If you haven't cleaned out the "closet" of your subconscious mind, what you think, say, and do is based on old beliefs, ideas, experiences, programming, and limitations.

Here's the great news – there's a solution! Clean out the closet of your mind to get rid of the old stuff that doesn't work and make room for the new!

The "Knowns" That Can Take Over 90% Of Your Life

Your subconscious mind is like a closet storing your life's experiences. Some are positive, some negative. Your subconscious is literal, taking in exactly what it is given, not knowing true from false. Recall having been told "No!" and how it affected your ability to explore your world or express your creativity. Maybe someone told you you didn't deserve to be rich or happy, or you observed life was a struggle. All that was stored in your subconscious and became "knowns" in your belief system, which operates 90% of your life.

Operating on a pleasure-pain principle, a "known" is always pleasurable, even a negative belief that doesn't feel good, because your subconscious knows what to expect when you operate from that belief. Its job is to protect you and help you survive. An unknown is painful, because your subconscious doesn't know the outcome. This is why people stay stuck – they don't like it, but they know what to expect!

Your conscious mind uses logic, reason, and willpower to create change. However, it represents only 10% of your mind. Ideas filter from your conscious mind and are compared with what's in your subconscious. If you make a conscious decision but there is an opposing belief in your subconscious, that decision is rejected and you won't get what you desire!

Remember *what you think leads to what you feel, what you feel leads to the actions you take, and the actions you take determine the results you experience.* As your conscious desires and your subconscious motivations align, you will get more of what you want, you will be in control of your life, and you will be free of the past! By removing blocks to your success, releasing old ideas and beliefs, and gaining freedom from fears, you can fill the space you've created with new, positive experiences to accelerate your success at creating enlightened wealth and abundance.

What's Hiding In Your Closet?

When you look into the closet of your subconscious mind, what do you find? Are you operating from limiting beliefs, responding to situations based on past fearful experiences? Much of your closet may be crammed full of stuff that doesn't even belong to you! Ask yourself: What am I ready to let go of? What do I no longer need? Then get rid of it.

Many tools and techniques are available to guide you in releasing old beliefs. For this article, I will present a few I have found to be most powerful.

1. Identify and Release Your Limiting Beliefs

Take a piece of paper and divide it in half lengthwise. On the left side write your limiting beliefs. Any time you say or think "I can't," "I don't deserve," "It's not going to work," you've identified a limiting belief. If you're not certain what they are, become conscious of what you're saying or thinking during the day. Tape your phone conversations. You may hear these limiting beliefs as "voices" in your head, reminding you of thoughts or ideas that someone told you repeatedly until you believed them.

On the right side of the paper, write a powerful affirmation in the present tense that is the opposite of your limiting belief. For example, if your limiting belief is "I'm not smart enough," your affirmation might be "I am a gifted, talented, intelligent person."

Tear off the left side of the paper. Rip up your limiting beliefs, thank them, and acknowledge that somehow your mind thought they served a purpose and helped protect you. Release them with love, repeating, "I release you. I release you. I release you." Burn the scraps of paper in a safe container, and watch your limiting beliefs disappear. Acknowledge that they are now gone.

Write your affirmations again and place them where you will see them. Say them aloud at least three times a day, especially first thing in the morning and last thing at night.

2. Morning Journaling

The first hour you're awake is a great time to release old stuff your mind has vented in your dreams. Each morning, take five minutes and write whatever comes into your mind. Give the negative, unwanted ideas, thoughts, feelings, and beliefs a place to go.

Fill up two pages. Open to letting all that's been clogging your brain flow out. When you're finished, write at least one affirmation on what you choose to experience that day, and visualize yourself experiencing it with all your senses.

3. Use the Power of Your Subconscious Mind

Hypnosis is a powerful tool for accessing and releasing your subconscious beliefs. It is a gentle process allowing your body and mind to relax so you can focus your attention, bypass the conscious mind filter, and allow the subconscious mind to be receptive to positive suggestions.

Hypnosis has been approved for years as a powerful healing tool and many professional products are available. The recording or book you select should have four parts: a relaxation process for your mind and body; a releasing of the old to create space for the new; a visualization to experience new choices; and affirmations. (All the CDs I produce include all of these.)

You can also use self-hypnosis by recording a tape to have a conversation with your subconscious mind. This will allow you to reinforce the choices of your conscious mind so your subconscious, unconscious, and conscious beliefs become congruent. Write down what you choose to release and bring into mind. Find a place where you won't be disturbed. Take some deep breaths, and feel your body relax. With every in-breath, feel a peaceful relaxation. With every out-breath, let go of anything you don't want or need. Count down from 20 to 0 knowing that with each count you are becoming more relaxed.

The releasing process can take different forms. Choose a scenario such as being bathed in a golden light that washes away doubts and fears. Or see a golden wave of light moving in through the top of your head cleansing and renewing every cell in your body.

Now, visualize what you choose to have with all your senses. Follow this with affirmations such as "I am strong enough," "I am good enough," "I am worthy," and expand them as you become more comfortable with the process. Then, count yourself out from 0 to 5.

Going Shopping For New Things To Fill Your Closet

Once the closet of your mind is clean, you are ready to shop. Discover new ideas and beliefs to support a healthy, positive, wealth-building self-image. Take advantage of the unlimited possibilities for living an inspired, abundant life!

1. Choose

If you're not consciously choosing what you want, your subconscious mind is choosing for you. If you don't like what you're experiencing, make different choices. Choose Happiness. Peace. Financial Freedom. Love. Health. Success.

Choose consciously, consistently, and congruently. Become aware of your choices and thoughts. *What you focus on expands and becomes activated. What you ignore fades away from lack of attention.* Write down what you choose and review your choices throughout the day. If negative feelings come up, thank them, and then ignore them, immediately refocusing on your positive choices.

2. Visualize

Spend time each day visualizing what you choose to have in your life. Make this vision as vivid as you can, and feel, hear, see, taste, touch, smell, and sense what you choose as your reality. Be grateful, accept that it is already present, and be willing to receive. Write a vision of your perfect day, perfect relationship, perfect work, or whatever else you desire, incorporating all your senses on paper.

3. Evening Journaling

Go to bed with powerful, positive thoughts by journaling these four topics before you go to sleep: 10 positive experiences from that day; 10 items to be grateful for; one thing you would do differently; and affirmations to focus on during the night. Your subconscious mind will kick in as you sleep to create more of what you draw to your attention. As you fall asleep, avoid negative thoughts. Instead, allow the major choices for your life to drift through your mind: Love, Success, Financial Freedom, Peace, Compassion, Health, Abundance.

Give yourself permission to live the abundant life you deserve!

Debbie Friedman, C.Ht. is a gifted Certified Clinical Hypnotherapist with more than 20 years in the field of personal growth. She is the creator of the 8-CD series *Cleaning Out the Closet of Your Mind for Wealth.* Debbie may be contacted at *(310) 230-0872* or *www.cleaningoutthecloset.com.*

Talking to Yourself?

Are You on the Road to Success or Driving Yourself Crazy?

By Diane Fontenot

It depends on what you are saying! Has it occurred to you that you are a very important person to talk to? Have you considered the connection between your success and conversations you have with yourself? Have you wondered which conversations are essential to your highest aspirations?

Your answers to these questions have an incredible impact on your life and successes. Your answers become important harbingers of your quality of life.

Without a doubt, the most important person you have conversations with is yourself! Why? Because the impact of your private conversations is profound. *Everything else* depends on what you first say to yourself!

The question becomes "Are you having a profound positive impact on your life - or a profound negative impact on your life?" Learning more about your private conversations and their impact on your life moves you rapidly toward your dreams!

Not sure about that? Let's see! You tell yourself you can do something, *or not*. You tell yourself you want to do something, *or not*. You tell yourself whether you will do something, *or not*. You tell yourself whom to talk with, *or not*. In fact, you tell yourself whom you have the right and the authority to speak with, *or not*. You tell yourself whether you are smart, confident, friendly, caring, *or not*. You tell yourself whether you matter, whether your dreams are possible, and whether you have what it takes, *or not*. In short, you tell yourself what you can and cannot do, whom you can and cannot do it with, and when, where and how you do absolutely everything you do or *do not do* in your life.

Though we understand the value of effective conversations with others in our personal and professional lives, we are often unaware or underestimate the extent to which we are affected by our private conversations!

What Are Our Private Conversations?

Private conversations, in the context created here, refer to the conversations we have with ourselves, whether automatic or intentional, ruminating or actual thinking and planning. Each of these private conversations has a different meaning.

1. Automatic conversations refer to those that just pop into our heads, whether or not we want, like, or agree with them.
2. Rumination refers specifically to automatic conversations that occur over and over and seem to last forever. They are nonproductive, catastrophic, fear-based messages that we participate in again and again.
3. Intentional private conversations, on the other hand, are the conversations we have on purpose! They move us toward self-mastery and our aspirations.
4. Thinking refers specifically to intentional conversations in which we apply knowledge, skills, rules of logic and reasoning, comparison and contrast, to draw conclusions or make decisions.

Private conversations are very important to us. They determine where we focus our attention, including whether we focus on the past, present or future. They help us understand the impact of focusing in different time frames and which is best given our current goals.

Powerful private conversations, conversations aligned with your aspirations, form a Language for Success. The basic premise of your Language for Success is that what you say to yourself matters. It is based on the tenet that you can choose which conversations to pay attention to. While you may not be able to choose every thought that pops into your head at any particular moment, you can notice them, evaluate their usefulness relative to your aspirations, and become more selective. When you master this process, you are then able to design constructive patterns of conversations, your Language for Success.

There are many personal examples of ways that I changed by developing my own Language for Success. I successfully changed my moods, my relationships, my career, and every aspect of my life by gaining a better understanding of the relationship between my private conversations and results in my life. My relationships with my husband, my sons, my parents are better than they were years ago. Once separated and near divorce, I am now happily married to the same person and our marriage is stronger than ever. I have three wonderful sons and a beautiful daughter-in-law, and relationships with all of them that bring great joy to my life! I have a career that I love and look forward to every day of my life!

I was prone to depression, experiencing sadness from out of the blue, getting into a downward spiral of increasing negativity. Now, I not only limit conversations that contribute to such negativity, but have replaced this mood with a very up-beat, positive one. I can now shift my negative moods, even when related to circumstances I am unable to change. Or perhaps I should say especially when I am faced with circumstances I am unable to change. Thanks to new private conversations, there are ever fewer circumstances that fall into the I-am-unable-to-change category.

I still experience great losses. My father-in-law died a few years ago. My Dad has dementia and Parkinson's disease. It is with great pain that I watch him change before my eyes. I miss Dad. My mother-in-law is in chronic pain. Yet I live a productive life, working toward my dreams, while at the same time providing time for Mom, Dad and my mother-in-law.

Language for Success is not a Pollyanna approach to a fantasy life that does not address obstacles, problems and other unpleasant, undesirable circumstances we sometimes face. We can deal powerfully and creatively with sad or unfortunate events and create a strong presence. We can enjoy our lives, creating success at every level. It begins with a Language for Success.

I have not yet developed the ability to have only desirable thoughts. I occasionally have ineffective private conversations. But I notice them more quickly and participate in them for much shorter periods of time. I rarely believe them. While I cannot yet eliminate all ineffective, negative conversations from my automatic private conversations, I can eliminate the attention and authority I give them. Instead, I replace them with uplifting, advantageous, private conversations. My life just keeps getting better and better. I love it! That makes it easy to replace them with my Language for Success.

What signs indicate that you do not pay attention to your private conversations? How can you tell that you may have ineffective private conversations? Notice how often you find yourself saying and doing things you do not want to say and do.

How Can You Alter Ineffective Private Conversations?

1. Notice what you say. Learn to pay attention.
   a. Allow time for reflection.
   b. Write automatically. Record every thing that comes to mind.
   c. Journal about things that bother you.
   d. Practice automatic writing and journal about your aspirations.
   e. Keep a notebook or index cards with you. Whenever you notice them, simply jot down thoughts you are having them.
   f. Or record your thoughts every hour.

2. Notice patterns in your private conversations. You will be amazed at your private conversations and how strongly you believe in them. For example, I often found myself saying, "I can't believe this is happening!" in response to *good* things happening in my life. Can you believe that? I could easily believe it when something bad happened! Now, it is easy for me to say, "Yes, it's happening. I love it and I believe it!"

3. Notice connections between mood changes and your private conversations. Are you fearful or inspired, doubtful or confident after having a little one-on-one conversation with yourself?

4. Distinguish between rumination, problem-solving, automatic and intentional private conversations.

5. Once you can begin to distinguish between rumination, problem-solving, automatic and intentional private conversations, you will better understand the relationship between the private conversations you are engaging in and their impact on your life.

6. At this point you can begin to design your conversations – conversations that lift your mood and inspire you. Eventually, you will have automatic, positive private conversations that profoundly affect your emotional well-being, actions and the results you are getting in your personal and professional life – your own Language for Success.

The progression goes like this: We have private conversations. They affect our emotional state. Our emotional states impact our actions. Our actions impact our results. Our results further impact our emotional state and eventually we get into repetitive patterns of conversations, emotions and actions. This combination often locks us into a set of recurring results. Is your sequence a downward spiral of negativity? Or a whirlwind of excitement?

We are not at the mercy of negative thoughts. Indeed, the more we accept this possibility, the more we realize we are at the mercy of little. We can learn to deal more easily with losses. We can master the ability to design private conversations that support our well-being, goals, relationships, and careers.

Fortunately, this is not rocket science. This is success science. Far more of us are interested in making our lives work than launching rockets. Language for Success matters!

Best wishes on your Road to Success.

Diane Fontenot, corporate and executive coach, writer, seminar leader and life-long educator, understands essential elements for success. She has summarized them in *Success Habits: Timely Tips for Sustainable Success*. Whether working with individual professional men and women or her corporate clients, Diane helps them master critical elements for success. Inspiring lifestyles and rewarding careers develop as her clients weave the Success Habits into their personal and professional lives. Want to know more? Contact Diane at *diane@janusresources.com. www.janusresources.com.*

How Healing Your Heart Can Heal Your
Mind, Body and Soul

By Dawn Camilla Clinton-Jones

In order to heal the heart, which can ultimately heal your mind, body and soul, you must graduate to a whole new level of consciousness. You must walk through the door of illusion and find your place in God's rich tapestry of this game called life.

How do I do this, you ask? How do I heal my heart and create the life I was born to live?

I will tell you! Below are a few of the universal and biblical laws I have tried and tested for years. Yes, I have actually used these principles to heal all areas of my life.

My name is Dawn Camilla Clinton-Jones. I have been doing transformational work for over two decades as a master healer, revelationist and life coach. I see core issues at a glance and would like to show you how to heal your heart and create the life you have always dreamed of. You deserve it!

My client experience is diverse – international undercover work for the government, celebrities, and prominent personalities in San Diego. Most recently I was asked if I wanted to be the personal psychic for a former president. I turned the opportunity down because I am more interested in helping people like you turn your dreams into reality.

Many people I know feel I live a dream life. And you know what, I do! I live the American dream. I own my own home and car. I have no credit card debt to speak of, and have a great loving relationship. Oh yes, I'm healthy and happy too! My time is my own. I can show you how to do what you want, when you want! How does that sound?

Life was not always this way. For years, I had no peace of mind. No matter how hard I tried, I never felt like I fit in. I always picked the wrong guy. I was passed up for a promotion and had a hard time communicating what I truly felt. I would always say the wrong thing at the wrong time. I didn't even feel like my own family understood me. Nothing really seemed to work in my life.

What I *did* know was that I was a good person who needed to find herself and her direction in life. Know the feeling? Very early on in my life I studied philosophy, psychology and yes, even religion. I took countless seminars, and read every spiritual, personal growth and development book I could get my hands on. Along the way I discovered I had a gift – a gift for helping people. I found my destiny.

I learned not to judge people. Through extensive research I have come to believe that karma and the seeming appearance of life-altering traumas and illnesses, in most cases, stem from our past life karma. Karma is carried over from one life to the next, until we overcome that particular test.

Dr. Brian L. Weiss states in his book *Many Lives, Many Masters* that everyone is born with a dominant trait such as greed, lust, hate, etc. You must overcome this trait or it is carried over to the next life as well as another one. The trait has a direct relationship to a debt you owe to other people. Not absolving yourself of the debt creates a compounded debt in your next lifetime. If you do not fulfill this debt the next one will become harder. If you do fulfill your debt, you will be given an easier life until you become what is called a "sage."

Each one of us also has a very specific purpose on this planet, one we must uncover and fulfill. It is my belief that this is part two of our test. When you are not "on purpose," life seems to be filled with drudgery. When you are "on purpose," attempts to succeed seem to fall into place almost effortlessly, giving you a passion that drives you to work hours on end.

How do you know if you are "on purpose?" Ask yourself one simple question: would you do it for free? I know because I tried several careers and businesses. I was always able to obtain a degree of success, but nothing of monumental proportion. For over twenty years as a sidelight, I performed God-sent healings with remarkable success. Yes, God has sent me hundreds of clients, and I have never advertised. No matter which area of a person's life I was dealing with, I was always able to come up with life changing results.

There are several levels of soul evolution. Newer souls have a greater need to be right. They are even willing to kill for it. Older souls are much wiser and have learned that education, communication and understanding regarding one's position is a better way to come to terms with some of the atrocities that men inflict on one another.

You may also agree to disagree. It is my belief that by patient listening and demonstrating compassion we can rise above any obstacle or perception of defeat. But there must be balance – balance in all areas of our lives – in order to create peace on earth. This is how we heal.

Life is not all about giving but also about receiving. I just felt the hair rise on the back of your neck. Allow me to explain. It is an absolute necessity to understand universal law. You must understand that once you have empowered yourself with certain biblical principles, you must also find balance with this universal truth. Learning to receive achieves balance. You must understand this is a piece of the puzzle. You must!

God does not want his children to be impoverished. You may not expect to receive, but when you do, do it with a loving, humble and thankful heart. If you get cocky, you *will* take a step backwards until you learn not to abuse this law. It is in this truth that we can heal all hearts and live in the miraculous menagerie of God's magnificent kingdom.

"As is above, so below!" The angels do not worry about jealousy, hatred or even getting sick. They do not worry about the next war, paying bills or the misdeeds they have done. These things simply do not exist. They already have found their higher purpose – God! Their connection with our heaven, which, by the way, "is" descending on earth, is their main concern. It is in this truth that you must let go of fear. *All fear.* Free yourself from guilt, but first you must overcome your tests.

This brings me to my final thought as to how your thinking creates your reality. Your thoughts have created the life you are currently living; no one else is responsible. If you have been unable to create a magical life, seek counsel. Seek to work with someone who can help put the pieces of your life back together. You do have a choice. You can be a negative martyr or live in the glorious brilliance of God's light. This will heal your heart which will heal your mind, body and soul. I promise.

Educate yourself to speak with intelligence and wisdom instead of ignorance. Lovingly eliminate that which no longer serves your highest and best good. Seek to find unlimited peace in your heart and create a purposeful, magical melody that soars throughout the planes of our great universe. Learn how to mediate. When you do, ask your higher-self not only to reveal your tests and lessons, but also ask that you may learn your lessons in a loving, healing and peaceful manner. After all, the Bible does say, "Ask and ye shall receive."

I might also suggest that you take the time to reconnect with nature. It is a source of tremendous healing for the soul and a great way to recharge the battery of your mind.

All my love and light to you and yours! God Bless…

For more information or to become a protégé of Dawn Jones and *Wand of Light* call *1-888-711-1964* or visit *www.walkingwiththewise.com* and complete the feedback page. The planet is in dire need of more lightworkers. Be sure to keep your eyes open for some of Dawn's upcoming books, *Touched by Angels ~ Saved by Grace, Walking Through the Door of Illusion, Photo Frame Your Life, How to Heal Your Life Through Color* and *Ancient Remedies, Products and Techniques for Healing Holistically.*

The Seven-Step System

to Take You From

Idea to Action in Five Vital Venues of Your Life

By Julette Millien

Are you turning your ideas into **reality?** Do you have great ideas, again and again... but take no (or ineffective) action? As an entrepreneur, you're probably bombarded with creative thoughts and ideas about how to make your business and your life more profitable, more gratifying, more balanced, and more fun. But do you ever *implement* those ideas?

Here's what usually happens: an idea pops into your head. You say, "Wow, this is GOOD!" You get all excited about it. Maybe you even share it with someone as you decide that you're going to make it happen this time. Then something comes up (isn't it a shame how life continues to "happen?") and your idea gets put off for a day, then two days. Before you know it, it's on the back burner, waiting for that glorious day when you'll have the time to develop it further. You know what that means, right? That fabulous idea goes so far into your subconscious thought that you forget about it. (It might even reoccur again one day as a brand new thought.) And then the cycle begins again.

In the meantime your sense of accomplishment, self-esteem and integrity takes a beating. Once more, you merely flirt with greatness. Once again, the awesome potential of your idea is reduced to just a dream – or worse, a vague feeling of frustration.

Why does this happen? As we speak to people all around the world, there are recurring themes: challenges with time management, a lack of optimism, poor organizational skills, and little or no faith in one's ability to complete a project. There's no big mystery here about *why* your exciting and even groundbreaking ideas get shelved. But this seven-step system will show you *what* to do about it.

Organize Your Writing in Five Vital Venues

Whether you try this seven-step system or not, at least commit to writing your ideas down – preferably as soon as you get them — but certainly by the day's end. To get the most benefit, get five notebooks and label them as follows: **Home, Work, Relationships, Self,** and **Community.** Write all your ideas connected with each of these five areas of your life in the appropriate notebooks. Why these particular venues? To live a balanced and truly rewarding life. This is something we all say we want, but do we live it? Or, are we focused on one, maybe two venues? Of course, we all are involved in some way in our home lives, work lives, relationships, our own selves and our communities – even if only as a user of services. But are we *intentionally and positively* involved with projects of our choosing in each of these five areas? If "yes," this is a surefire path to deep and lasting happiness.

My projects in the five venues are: 1) **Home:** Designating myself general contractor for the renovation/design project to create a joyous home for my relatively new family. 2) **Work:** Getting my book *The Write Way to Action* ready for e-commerce by June 2003. 3) **Relationships:** Improving the quality of specific family relationships by working together on our new web site, networkoffamilies.com. 4) **Self:** Rededicating myself to a healthy approach to diet and exercise so I can look fabulous and feel great for my family reunion in August. 5) **Community:** Procuring a grant for our nonprofit arm – Agape Community Development Foundation – to permit us to offer more self-esteem workshops for the youth in our community. By working on all of these projects, my life has never been more deeply joyful.

Take a five-minute break from this reading and consider five projects you can work on simultaneously that will bring the highest level of joy to your life.

What You Need to Bring to the Table

Every time you get an idea, jot it down in one of the five notebooks. These ideas will grow and cross-fertilize. Each time you review them, something else will occur to you. To get the seven-step system going, pick the one idea you're most excited about in each notebook and make it happen.

The system works best with three areas of commitment: 1) organization, 2) acknowledging your present knowledge (AYPK) and 3) committing to taking action.

Your tools of choice are the five notebooks, five-pocket file/folders (for clippings, pictures, etc.), a highlighter, a pen, and a nice quiet spot where you can have private brainstorming sessions (PBSs).

The Seven-Step System

1. Visualize

After picking an idea, sit quietly and let yourself visualize your current knowledge on the subject. Allow yourself to see images of your vast knowledge in your mind. Don't fight the shape the images take.

Imagine you are stress-free. Yes, this is *make-believe* (you've got to *believe* whatever you set out to *make!*). Just sit still, tighten your muscles (your fists, pelvis, legs, face, etc.), and then release them. Do this as many times as necessary until you feel a noticeable difference in your stress level. Now close your eyes for three minutes and imagine being totally at peace – no troubles, no pain, no anxieties From this state of calm, think about a time when you were at your best. If you can, think specifically about the subject you've chosen. If that idea is too new, think generally. When were you your best self, whatever that means to you? Remember how you felt, what you looked like, and what you sounded like at that moment. What were your thoughts and feelings? You probably felt resourceful and capable of finding creative solutions.

2. Write From That Resourceful Perspective

If your topic has to do with communicating an idea to people, think of a time when you connected and felt the passion of your idea as you spoke. Write everything you know about your topic. The exercise is to write what you *know*. (*Doing* it is a whole other discussion! See step 7.)

You might begin this process by first making a mind-map. This means brainstorming without attempting to structure your thoughts. Simply write your topic in the middle of the page and position every thought or phrase that pops into your mind somewhere on that page. You can draw lines connecting the central topic to the ideas if you'd like. The goal here is to map out a picture of your knowledge.

Then just write, freely and completely, without editing, judging or blaming.

If you are a business owner, this is a critical step for all aspects of your business. Even if you're not developing a new project or idea, you always need to be very familiar with what you *do* know, in order to assess the holes in your knowledge. Then you'll be able to intelligently engage professionals to assist you with very specific tasks.

Write for as long as it takes in order to get a full picture of your knowledge base. Try to recapture that rush of emotions and thoughts that accompanied the idea when it first occurred. Get it all on paper. If you did some writing before, take a look back and see what else occurs to you now. Remember, you're not structuring – just flowing with the energy of each thought, whether or not you see the connection. When you feel somewhat empty but light with excitement, you're ready to move on to the next step.

3. Read What You Wrote.

This is where you will begin to add some structure. Let yourself be receptive to all the wonderful ideas on your paper. If other ideas pop into your mind, jot those down too (possibly using a different color ink). This is where you get to cross-fertilize these great ideas. Parts of this entry can even be read out loud for others' input. Remember, you don't want nay-sayers to give feedback. No judging of ideas is allowed at this stage, only cross-fertilizing.

4. Highlight and Visualize

As you review your writing, look for action steps. Each time you mention *doing something* or taking some specific *action*, highlight those words. Review these highlighted items and visualize what it would be like if they were done. What would be different in your life? Visualize the benefits you would receive as a result of taking these actions.

5. Rewrite Action Steps in the Back of Your Notebook

www.mentorsmagazine.com

Move the highlighted action steps to the back of your notebook or journal. Write one action per line. (Dedicate about 8 to 10 pages to writing your action steps)

6. Add Dates.

Next to every action step, place a date when you expect to complete the item. Also place a small circle next to each item. Example:

Action	To be completed by:
0 Call plumber Re: XXX	02/15/03
0 Begin tile work - wall	03/12/03

7. Do It

When you have completed the item, place a mark or date on the line. After accomplishing something, acknowledge and celebrate. Give thanks for your commitment to taking action in your life. Keep the process going.

Continue writing in your notebook as you take actions, learn new things, and have different thoughts about the process. This book is the place to record all your thoughts and feelings pertaining to this project. If you get stuck, write about that too. Your activity level may be uneven; that is OK. As a result of focusing on your areas of interest, you may find lots of information coming your way – articles, quotes, news reports, people, etc. This is to be expected. It's the power of focus and organization.

If you make this seven-step system a part of your creative process, you will make use of your wonderful ideas. You will take action, discover hidden talents, and find joy – the joy that comes from accomplishment. Imagine this state of joy multiplied by five! By implementing a project from each of the five vital venues of your life, you will experience the awesome joy of success through service.

Use the following diagram as a visual reminder to TAKE ACTION in your life! Enjoy the process!

Julette Millien is passionate about helping people take action with their inspired ideas. Julette provides a loving and firm push to action through e-coaching, workshops and personalized consultations. Visit *agapeinc.com* for free feedback or call *888-721-2235.* Do it today; experience the joy of success by moving from idea to action.

Coaching the "Whole" Manager/Executive

By Dawne Era

Coaching for performance improvement works best when I know the "whole" person – emotionally, mentally, physically and spiritually. This is true at any level of management. It's as true for coaching new executives who need to get up to speed as it is for coaching a current top-performing manager to peak performance. I rely on my knowledge of the "whole" person to optimize my performance as a coach and to make the process a "success " for my client.

A case study of this approach involves an executive who felt overwhelmed and disorganized. His peers and direct reports confirmed that his perception was accurate; they rated his leadership as less than organized. A cognitive coaching approach might have included identifying work-related problems, utilizing stress management techniques and developing organizational skills. Fortunately, he agreed to look at every area of his life to uncover the deeper information needed to create an effective action plan. The underlying cause was discovered to be linked to his sister's death two years earlier. She had been his best friend; his sense of loss led him to immerse himself even more deeply in work, but interfered with his productivity.

At the same time, he stopped exercising because he could not go to the gym where they had often worked out together. He then developed insomnia which he treated with a combination of alcohol and sleeping pills. His social life became non-existent. His family and friends had to be careful to no long mention her name in front of him. On some level, he knew he was still grieving deeply and needed help. Through our exploration, he was able to connect the loss of his sister to his performance problems. This allowed us to take the next step and develop an action plan that included grief counseling, an exercise program, a meeting with his physician to discuss his insomnia, and starting a journal to stay in touch with his feelings.

Although this is an example of deep grief significantly impacting an individual in all areas of his life, lesser events or imbalances in any area of life always impact the "whole" person.

All of my clients, even those with some initial reluctance, have reported great benefit from looking at the "whole self " as it relates to their behavior and performance.

I use two validated assessments:

- A 360° management skill assessment to get a clear picture of how the individual's management competencies are perceived by boss, self, peers and direct reports, and

- A personality assessment so that I can better understand who the person is and whether they have the energy and motivation necessary to work through a behavioral change process.

A client's "life" assessment explores the individual's emotional, mental, physical and spiritual capabilities. Imbalance between or within any of these areas will impact the ability to reach top leadership performance level. It may be helpful to take a brief look at each area and how it contributes to optimal performance on the job:

360° Feedback Assessment

Multi-rater feedback instruments are increasingly replacing the traditional "boss-down" management performance appraisal. One of my clients reported her stress vanished when her organization implemented "360's" and she no longer had to do individual appraisals.

My clients have been very receptive to using a "360" during the coaching process. As a coach, this invaluable tool gives me information I would not otherwise have and significantly increases the value of the process for my client.

I use Profiles International's *Checkpoint 360°* because it is a validated comprehensive measure of management skill and knowledge, is administered and completed on-line, and, most importantly, has a follow-up Skill Builder development tool specific to any identified area of competency development.

Personality Assessment

I use Profiles International's *The Profile* which measures thinking style, occupational interests, and personality traits. Overall, this gives me a very accurate portrait of who the person is and allows me to tailor the coaching process to the individual. Additionally, my clients gain some level of self-awareness and validation from their report.

Emotions

Emotional intelligence, which creates emotional well-being, lends a functional advantage to every area of life. In the workplace, this becomes competitive advantage. It is defined as "the ability to recognize emotions, name them and control them enough to enable us to choose how to behave" (Source: E I Advantage, Mcbride and Maitland).

As the basis for every area of development, emotional intelligence is, by far, the major focus in my coaching practice. Most of us have not been taught that recognition and expression of emotions makes us more effective, or that we must consciously and actively pursue the learning process in order to develop these skills.

Physical/ Mental/Spiritual or (Body, Mind and Spirit)

We all know that physical well-being is a key part of our overall functioning, yet it remains an area that often gets little attention. Exercise, eating, drinking, and sleep habits are important to explore. I had one client decide that it did not make sense for her to work on identified management skill gaps unless she immediately pursued an exercise and diet program. She suddenly understood the impact her weight, and resultant poor energy, was having on her ability to manage others.

The Profile gives me information about an individual's cognitive style – ability and speed of information processing. I have found this to be particularly important with clients who are very high on this scale. Most often, they have problems communicating and are unaware that it is due to their ability to process and output information at a rate that confuses others. With self-awareness this can be quickly corrected. Cognitive performance can be impacted by many things including diet, physical fitness, sleep habits, and the ability to deal with stress.

Whether religious or not, we are all spiritual beings. When I ask the question, "What does your spirit look like?" everyone has always had an immediate answer. When emotional awareness increases during the coaching process, as it always does, spiritual growth occurs as well.

Why Do I Coach?

I have lived much of my adult life as an admitted self-help/personal growth junkie. I have a strong belief that each individual on this earth is here for a purpose and many of us need to find our self-worth through self-discovery. We are all connected and that knowledge allows me to honor my clients. I know they already have everything they need to live their life of purpose. It is thrilling for me to see my clients' growth. And best of all, as any good coach or mentor would admit, I always grow right along with them. Here's an example:

One of my clients, a Global Head of HR for one of the world's largest companies, had difficulty influencing his team, his peers and his boss. Before a major presentation of his vision to what he described as a "hostile team," we sought to enhance his influence by increasing his emotional intelligence. We worked on body language awareness (particularly improved eye contact), improved listening skills, and mapping out an "inspiring" speech. Because I was not able to attend his presentation, we asked for feedback from key people in attendance. I will never forget his telephone call to me and the sense of accomplishment in his voice as he said, "It was a great success. Immediate feedback was extremely enthusiastic and rather than the complete non buy-in I expected, I believe 80-90% of the team support my vision! Thank you so much!" Do I accept the thanks? Of course, and I give thanks, too, because I am fully aware that coaching is a team effort and that I learn as I go along!

Looking at the "whole" person creates endless opportunities for growth and feelings of positive self-worth. My career as a Management/Executive Coach in the global market allows me to model "positive presence" and continue my own ongoing growth process as my clients are pursuing their development and achieving their goals.

My story, which will be fully told in the upcoming book *Growing Positive: If I Can Do It – You Can Too* is meant to inspire others to move beyond life circumstances, mental negativity and anything else that keeps them from living life positively and with purpose. It is not always a pretty story. Mine started with a poor and dysfunctional home-life, teenage pregnancy, divorce, economic struggle, family conflict and estrangement. But I am thankful that it is my story, for it has made me who I am today. I know my purpose in life is to make a difference in the lives of others by inspiring them toward self-acceptance, personal growth and pursuit of their own life purpose. It is an extra benefit that their success allows me to continue my own growth.

Dawne's "whole person/heart centered" approach toward self-awareness and full potential has inspired her own growth and work with clients throughout her career as Psychotherapist, Executive Coach and Business Owner.

Dawne Era, President, Performance Check, Inc.
dawne.era@cox.net   401-739-0327

You Have The Power
To Choose

By Susan K. Perry

Obstacles are those dreadful things you encounter when you take your eyes off your goals.

The Dalai Llama reminds us of Henry Ford's insight that our primary goal in life is the desire to be happy and to avoid suffering. I know you can overcome obstacles.

My experiences and study of spiritual leaders have given me some unique insights to obstacles handling. I want to help you avoid the suffering obstacles can present. I will make it easier for you to define your goal, make a plan and reach your goal with abundance and peace.

You are where you are today because of choices you've made or let others make for you. Are you where you want to be? If not, why not? What is trapping you, holding you in an abusive or unhealthy situation?

Most likely it is fear. When you are trying to *control* fear. You are keeping it in check, just beneath the surface where it is ready to erupt at the slightest provocation. When you try to *manage* fear, it keeps you off track by telling you to focus on the circumstantial issues of life rather than the actual fear itself. Fear is making your decisions for you passively, unconsciously, reactively. On the other hand, when you *master* your fear, you acknowledge it, stare it down, allow yourself to feel it and move through it without getting stuck in it.

Wishing changes nothing. But using your greatest power – the power to choose, you can make a decision and a commitment. That changes everything. It is the difference between wishing and making those wishes come true.

The power to choose can never be taken from you, but it can be neglected or ignored. If it is used, it will make a major difference. Perhaps it will not change history, but you will definitely change your future.

Throughout your life, your dreams don't disappear. As you go along, they surface every so often to tug on your heartstrings and remind you what you haven't achieved yet. Listen to them. But how can you achieve them?

You've heard "If you keep doing what you always do, you'll keep getting what you've always gotten..." Have you repeated the same behaviors? Hello!? Have you hit rock bottom? Well, I have, and many other successful people have, too.

Think about the words "rock bottom." Rock is solid. The Bible describes houses that will never be destroyed as being built on rock. So, if you have hit rock bottom, it's a firm place from which to re-evaluate your life. There is no way to go but up!

Every day brings us a choice: to practice stress or to practice peace. Finding inner peace doesn't require hours of staring at your navel or twisting your body into a pretzel. It just takes willingness and common sense.

You realize there is so much good going on around you, and you know you are meant to share it, but you find you have just too much to do. Life is a precious gift to be savored, not an endless series of tasks to complete while you complain about being "too busy." Yet if you don't take the time to plan your life and make sure you are spending time on what is most important, it is easy to feel overwhelmed. Remember this: your to-do list is immortal. It will live on long after you're dead.

You want success in your life. What makes people successful? Successful people have a purpose so strong that they *formed the habit of doing things that failures don't like to do.*

You weren't born to work yourself to death. You were born to fulfill your desire for experiences. Success is not easy, but remember, no one becomes successful by accident. Success requires making a plan and sticking to it. It is simple, but it requires commitment and work.

The good news is that once you begin, the results start coming almost instantly. The miracle of successful living is that the smallest step towards success attracts even more success! I would like to share something very different and very special with you, and it's going to change *everything around you.*

You Need a Compass, Not a Roadmap

- Define Your Destination – Your Goal. See it as a mountain off on the horizon. What makes you really excited? What would you love to do or be if money were no object?

- Write down *why* you want it. When the *why* is big enough, the *how* doesn't matter.

- Commit to it. It *is* where you are headed. It's not an "I hope it will happen" or "I hope I'll make it." It *is* where you are going.

- Experience it. Set your sights on it. *See it,* feel it, smell it, taste it, dream it, live it. Surround yourself with pictures of it.

- Determine what it would take to get there. Don't expect to go from A-Z. Remember B-Y. All the stoplights in a city aren't green at the same time;

yet when you get one now, then one at the next intersection, etc., you will be able to make it across town.

- Decide if you are willing to pay the price. Everything has a price. Especially doing nothing. Don't wallow in self-pity.

- *Focus! Why* do you want it? Don't ever let your sights off it. See it. Be consumed with it. If your child or your dog were trapped under a burning tree branch, would you worry about the logistics or how you might get burned yourself, or would you go after them? Of course you would take action. *Make it happen.*

- Know you can do it. Write it down! You won't believe what a difference this will make.

- Tell people you are doing it. This helps it sound real to you, and they will help keep you accountable.

- Every day take at least one step towards it. No matter how small, do something towards achieving your goal.

- When people ask how they can help, tell them. Be specific. Ask for exactly what you want.

- Keep your direction. If you go off road to explore, realize it, then get back on the road. Do you still see the mountain? Do you need to alter your course?

  Don't let people who feed your ego get you off track. They may give you praise on something that is off your path. Enjoy it for what it is, someone else's opinion. Then, get back on the path to your goal. Stay committed.

- Eliminate unnecessary clutter from your daily activities – television, endless internet surfing, games, telephone, gossip, anything that is non-productive or not in line with your goals.

- Every day, do something you think you can't.

  Realize that not every goal will be fully achieved. Not every job will end successfully. Not every relationship will endure, hope be achieved, love last, endeavor be completed, nor every dream realized. But when you fall short of your goal, perhaps you can say, "Wow. Look at what I found along the way! Look at the wonderful things which have come into my life because I tried to do something!"

Keep the Faith

- In God or Higher Power (He wants you to have a life of abundance)

- In Your instincts (Have you ever ignored them? What happened?)

157

- In Your judgment (Don't just re-act and you will make better choices.)

- In Your abilities (You certainly have them. Keep them in mind.)

- *Know* it will happen. (What you think about, you bring about.)

- Trust that *your* needs *will* be met (Let Go and Let God).

- Worry is like a rocking chair. It gives you something to do, but it doesn't get you anywhere.

- Keep a sense of humor.

"Life is ever-changing. Nothing in this world is an accident. Through unexpected incidents, the universe tries to teach you something. Learn the lessons."

Set Boundaries

- Be willing to eliminate negative people, gossip, and mechanically going along with other people's wishes when they aren't inline with your journey.

- Learn to politely say "No" to people who want you to help out on "just one more committee," or drop what you're doing to do something they can't do. Try, "I'm so honored you thought of me. Right now isn't a good time, but please consider me again after I'm finished with my project, etc."

- Do not try to excuse or justify your goals to anyone. You don't try to tell them what their goals are, do you? (If you do, realize it's the counter-productiveness of co-dependency and is harmful to you both.) Some hold others back to try to make themselves look good in contrast. Think, "I no longer want to be your victim. You can play the game without me."

- Don't accept other people's nay-saying. People told the Wright brothers they were nuts. Benjamin Franklin and electricity? Robert Fulton and the steam engine? If it's *your* goal, *do it*. Edison and Bell both said that they had no failures; they only learned one more thing that didn't work! Remember that when you're on the phone in the evening making flight arrangements. The only failure is in not trying!

Priorities

Yes, we all have lots to do. Some days it's like a three-ring circus. It's imperative to decide which are *really* our priorities. Try:

- A-list – you will not live without doing this (faith, family, health)

- B-list – you really will do these (career, fulfillment)

- C-list – you'd like to do these if you have time (friends, hobbies, outside interests)

- D-list – someday, you'd like to do this (travel, adventure)

Serenity

- Allow yourself to live in the *present*. Like a child, when you're in the present moment, past and future fade away. There are no mental conditions for happiness. The simple pleasures of a sunrise or a sunset, the breeze on your face, or a smile that seems to reach into every cell of your body, are always available.

- When you're able to let go of thinking and relax, the clouds part. You automatically become like a child again, and feel the radiant joy of the inner sun. When that sun shines you feel whole – a part of something that extends far beyond your separate self. The only reality that exists for you is in your own mind. Grant yourself grace.

- Use your greatest power – your power of choice – to realize abundance in your life.

- God in His faithfulness gives each of us what is best for us. It is in surrendering to His will that you will discover peace and abundance. You will realize your worth is not found in your bank balance, but in your heart. This is my sincere wish for you.

Susan Perry, RN, has over 20 years experience in nursing. An award-winning, published author since age 15, Susan has recently begun work on book, *NO IS a Complete Sentence!* as a result of a severe domestic violence. During this time, she lost everything except her integrity, spirit, determination and her faith in God.

As a woman who has been there, from the depths of despair to the mountain tops, her writing is directly from her heart to yours. Susan is dedicated to enriching others' lives, helping them find their passion and living it, and to promoting physical, mental and spiritual health and abundance living. Visit *www.SusanKPerry.com*

Why Cats Don't Bark
Unleash Your PowerZone: Intuitive Intelligence – The Other IQ
By Edie Raether

"I did not arrive at my understanding of the fundamental laws of the universe through my rational mind. The intellect has little to do on the road to discovery. There comes a leap in consciousness, call it intuition or what you will, and the solution come to you."

– Albert Einstein

Unlike traditional IQ, with a century of research behind it, intuitive intelligence is a new concept. It is a different kind of intelligence. In recent years, it is gaining in respectability largely because psychologists are recognizing it as a natural mental skill which helps us make decisions, solve problems, generate creative ideas and even forecast future events. We are beginning to realize that intuition is not just a mysterious gift or an accidental insight.

The advances in transpersonal psychologies, brain research and the remarkable acceptance of Eastern medicine and philosophies have led many researchers to believe that there are untapped powers and wisdom deep inside of us. They are beginning to agree that there is something inside of us that understands who we are, what our purpose is, and what is necessary for our protection, growth and development. In fact, in interviews eighty-seven of ninety three Nobel Prize winners claimed that intuition was primary to their success. Webster defines intuition as "quick and ready insight... The act or process of coming to direct knowledge without reasoning or inferring." Psychologist Carl Jung calls it "one of the basic psychological functions that explores the unknown and senses possibilities and implications... Not readily apparent."

Intuition is unconventional wisdom, unfiltered logic and a direct knowing that provides sensory feedback and is, in fact, a sensory fact-finding system. Buckminster Fuller called intuition "cosmic fishing." Whether you call it God's telephone, reason in a hurry or psychic telegrams from the subconscious, it is difficult to quantify because it applies to a broad range of human sensory experiences. Unfortunately, millions of women were once burned at the stake as witches because of their misunderstood gift of intuition, which is actually a reliable cognitive tool within each of us and a skill to be refined and developed. While not advocating an impulse revolution, igniting your intuition will automatically provide you with the energy, drive, determination and discipline to create your destiny. The fulfillment of your dreams and goals will become so self-rewarding that without conscious will or effort that pattern of success will become self-sustaining. You will become spiritually intoxicated.

As you get rid of the emotional cataracts and your vision becomes clear, you will find the walk upon your path effortless as you proceed with ease. Fears will dissipate as you relinquish yourself to a greater cause or your reason for being. You will feel in sync, not out of touch. You will experience your work as an extension of your self or your very soul, feeling one with the process of becoming. You will achieve a level of unconscious competence where excellence and peak performance feels effortless as the energy is allowed to flow through you. Perhaps that is why Michael Jordan refers to this state as being "in the flow." Other sports use different buzz words, although the experience is the same. In golf, it is referred to as being "in the zone." Tiger Woods would qualify. In the current world of musicians, Wynton Marsalis seems to become one with his instrument, as does any exceptional musician. The question is, can we all achieve this supreme level of mastery? I believe the answer is "yes," if we are in sync with our instinct and we learn the mind-empowering strategies that provide access to the inner unconventional wisdom of our intuition and instinctual intelligence.

The futurist and author John Naisbitt has also recognized the increasing importance and value of intuition in the new information society precisely because there is so much data and we are all suffering from information overload. Our intuitive abilities provide an informational bypass to make spontaneous decisions that are razor sharp and to develop problem solving skills that encompass the big picture and visionary thinking while never losing sight of crucial details. Intuitive intelligence is holistic, perceptually accurate, and reveals the gestalt of our reality. Learning to trust this unquantitative process is our challenge, and trust we must, for our intuitive abilities strengthen and develop only as we trust and believe in the process. The intuitive mind is like a rebellious child if you do not support and – believe in that child's abilities, she will prove you right. To discover our core genius and harness the power of your inner wisdom you must ignite your intuitive intelligence.

Actually, the lessons on how to unleash our PowerZone, our intuitive intelligence, was revealed long, long ago in a book called the *Holy Bible*. Here are the steps to helping you get in sync with your core genius and intuitive intelligence.

1. *Be ye as children.* Be open, curious and attentive. See the world through the unfiltered eye with the awe and wonderment of the child.

2. *Be still and know.* Take time to pray, meditate, and listen to your inner guide. Silence is more that golden, it is essential to our spiritual

growth and provides fertile territory for moments of inspiration and creativity, which are crucial to thriving in today's competitive market place.

3. *Seek... and ye shall find.* Our eyes must be open to possibilities. We must expect miracles and positive outcomes. We must also be focused and clear on what it is that we seek. Be a possibility thinker. In fact, dwell... in possibility. Expect a miracle! The power of positive expectations is so well stated by the following: "When I was a boy, my mother said, 'if you are a soldier, you will be a general; and if you are a monk, you will be the pope.' Instead, I was a painter and became Picasso." May you unleash the Picasso in you.

4. *Ask and it shall be given.* Questions shape our destiny. Questions also activate the brain into an automatic retrieval of information and subconscious processes. It is imperative to first ask "what" questions, which stimulate visionary, big-picture thinking. Then ask "why" questions to gain an understanding of purpose and meaning. "How" questions address the skills necessary for the achievement of your vision.

5. *Knock... And the door will be opened.* We must be proactive and take meaningful action. As Jack London said, "You can't wait for inspiration. You have to go after it with a club."

6. *Oh, ye of little faith!* Trust and belief in the intuitive process only makes it more active and accurate. St. Augustine said, "Faith is to believe what we have not seen, and the reward of that faith is to see what we believe." Research has proven that intuition is more accurate with a state of positive belief and activity. In other words, if you don't use it, you lose it.

I believe our intuition is a gift from God. I also believe that pure intuition is 100% accurate when it does not become contaminated by cultural override or confused with worry or wishful thinking. It is through our personal alignment with our divine nature, our core genius, that we can remain in sync with our instincts and our intuitive intelligence.

While all living things grow into their nature with a supportive environment, we must also have the courage to be different to make a difference. We must transcend from success to significance. As we gravitate toward our own uniqueness, we must respect the direction of our "future pull" which is our present self becoming our future authentic self. Singleness of purpose means avoiding exterior clutter like power, prestige and possessions, which may interfere with the chief purpose of our lives.

Shakti Gawain explains, "Every time you don't follow your inner guidance, you feel a loss of energy, loss of power, a sense of spiritual deadness."

Activities and life experiences which derive from our purpose are not burdensome because there is harmony between what we feel we are supposed to do and what we want to do. Unfortunately, we are often derailed and live in someone else's comfort zone, than our own. Our parents often encourage and coerce us to manifest their own unfulfilled wishes and destiny which, if we obey, is a violation of the soul.

We live in a world of distractions. Our lives are filled with work and family responsibilities, our own desires and goals, community concerns, and global pressures. Most of us get caught up in the demands society places on us and end up in the enter lane of the rat race. On the surface we may appear happy, confident and in control, but inside we suffer from the tensions imposed by 21st Century living.

We move so fast that we lose opportunities to discover and express our authentic self. We grow out of touch with ourselves and settle for just going through the motions. We lose sight of our purpose. We become strangers to ourselves – all shell and no substance. Knowing yourself, what you do well and what you don't do well, what motivates you, what you value, who you want to spend time with, what makes you happy or sad, is your chief occupation in this life. "The purpose of life," said Eleanor Roosevelt, "is to live it, to taste experience to the utmost, to reach out eagerly and without fear for newer and richer life experiences."

Until we do the work of excavating, claiming and expressing our uniqueness, we run the risk of putting our life script into someone else's hands. Joseph Campbell, in his book *Myths to Live By*, warns, "The world is full of people that have stopped listening to themselves or have listened only to their neighbors to learn what they ought to do, how they ought to behave and what the values are that they should be living for." Unfortunately, for many people, Campbell is right.

In the extremely interesting book, *The Cell's Intelligence,* we read that "if the cells of the brain do not get to express their mission and purpose in a balanced way, they... rebel by manifesting diseases such as tumors."

We are obviously much, much more than biochemical machines and mere bundles of DNA. We are specks of Divine Intelligence in human clothing. In her companion book to *The Artist's Way*, Julia Cameron gives her interpretation of why we must express our purpose. She says, in *Veins of Gold:*

"All of us are far richer than we imagine. None of us possesses a life devoid of magic, barren of grace, divorced from power. Our inner resources, often unmined and even unknown or unacknowledged, are the treasures we carry, what I call our spiritual DNA... The stamp of originality, which is the blueprint of our unfolding."

Human curiosity, intuition, practicality and logic are the fulcrums of personal and professional achievement. They are the revitalizing forces for converting raw human energy and potential into sound judgments and creative ideas. Managing our logical side and our intuitive nature will take all of the cunning, patience and open-mindedness we can muster. Intuition cannot be ordered, commanded, contrived or predicted. We simply have to be ready for it. Rest, quiet, and relaxation siphon off the busy chatter of daily distraction and allow us to hear our inner wisdom which seeks conscious expression and the manifestation of our soul.

Jack Schwartz has a theory that at the moment of indecision there is simultaneously a solution. However, it may take years for us to discover that awareness and act on it. The result is learned helplessness or mediocrity. People stay confused and unfulfilled, victimized by toxic logic. That happens when we take the maxim "look before you leap" to absurd extremes. Sometimes we just have to take an intuitive leap and trust that the net will be there. To be fully intellectual beings and experience those "leaps in consciousness" that Albert Einstein believed are necessary for bringing solutions to us, we will need to develop our intuitive abilities as well.

Edie Raether, M.S., CSP

A change strategist and Fortune 50 favorite, Edie Raether is an expert on innovative thinking and intuitive intelligence (the other IQ). As an international speaker, performance coach and author, Edie promises a positive ROI on your intellectual capital.
View her live at *www.raether.com* (919-557-7900)
edie@raether.com

Align Your Beliefs for Success

By Mandy Myles

People commonly recognize *skill* as a primary component of success, but it is a little known fact that *beliefs* can be an even more significant determining factor. Most of us have experienced times when we felt that we were too old, too young, didn't have enough money or in some other way were not good enough to have what we really wanted. We must rid ourselves of these thoughts. They shred our ability to succeed into tiny pieces. Doubt and fear replace any confidence we start with and the odds stack up against us.

Beliefs directly affect your actions, which then affect your results. For example, if you start with a belief that you are a good athlete, then you are more likely to become one. If you believe you are not, you will convince yourself, and it will negatively affect your performance. Luckily, you can change your beliefs. Once you change your beliefs, your actions and results change as well.

The power of belief first showed up for me personally in childhood during my gymnastics career. I started training at the age of five with my head coach Dennis. I competed under his coaching until I reached Olympic-prep level at age thirteen. Overall, he instilled in me the belief that I could do anything I set my mind to. He showed me that I could do anything he believed I could, whether or not others had done it at my age yet, and I did extremely well.

Then came some difficult times. The gym had grown significantly. Dennis stopped his personal coaching in order to oversee the new coaches he hired under the expanded format. My newly assigned coach was strict and very demanding. This in itself was not bad. However, her daily comments did not encourage my strengths as Dennis had; instead, she berated weaknesses. Her criticisms specifically focused on my floor routine: "You have no rhythm and can not dance. You will never be good at floor exercise!" I remember her exact words to this day.

I believed at the time that my tumbling skills were strong and my dancing skills needed work. As an impressionable child, I was struggling every day with the conflict between her negative influence and my desire to believe I could succeed. Deep down I believed if I tried harder, I could make significant change. However, over time, my coach's constant negativity began to make me doubt my abilities as a gymnast. I began to fear failure. My performance soon reflected my flagging self-belief. Eventually, my emotional and physical condition also weakened. My lack of confidence began to lead to injury.

Thankfully, Dennis saw the pattern and decided to place me under a different coach, alleviating my stress and frustration. My new coach, Cheryl – like Dennis – believed in my abilities and re-taught me to do the same. She encouraged me constantly, correcting my thinking until I believed in myself again. My restored confidence improved my actions, which then improved my results. Good results were the product of positive beliefs.

The lesson I learned by changing my beliefs led me to pursue the one area for which I had received criticism – dance. This was done out of pure love and enjoyment of the sport. I wanted to keep challenging my body and training at something that I loved to do. My new belief and skill set gave me the courage to audition at a dance studio closer to home. I joined the studio and became one of the top dancers in our company productions and competitions. I would never have auditioned if I had not been encouraged by my childhood gymnastics coaches, Dennis and Cheryl. I danced for four years. My dance instructor advised that with a little more training, I would be dancing at the professional level. However, I was by then simultaneously competing in track, volleyball, and rodeo. I had to choose among these sports and decide what kind of life I wanted to lead. My love for horses won out, and I chose rodeo.

I share this personal experience with you to show the incredible power of believing in yourself and remaining determined. I could not have achieved the outstanding results I have accomplished had it not been for my re-established positive belief structure.

The theory of "Survival of the Fittest" is based on the ability to change and adapt in response to changing pressures and demands. It is essential to survive in any environment. Today information is changing rapidly. Have the ability to change with it. I now make it a point to adapt my beliefs based on what is working and what is not. I am open to learning and growing as much as necessary to ensure success.

What are your beliefs? Are you willing to change them in order to get the results you desire and deserve? By analyzing past results, you can unveil the beliefs you have been focusing on. You can then begin to determine what you must focus on now in order to attain future desired results. How can we change your focus in order to reach your desired outcome?

There is a way to re-program your mind for empowerment, giving you an identity that produces desired results rather than dwelling on shortcomings. One way is by asking empowering questions. Questions formed in an empowering way have the ability to change your life immediately. What are the questions you ask yourself daily? Do they give you the ability to move forward, or are they holding you back? For example, do you find yourself asking, "Why can't I do this?" or "Why is this so hard for me?" If so, imagine asking in a different way, "How can I do this better while enjoying the process?" This simple manner of rephrasing questions changes the perception of your circumstances. The quality of your life then changes. It gives you the ability to think of creative solutions instead of taking away your power of quality decision making.

Think about one area of your life you would like to improve. What do you believe to be true about it? If you don't know what your beliefs are, then think of a time when things did not go as you planned. As this was taking place, what were your thoughts? What did your "inner voice" say to you? (If you just now said to yourself that you don't have an inner voice, it was your inner voice you just heard!) By listing these thoughts (beliefs) you become aware of what is influencing your behavior. Eradicate all negative beliefs as they undermine success.

If fear is holding you back, ask, "How can I look fear in the eye and show that I am no longer controlled by it?" Use your identity (from empowering questions) to allow yourself the freedom to do what you want most. Do something every day to get you closer to your goals. Every action step counts.

Have measurable outcomes. Writing them down gives you clarity to determine whether or not you have reached them. For example, let's say your goal is to keep your family happy. You must know precisely what *makes* them happy along with how you will know they *are* happy. What are the indicators? The more clarity you have, the greater the chances are you will accomplish it.

Surround yourself with success-minded people of action. They put their formula to work for them. You want to have people around you who support and encourage you to do your best. Do whatever it takes to get away from negative influence. You are an image of your current environment. You are choosing your probability to lead a fulfilling life when you consciously or subconsciously choose your environment.

My Formula for Success:

1) Attain precise clarity of desired outcomes – visualize what you want and why you want it while you are in an empowered state and write it down.
2) Beliefs – ensure the identity needed to hit your target.
3) Skills/Actions – continually work on skill mastery.
4) Results – measure results and adjust future actions until you get the desired results.

Take what you know and build on it. Don't wait for perfection before choosing to act. Waiting can lead to doubt and fear, paralyzing you with inaction. Actions create results. If you are not getting the results you desire, assess your belief structure and change those beliefs that are not aligning you with your goals, keeping you on target. (If they are aligned, then all you need to do is change your action steps). *Do not* stop taking action. If you find you are still not getting desired results, then measure them more frequently allowing refinement of your system more quickly, improving your ability to see and mitigate obstacles.

We all have beliefs that restrain our abilities to attain or maintain success in some area; they can also annihilate gratitude and appreciation of life. With beliefs, skills and environment in alignment, you will achieve your heart's desires.

Results Coach, Mandy Myles supports clients with visualizing, measuring and achieving their ultimate desired results. She specializes in business success, personal growth, and athletic peak performance.
For more information go to *www.myresultscoach.com*, or contact her directly at *mandymyles@earthlink.net*.

Business Tips
for Success

© 2003 Kim Muslusky

Keys To The Vault

By Keith J. Cunningham

Raising money can be frustrating, confusing and traumatic for most people. Having structured and negotiated deals worth over $1 billion, I am convinced this intimidation stems from an inability to understand the psychology or the point of view of the investor.

Usually, people trying to raise money fail to do the necessary work required to successfully raise all the money they want and need. In other words, people tend to think that if they have a better idea or have created a better, faster, cheaper, revolutionary, higher quality gizmo or service, then it must be obvious to everyone and a forgone conclusion that it will be successful. *Of course* everyone will love it and the big bucks will start rolling in!

In reality, most entrepreneurs fall in love with their ideas or inventions to the point that they are blinded by their own brilliance and thus are incapable of seeing the risks and potential downsides or problems.

There is no shortage of capital available. The last figures I saw indicated that about $175 billion was under management by U.S Venture Capital funds and $72 billion was waiting to be invested in deals. Investors *must* invest and lenders *must* lend. That is what they are in business to do. They make no money unless they put their money to work. And there is no shortage of new ventures being created that are looking to get funded.

So why is it that only 1 out of every 100 deals that a venture firm or an angel investor sees gets funded?

The answer is not hard to understand: most people trying to raise capital are not on the investor's wavelength: they don't know what an investor is looking for or even how to talk to him.

The best way to approach this problem is for *you* to write down the following on a piece of paper: "I have $10,000,000 to invest and *I must* invest it!" Now, suppose an entrepreneur brings you a deal and wants you to invest in a new company. What questions will you ask? What specific issues will you want addressed? What are you looking for? What would be important for you to learn that will give you confidence that this deal will work?

The answer to these questions should be addressed in a well thought-out, comprehensive business plan. Your business plan is a great sales tool and is your road map for your new venture. An effective business plan should answer/address fifteen key points:

1) Who are you? Who are the players, the management? What is your experience? Have you "been there, done that?"

2) Where are you? What is the status of your venture? Do you have a working prototype or has anyone tested your product/idea? What milestones or benchmarks have already been hit?

3) Where are you going? What is your goal?

4) What is it? What is your product or service? This must be very easy to understand, even if it is complex. Investors will not invest in something they do not understand.

5) Who wants it? Who is your target market?

6) Why do they want it? What is the problem being solved? Where is the pain? What itch are you scratching? What is your value-add proposition?

7) How many might want it? What is your potential market size?

8) How do you know they want it? What testing/research/studies have you done that confirm your belief that "if you build it, they will come"?

9) How will you tell them about it? What is your marketing plan?

10) Who else has it? Who is your competition? Remember, everyone has competition.

11) How are you different? What is your niche? What will keep your competition from duplicating your idea and crushing you? Do you have any Intellectual Property? Patents?

12) What are the risks? What could go wrong?

13) What are the rewards? This is where you talk about the numbers/projections.

14) What do you want? What is the deal? You should propose a deal and an amount of money… enough to get you to the next significant milestone. **Good** = "We need $3 million to reach our next milestone." **Bad** = "Whatever you give us is fine."

15) What is the exit? How does an investor cash out of this deal?

It is not at all uncommon to spend six months researching and preparing a business plan. Remember, your goal in writing a business plan is to get funded. You will not even receive a return telephone call, much less get a face-to-face meeting, if you haven't done your homework.

Common Mistakes

Most new entrepreneurs make two common mistakes in raising money. First, they believe that since investors are "numbers guys," the projections are the most important thing. Nothing could be farther from the truth! Any fool with Excel can string together a set of projections. The numbers are a reflection of management decisions. Good decisions = good numbers. The people making the decisions are the management team.

All deals hit bumps, detours and roadblocks. No business plan has ever been perfectly executed. The unforeseen and the unknown always arise. Murphy is alive and well. Who deals with these problems? Management! People make the deal work. *Money follows management* is the mantra on Wall Street, and money loves a track record. For example, would you be willing to invest in one of Bill Gates' new ventures? I know I would love to be a partner with Bill because he has demonstrated that he knows how to successfully start and run a company.

The second biggest mistake most entrepreneurs make is their fixation on the brilliance of the product. They fall in love with the idea or the gizmo. Investors know that a great product is not necessary and it does not insure success.

Apple Computer is generally acknowledged to have a better operating system than *Microsoft,* and yet *Microsoft* is worth 100 times more than *Apple.* All of us can think of places we would rather eat than *McDonalds,* but you can't name a restaurant that has made more money over the years than *McDonalds. Southwest Airlines* makes a lot more money than *American* or *United* or *Delta* or *Singapore* even though each of these other airlines offers first class, reserved seating and meals.

Marketing

You must have a strategy to tell your customers what your value-add is or what problem you are solving. This is called Marketing. It is differentiating you from the competition. It is filling the need. It is finding your niche. *McDonalds'* niche is not hamburgers but rather consistently inexpensive food, with fast service in a clean environment. *Nike's* niche is not tennis shoes but attitude. *Eastman Kodak's* niche is not film but

memories. *Federal Express'* niche is not delivery but "One World. On Time."
In each of the instances above, the niche that these companies have found is
not necessarily the product but rather something intangible and emotional
related to the ownership or use of the product. This intangible has
differentiated them from the pack and made them outstandingly successful
companies. In other words, *success is not a result of what you do, but rather how
you do it.*

The key to successfully building your business is not found internally in
the idea, but rather externally, with the customer. The key to making a billion
dollars is simple:

1) Find out what they want.
2) Go and get it.
3) Give it to them.

Most entrepreneurs begin with number 2. They "go and get it" without
first finding out what the customer wants or where the customer is in pain.
Which is why most businesses fail in the first two years. The unsuccessful
entrepreneur focuses on the product and not on the customer's wants and
needs. Since the customer is the person who is writing the check, it only makes
sense to focus the bulk of your attention on what they want and need.

If you will find out where the market is in pain, find out where they need to
be scratched, and ask them what they want, you will significantly improve
your odds of getting the funding you need and ultimately of building a
successful and profitable company.

Investors want to know the answer to three basic questions:
1) Are you financable? Have you and your team "been there, done that?"
2) Is the deal financable? Is there a need in the market?
3) Is the risk financable? Is the amount of risk and the amount of return or
upside congruent?

Writing a great business plan, recruiting your team, finding the pain in the
market and structuring the deal so that the investor is adequately compensated
for the risk are The Keys To The Vault.

Keith J. Cunningham has negotiated and raised in excess of $1 billion.
He teaches and mentors individuals about how to produce the results
they want in their life. To find out more, go to *www.keystothevault.com*
or email him at *keith@keystothevault.com*.

When
Customer Service
Comes Off the Rails

By Gray Elkington

I'm standing in a train station on a weekday morning waiting for the 11:13 to London. The platforms have largely cleared after the earlier rush, but still there are people milling around – those taking a train and those who have come to see them off. Suddenly the peace is interrupted by a loudspeaker announcement: "An Intercity train is about to pass through the station. Would all customers on Platform 4 please stand back behind the white line." Some moments later an Intercity train approaches the station like a Japanese bullet train, with a frightening roar building in intensity, throwing up dust and waste paper which is sucked into its wake as it passes. Anyone standing too close to the line might follow the swirling paper over the edge of the platform. This is life and death stuff. When I heard the announcement, I admit I smiled wryly if not a bit wearily, for whoever wrote the warning was slavishly following the policy of Railtrack (the station operating company) of becoming more "customer focused." In doing so they had potentially and unwittingly consigned to oblivion those four or five people on Platform 4 who were there just to see someone off. Not being *customers*, they were not – strictly-speaking – the target audience for the announcement.

Splitting hairs? Yes, and this is about the benefit to your bottom line from doing just that. When it comes to all-important communication, such fine distinctions will distinguish the winners from the "also-rans" in business, in politics, in every walk of life.

Loose Lips Sink Ships

Some of us remember the expression "Loose lips sink ships" from wartime. It meant careless talk costs lives. Now it's a case of "careless talk costs money." You can hear money being poured away wherever you hear vacant customer servants locked on to automatic pilot. Of course we can all sense the meaning behind words, but when it comes to careless talk within customer service, I find my hackles rising.

My interest in this started in the early 1980s. This was the beginning of the communication development boom in the West. By the 1990s I found myself showing senior managers how to cascade good customer service communication down through their organization. The ideas I was proposing were powerful ones; indeed, the British nation was left spellbound by a BBC documentary about the revolutionary communication techniques we employed in our company. And the Guardian Newspaper (a major British national broadsheet) exclaimed, "Can anyone explain it?" referring to the voting swing in a parliamentary constituency where some friends and I had been active, applying our powerful communication techniques door-to-door as well as on radio and television.

Communication is a delicate art – even more so when people's antennae are extended such as when they stand to win or lose something of value, as in a general election. Of course, my antennae are most commonly extended in business when parting with my money.

And I don't like what I'm sensing.

When "How May I Help You?" Conveys the Opposite

Sometimes a sales person or customer service representative can appear to be speaking some well-chosen words but my impression is of someone who doesn't really care. Certain seemingly harmless words (think of the railway station example) are giving the game away, just as plainly as certain body language does.

What hurts me as a trainer is that some of the ill-chosen words mouthed by customer-facing employees come directly from what they were taught in their service trainings. You can hear the pain in their voices as they dutifully expel some prepared greeting from their mouths. "How may I help you?" said with the wrong intonation is best not said at all.

It would be nice to start over with a clean slate. In a way that is what I am doing, training the Chinese to avoid the pratfalls I've observed in the West. Well educated but still largely unspoiled by the worst of Western training, the Chinese are eager to advance their customer service communication. They may have some things to learn in this area, not surprising for a country emerging from an era where you got what you were given, but they have a tradition of respect for others and service which will act as a springboard to global competitiveness. Providing they avoid the idiocies drummed into the heads of customer service representatives the world over, they really will be a formidable competitor.

Back in the West, announcements such as the British railway example continue to create a subliminal feeling of worthlessness within people, of being unloved. By itself this example may be insignificant; however, it is disturbing when seen as part of a general laziness regarding the impact of communication.

The "Insignificant" Words Can Be The Most Damaging Ones

One problem seems to be that communications are sometimes written by managers who are remote from the realities of the front line. They may get the main sentiments right and the important words may be carefully chosen. But the devil (and the comparative advantage) is in the detail. It is often the padding, the common-or-garden vocabulary which carries the subliminal message "We really don't care" – whether this is true or not of the speaker.

You may have noticed one common example if you spend time on aircraft – the prepared statement read by attendants on some flights. As your plane lands on the runway, you will hear a welcome to your destination ending with a "Good-bye," despite the fact that you may yet be some time away from arriving at the terminal gate. To my mind, "Good-bye" means finish, end of contact. Even as a seasoned traveler (I know they're not really going anywhere) I still feel "deserted." It's an ill-thought out statement they recite and unnecessary since they, of course, have the chance to say good-bye as people step from the plane. Such a harmless word normally, "Good-bye" becomes an arrow through the heart when spoken in the wrong context.

Airlines may not be your industry, but here are two other examples where seemingly insignificant words may be used in your company right now in the wrong context and doing damage.

When "Thank you" Is Not The Right Word

The first instance is when your people, for lack of imagination, resort to thanking the customer for their business. This point will take some reflection because it has been so ingrained into us from childhood to say "Thank you." But think for a moment who is getting the gratification in the context of a "thank you" from a sales person or service assistant. If I am serving you and I thank you, then I am thinking about what *I* have gotten out of the transaction! Now, before I am taken too literally, remember I am not talking about a world where there are good and bad behaviors, but instead a world where nuances in communication will leave their mark, if repeated, *indelibly*. If the first call center operator says, "Thank you" for my business and the next one instead uses the short time available on the line to give me some added advice about using the product or service, then, at some level of consciousness, I will find myself returning to the second and not the first. Splitting hairs? Sure. However, maybe you can begin to see that those who pay attention to such niceties will inexorably win over their customers. With their feeling for subtleties, China will learn to exploit such nuances. With their thirst for education, how long will it be before they outstrip the West in customer service?

I Don't Want to Be Your "Customer"

Secondly, when communicating with us, your customers, don't – for goodness sake – call us "Customer" to our faces. The use of the word on the station platform had the potential to cause double offense. Not only did it carry the implication to non-customer bystanders that their safety was not the concern of Railtrack. But it also offended me (at some level) to be described by reference to the company's agenda rather than my own. Granted I was a customer of theirs. I had bought a ticket and was therefore covered by their announcement. But I was no longer what I felt I was, that is a traveler or a passenger (on a passage). I was now a Railtrack "customer," defined by them and clearly labelled. In doing so, they unwittingly showed their true colors and, reading between the lines, I felt that their interest in me was my "custom." Find me a method of transport where I am treated as a person rather than a wallet ("Would *everyone* on Platform 4 please stand back behind the white line" would have done nicely); then I'm theirs for the taking.

Postscript: A few months later Railtrack ceased to exist. Their demise was tellingly unlamented.

Gray Elkington, a corporate communication speaker and author (Macmillan/Que), helps organizations with their human issues. If you come across any customer service horrors, please send them to him c/o Paola Gay at *pgay@unileader.com* (+34 93 270 1656). Also by the same author and available free from *www.unileader.com*: "How *Customer Loyalty* is damaging your business."

Opening New Markets Through Partnering

By Brian Smithies

Have you ever looked across the Atlantic or Pacific Oceans and thought "if only?" "If only I could get a foothold in Europe, North America or the Pacific Rim." At the moment, global trade seems to be largely the preserve of large corporations despite the Internet and the promises of e-commerce. But need it be so?

The answer is, of course, no. If you're interested in finding out more, read on. First, ask yourself this question: What is stopping you from expanding into the European, Australian, Japanese or US markets?

We've asked this question to quite a few companies around the world. The answer is normally a variant of "We don't have the money to make the investment," or "We don't understand the complexity of the trading environment," or "We don't understand the local culture." More often than not, it is a combination of all three.

These are all valid business reasons. However, in our experience, when you really get down to the bottom line, in a lot of cases it's just simply that you don't have the time. You are too busy just doing business in your own market – a market that's increasingly being filled with foreign goods and services. Things are getting more crowded, that's for sure.

Here at Longwater we believe that there is really no reason companies can't trade globally if they have the desire. Our philosophy is simple: "Find like-minded people, share some of the revenues, and open the new market."

To help you understand our approach and how to find the right people to help you grow your business outside of your home territories, let us share with you Brian's experience a few years ago.

He was contracted to help a small UK company of some 35 people find new ways to sell and market their products and services on the international stage. Part of the plan was to open new offices in Asia and the USA. The budgets for this were very restrictive.

Brian could see from the beginning that achieving the desired business and financial goals was going to be very tough, especially given that large up-front expenditure on office space, staff, advertising and all of the other "traditional" start-up costs was out of the question. After a great deal of careful assessment, lots of discussions and many late nights, Brian came to the conclusion that the only way the company's goals could be achieved was to find like-minded people in the target market. They needed business people who shared the same common goal, that of:

"Making SALES & PROFIT together"

Brian talked to many entrepreneurs and business owners who were surprisingly receptive to this approach. He found that they had the same key issue, finding a cost effective uncomplicated way of selling and promoting their products and services into foreign markets.

Some of you may at this point be asking: "So what's new here? It sounds like common sense to me." We couldn't agree more. But before we look further into this model, let's analyze what Brian had discovered.

He had uncovered a practical way to bring like-minded people and organizations together to share the risk and rewards. He had also created a strong united force in business development, one half with a product, the other with the knowledge and means to sell that product into a new market.

To conclude our story, I am pleased to say that Brian did find many organizations with whom he could partner, who had the skill, drive and ambition to make the venture successful. The business eventually was sold for many millions of Pounds.

The key lesson learned was that you do not need to have new premises, spend large amounts of money on country specific sales staff, marketing, consultant's fees, office space, etc.

Brian eventually spent one-tenth of the proposed original budget and the company attained 900% growth through partnering with professionals in each country – professionals who knew all the trading laws and even more importantly knew how to SELL into their own markets.

So now back to the question of common sense. If it was so obvious and easy, then why aren't more people doing this already? There are probably as many answers to this question as there are individuals. But in my experience the two key factors preventing this type of innovation are:

- The lack of understanding, or more importantly, willingness to understand.
- The lack of trust, or more importantly, willingness to trust and be trustworthy.

It boils down to what we call "hard ball humility." If someone approaches Longwater to help them open a new market, then we are humbled. Humble that someone will trust their future success in our market to us. But likewise we need our potential partner to understand that we know the market and the local trading environment. That's what we are bringing to the deal. Any relationship going forward must be truly two-way. To quote Stephen Covey, it must be: "win-win or no deal." Our key criteria are Trust and Integrity. Without these we are just not interested.

This doesn't mean that you should not engage in the normal business practices of conducting your "due diligence" and having a very well thought-out contract in place. In fact, I would see these as being prerequisites to any new partnering. After all, things can go wrong, and one thing business life has taught me is this: "When we're all friends, no one needs the contract; but if we stop being friends, then the contract is most definitely our shelter in the storm."

Here is a piece of practical advice: when drafting the contract, include the concept of "mutuality." This is something both parties should insist on. It is only fair to protect both parties.

Regrettably this does not come easy to some, and may lead to a deal falling through. In this case ask yourself "Was this a deal I really wanted to be part of?" Our own bottom-line is that "mutuality" is essential to underpin a true win-win partnering relationship.

Having now examined how "partnering" can work, let us ask you the question, "Is partnering something of interest to you?" If so, then this last section is for you.

Over the last few years we've helped a growing number of foreign companies enter the UK and European Union market.

We believe that "partnering" is the "philosopher's stone" of business growth and entry into foreign markets. Here are the five key principles:

1) **Principle 1.** *Equality* - Any partnering deal must be a partnership of equals. There is no mileage in a one-sided deal. We are often surprised how many companies are motivated by greed and would rather have no deal than let a potential partner profit from the association. This is the kind of "partner" we don't deal with!

2) **Principle 2.** *Optimization* - Be prepared to optimize, not maximize. An optimized deal is one in which both partners feel that the outcome is "win-win." While you clearly have to look after and protect your own commercial interests, bringing a new product to market carries risk. It can be expensive and time consuming. Don't try to maximize your upside at the expense of your partner. This approach is invariably a deal killer.

3) **Principle 3.** *Transparency* - Both parties should be prepared to be transparent in their dealings. Nothing inspires confidence as much as a demonstrable willingness to be seen to be honest!

4) **Principle 4.** *Diligence* - Don't do anything without a contract. Remember that while we're all friends, there's no problem. Taking normal business precautions is an unfortunate necessity.

5) **Principle 5.** *Expectation* - Be clear about expectations. Nothing causes a deal to go sour quicker than a set of mismatched expectations. At Longwater we use our own Aspirational Sales Planning method to establish these expectations.

We have shown time and time again that if you adhere to our five principles, then the stage is set for a very profitable mutual relationship.

Brian Smithies has gained an International reputation by helping others understand and implement Global Partnering, Global Sales, Marketing, Entrepreneurship and Coaching by helping others achieve their business and personal aspirations, using his own tested methodologies of bringing like minded people together to achieve a common business goal – that of "Making Sales & Profit Together." He is a highly motivated speaker, who inspires and motivates others to achieve their objectives. He is the author of *Opening the Door to New Opportunities* published June 2003. He is a Co-founder of the Longwater Network. He can be reached at BrianSmithies@aol.com or through *www.briansmithies.com*.

Beyond Print:

Influencing The Buying Decisions Of 59% Of Your Customers With Email Campaigns

By Corey Rudl

Direct mail has long been a standard weapon in the small-business marketing arsenal. From black-and-white flyers to full-color catalogs, direct mail is a comfortable vehicle for most business owners to get the word out about their products, services, and special offers. But if you're relying on direct mail alone to let prospective customers know about your offers (or you're planning to), you could be neglecting a cost-effective method of promoting your business. And this could mean that your business gets left behind.

Direct mail can be a very powerful way of contacting your customers, but let's face it: it's not cheap. Every time you promote your business with a direct mail campaign, you spend time and money on design, printing, paper, and postage.

Think about how often you can realistically afford to contact a group of thousands of people if you rely on direct mail alone. Once a month? Once every six months? Once a year? In today's competitive marketplace, that may not be enough to really establish your presence in your prospective customers' minds.

That's why more and more businesses are adding email promotions to their marketing repertoire, regardless of whether or not they have a Web site.

Create a Flurry of Sales — Online or In-Store

Email promotions are really a natural extension of the direct mail concept. And with more and more people using email on a regular basis, email promotions have become an easy (and effective!) way to contact customers. So effective, in fact, that I use email promotions to generate over $2.4 million every year.

Whenever I mention this to people whose businesses are 100% offline, I tend to be greeted by a raised eyebrow or two. After all, email promotions have traditionally been viewed as a tool to generate online activity. But a recent DoubleClick study shows that email can have a major impact on offline purchasing decisions, too. The study showed that 59% of people reported making a purchase in a retail store as a result of an email promotion. And 34% made purchases by phone.

These numbers may seem surprising, but they're easy to understand when you think about your email promotions as simply another form of direct mail. You can send your customers email versions of your flyers and catalogues, in full color, without any of the costs associated with printing, paper, or postage. You can even send coupons that your customers can print out and bring in to your store.

And what makes email marketing even more powerful is that your customers can easily pass your promotions on to their friends, just by hitting the "Forward" button. How many people would go to the trouble of saving a flyer to pass on to a friend? And even if they did, they could only pass it on to *one* friend.

On the other hand, if you offer a great promotion or coupon that really interests your customers, the odds are in your favor that they'll forward it to a few of their friends, too. They just hit the forward button, and your message is on its way to even more potential customers – and you don't have to do a thing!

Building a Priceless Email List

Collecting email addresses is a little more work for an offline business than an online one. If your business has a web site, it's easy to automatically collect the email addresses of customers and visitors to your site. If you've got an offline business, your best bet is to have a sign-up sheet in your office or store. When people make purchases, ask their permission to add their email addresses to your customer database. Run a contest and put a space for email addresses on the entry form.

Whichever way you choose to collect email addresses, you'll have the greatest success if you give people a good reason to share their email address with you. The contest entry form works because people are motivated by the opportunity to win prizes. There has to be an obvious benefit to giving you their email address, like a chance to receive special discounts or an invitation to a special event.

Remember that you should never send email to people who haven't given you permission to do so. That's called "spamming," and not only is it ineffective, it can also result in serious consequences for you and your business.

Creating Your First Email Campaign

Whenever I'm talking with someone who insists that email marketing doesn't work for offline businesses, I always ask if they've ever actually tried it themselves. Most admit they haven't. When I ask them why not, the answer is almost always the same: They think that the process of creating and sending an email promotion is too complicated or too difficult.

Those of us who use email as a marketing tool know that nothing could be further from the truth. Once you've learned the basics, the process is a breeze. And there are new tools being created all the time that make it even easier.

If you've got a direct mail campaign in place, you're already well on your way to creating an effective email campaign. Think about ways you can translate your print materials into email promotions. If you're sending letter-style direct mail promotions, it's very easily to simply duplicate them in email format.

And since you should see most of the response to your email promotions within 48 hours, you can be constantly testing and modifying your efforts to see what works best!

If you're new to email marketing, I recommend you get some help from MyEmailManager.com. It's a simple program that works really well for beginners because you're actually given email templates to use, making it easy to design coupons or promotions with all the benefits of HTML (like full-color product shots, direct links to products, etc.) without any special technical knowledge.

Developing Valuable Relationships

The frequency and informality of communication that is possible when you use email promotions allows you to develop valuable relationships with your customers. In addition to promotions, to establish your credibility in your industry you can provide them with quality information about subjects that interest them.

For example, if you are a jeweler, every time you send an email to your customers, you could include a "Money-Saving Jewelry Tip" in which you share a tidbit of knowledge about what to look for when buying jewelry, like how to assess the quality of the piece you're considering purchasing, or the best way to protect jewelry you already own.

Your customers will appreciate the knowledge that you share with them, and they will begin to see you as an important resource. So the next time one of your customers is looking for that perfect pair of earrings, who do you think they'll call?

Final Thoughts

Email promotions are an important addition to the marketing arsenal of every business. As an extension of traditional direct mail marketing, they can be tailored to create sales in-store as well as online – without many of the costs associated with mailing a printed promotion.

The low cost of email marketing allows you to contact your customers on a regular basis, and establish yourself as a resource, not just a salesperson. And the relationship this allows you to build with your customers will be invaluable in today's highly competitive marketplace.

The time you spend developing your email list and creating your promotions is a solid investment in the future of your business. Once you've collected names and email addresses, they're yours forever. You never need to pay a penny to advertise to them, and the best part is that each time you send them a message, they become more comfortable with the idea of making a purchase from you, instead of your competitors.

And email marketing is getting easier all the time. It's just not as scary as it used to be, since there are so many great tools out there for you to use. But don't try to go it alone. Find a great email service that provides you with templates and other resources to make it as easy as possible to get email promotions working for you.

Internet marketing expert Corey Rudl, founder of *MarketingTips.com* is world-renowned for his opt-in email marketing expertise, having generated over $2.4 million with responsible email promotions in 2002 alone. He is also author of the best-selling "how-to" guide *Insider Secrets to Marketing Your Business on the Internet*. Ask for a FREE copy of *The Insider's Quick-Start Guide to Email Promotions* by emailing *mentors@marketingtips.com*.

More Sales Now!

By Eric Lofholm

Professional selling is one of the most interesting professions in the world – unique because it offers all of us the opportunity to earn what we're worth. Because of this fact, getting good at sales is vital because our skill sets directly affect our income.

Napoleon Hill, author of *Think and Grow Rich*, said, "One good idea is all one needs to achieve great success." This idea is true in sales when restated in this way, "One good idea is all one needs to greatly increase sales results."

For example, a few years ago I averaged two referrals per sales appointment. Then I learned of a way to increase my referrals-per-meeting average. I implemented this single idea and my referrals-per-meeting average went up dramatically. In one appointment I got a whopping 67 referrals! I estimate that I earned more than $100,000 in commissions from the extra referrals I got using that one idea.

Right now, in this moment, you are just one good idea away from significantly increasing your income. That's what this book is for – to generate sales ideas that will help you create the results you want.

The first idea I'll share with you is a way of thinking. I use the thought process I am going to now teach you every day. Once you learn this thought process, you will have it for the rest of your selling career. The thought process is called the *baseline strategy*.

Your sales baseline is a combination of all of your selling skills and selling actions right now. It is a compilation of your skills in the areas of goal setting, time management, handling objections, presentation, and phone management. Your baseline is everything you bring to the table as a sales professional right now.

The baseline strategy means you should keep doing whatever you are doing as a sales professional to create results and add one new idea or one new strategy. For example, let's say that at the end your sales presentation, you are not currently asking for referrals. If you added that one item to your presentation, you would continue to create the results you already are achieving, plus reaping the benefit of whatever referrals you get.

1. Create a Testimonial Book

I have closed hundreds of sales with the help of my testimonial book. It works because one of the most powerful ways to influence someone is with a testimonial from a third party. Major advertisers pay millions of dollars to celebrities and athletes to endorse their products and services. However, you don't have to pay anyone to endorse you. Simply go to your satisfied clients and ask them for a written endorsement. Once you have the letters, display them nicely in a binder. (You can purchase protective plastic pages at your local office supply store.)

Ralph Roberts is America's number one real estate salesperson. Ralph calls his book his "presentation folder." Here is what Ralph has to say about his presentation folder in his book *52 Weeks of Sales Success:*

"My presentation folder is a large-format zippered leather binder in which I have mounted photos of my family, a picture of my "U WIN" license plate, copies of awards or honors that I've received, even photos of my Corvette and of my wife and me in our hot tub at home. When I meet new clients I tell them my personal story, flipping through the pages of my folder to illustrate... Today I'm training all my assistants to develop their own presentation folders."

I taught Bill Mayer the strategy of creating a testimonial book. Bill implemented this one idea. He shared with me that he immediately closed a sale and he didn't believe the sale would have closed if he didn't have the book. His commission was over $20,000 on this sale alone!

Here are some hints on how to create a book able to boost your sales:
- Put a cover on the testimonial book and call it your "Raving Fans Book."
- Put pictures in your book showing that you are successful.
- Purchase a quality binder. (The nicer the binder the more impressed your prospect will be.)

Some ways you can use your testimonial book:
- Incorporate the book into your sales presentation
- Whenever you interview for a job, bring the book with you.
- Let clients look at the book while you are filling out paperwork.

2. Referrals

For many salespeople, referrals provide a huge opportunity to increase results. In general, salespeople are either really good at getting referrals or really bad. The ones who are really bad tend to be bad because they don't have a systematic way to get referrals.

One of the best ways to improve results in the area of referrals is to have a referral system. A great way to develop a referral system is to find out what others in your industry are doing and model them. The example that I gave in the beginning of the chapter of increasing my referrals from two per meeting to ten per meeting was learned by modeling a top producer in my industry.

Who is effective at getting referrals in your industry? If you don't already know, find out. How? Ask everybody and anybody who might know. Find out what they do to get referrals.

Many of my coaching clients want me to help them improve in the area of getting referrals. The first question I always ask them is, "When you go on a sales call, what is your outcome?" The most common answer is, "My outcome is to make a sale." I then ask them if they have any other outcomes. They almost always say no.

This is why they are not getting referrals. You get what you focus on. If you have an outcome to get three referrals on your sales call, chances are you will. From now on, define your referral outcome for each sales call. If you haven't been getting any referrals at all, set your original goal at getting one per sales call. Raise your goal each time you establish a new high.

3. Use the Law of Averages

Sales is a numbers-driven industry. Your sales results can be broken down into ratios of results. If you make 10,000 calls and you set 500 appointments, your close ratio on appointments is 1:20 – you set one appointment every twenty calls. Step one is to know the ratios in your business. Step two is to run the numbers. As an example of running the numbers: suppose your goal is to set five meetings this week and you know that you usually close one of twenty calls. This means you need to make one hundred calls to set five appointments. Your job then would be to make sure that you make 100 calls this week.

Prior to the beginning of each month, I identify my sales goals for the upcoming month. Based on my goals and based on the numbers in my industry, I create an action plan to achieve my goals. For example in my company we average $500 in revenue per sales call. If our goal is $30,000 in revenue from these sales calls, then we need to run 60 appointments. If I didn't know that we average $500 per sales call I wouldn't know how many sales calls we would need to do to hit our goal. If you don't know the numbers in your industry, it could be greatly affecting your overall results.

4. Sell the Benefits

I often ask my audience in my sales mastery seminars, "In a hardware store, what do drill salesmen sell?" The audience will usually say, "They sell drills." Then I tell the audience that drill salesmen don't sell drills, they sell the holes the drills will make. People want benefits.

Because I am a sales trainer, I will often sit through sales presentations to see how others try to influence me. In many of the sales presentations I've sat through, the salesperson has made the mistake of either not selling the benefits of the product or service, or they tried to sell me the benefits that interested them.

This raises an interesting question. How do you know what benefits the customer is interested in? The answer is: first you must *ask* them and second, you must *listen* to the answer. That is the reason why we have two ears and only one mouth. Many salespeople can double their sales by (a) listening better, and (b) by learning how to find out what benefits interest a given customer and then selling him or her on those benefits.

There are two types of benefits – direct and indirect. Direct benefits are measurable and tangible. When you purchase a car, one direct benefit could be a 10-disc CD changer. An indirect benefit is one that you receive as a result of having the car you might feel more confident in you new convertible, for example.

Which is more important, the direct or indirect benefit? You're right – the more important benefit is the one customers feel is more important to them.

Go to *www.ericlofholm.com* to receive your free copy of Eric's E-Book, "21 Ways To Close More Sales Now!"

Eric Lofholm
President
Eric Lofholm International Inc.
4950 Waring Road Suite #5
San Diego, CA 92120
(888) 307-2537 ext 16
(619) 286-2459 ext 16
www.ericlofholm.com
www.saleschampion.com
www.freegoalsettingbook.com

Mentor Your Way to Millions

By Greg S. Reid

It is a powerful message, and in today's business environment, I believe it's time to dust it off and share it with others once more. You've heard it time and time again: "To get what you want out of life, you must help others get what they want first." Or told in an original way... "The greatest success we'll know is helping *others* succeed and grow."

Re-acquainting yourself with this principle is not only a good way to live; it's a great way to do business! Over the years, I've watched many start-up companies come and go. Their failures and set-backs got me wondering. What happened? Where did they go wrong?

But then I began to ask a bigger question, rephrased in a more positive manner. What did all the *successful* businesses do right? The answer is right there in the first paragraph, summarized like this: The more we mentor others, sharing what we know, the more it increases our chances to succeed at any endeavor. Say you own a business, large or small. If it is your true desire to help everyone in the business to succeed, from the receptionist to the CEO (yourself), you will! Just help others get what *they* want first... and your own success soon will follow.

Right now you're asking yourself, "How can I do that?" Simple, really. First, find out what motivates the people around you and commit to helping them achieve those things. Let's take your receptionist to illustrate. We'll call her Nancy. You recognize that the receptionist is one of the most important positions in any organization. She probably interacts most with your current and potential customers. A happy receptionist is a positive ambassador.

During the one-on-one orientation meeting you have with every new staff member, you ask her, "If you could have anything you want out of life, what would it be?" She tells you she wants to go back to school to study nursing. Once she's shared it with you, congratulate her on selecting a great career path and tell her you're going to help make her dream a reality. Now, Nancy is no fool. (Of course not! You don't hire fools!) She may ask why you would support her in something that will eventually cause her to leave your organization.

Tell her she's a valuable employee and you'll be sorry to see her go one day. But you realize that by helping her achieve her true goal in life, you make it easy for her to give 100% the entire time she's working for you, and will assist you in finding a good replacement.

Imagine Nancy's excitement when, a few days later, you show a genuine interest by giving her a variety of brochures you've requested from local nursing academies You tell her she can take a few minutes each day on the company phone to contact schools to set up a class schedule.

Now Here is Where the True "Mentoring" Comes in.

Take a moment to share your experiences with change. Reflect on how *you* felt, the fears *you* faced, when you gave up your job to start the company she works for now. Detail how you overcame obstacles and shut out the noise of the nay sayers who told you why your idea was crazy.

Let her know you're there for positive support, a constant reminder that she can achieve her dream. Reinforce the message that if and when she needs guidance, encouragement, or a shoulder to lean on during her transition, she can count on you!

Consider how great Nancy will feel walking into the office each day, knowing that at the end of regular business hours she'll be heading right toward her life's goal: to become a nurse and help others. How will she answer your company phone from that day forward? What do you suppose her tone of voice and enthusiasm level will be when someone asks her about the place where she works? Think of the terrific first impression she'll make on the job applicants and potential customers with whom she comes in contact every day!

It paints a really pretty picture, doesn't it?

"Mentoring your way to Millions" is a win-win proposition. The more you help others identify and pursue their dreams, the greater support and backing you will get from them in return.

It just makes sense! No one wants to be a cog in the system, a faceless wage slave, day in and day out. When you show your people that you recognize their worth and support not only their goals in the workplace but their hopes and dreams outside the system, they will do amazing things. They will rise above adversity and give their all to you and your business.

Why? Because you have given them something all too rare in life: Unconditional Support!

Step back and imagine, if you will, your company filled with people who feel important and appreciated. People who actually *want* to come to work each day. What if your job became making the rounds, checking that everyone was on track with their life goals as well as their job assignments?

It Can Happen! Here are Some Real-Life Examples.

At WorkSmartNotHard.com., my advertising promotional company, I created a mission to increase our customer base. In order to succeed, I knew I needed to help others on the staff reach a dream of theirs **first.** I realized that almost everyone there either needed a new car, or could hardly afford the one they had. So, I established the *Success Club*. Here's how it worked.

When sales executives reached a rolling 7-week sales volume average of $5K and generated ten *new* customers, the company made their monthly car payment and publicly celebrated their achievement. The clear incentive and the recognition got the staff really "jazzed" and the project kept snowballing. We doubled our client portfolio in a year and net profits rose 15%, even after sharing the wealth through the car payment bonus program. They were no longer working for "the man." They were working toward their car.

At the executive level, we started the President's Club. That targeted a rolling 7-week volume of $8K plus generating fifteen *new* customers a week. When employees hit that goal, WorkSmartNotHard.com paid the individual's rent as well as the car payment!

By giving credit where credit is due, sharing the wealth, and empowering the sales crew to reach their goals and improve their lives, the company became a success story. Now, as you can read, I'm no rocket scientist, just living proof that "Mentoring your way to Millions" really works!

Let's Look at Some Other Examples.

In my hometown, San Diego, I have witnessed both the local family-owned convenience store and a huge corporation, Qualcomm, work along the lines I've described. Both have achieved great success.

The convenience store succeeds because of family dynamics. The people genuinely care about each other and want to help each other accomplish both personal and business goals. This is one reason why so many small family-run companies have survived so long.

In contrast, the people at Qualcomm aren't related at all, but the company finds other ways to foster a cooperative, nurturing environment. Employees are constantly sharing stories about how they are treated as individuals, not mere numbers. The company offers them incentives such as health clubs, day care, stock sharing, community awareness programs, and higher education opportunities. In other words, Qualcomm does whatever it takes to make people feel they're part of their family, an important piece of their organization, even in an *enormous* corporate environment.

"Mentoring your way to Millions" is a rewarding, positive process that results in dedicated employees and satisfied customers. Did I forget to mention the customers? Once you've mastered the principle of giving others what they want first, you'll find that success is guaranteed.

My approach to business deals with customers is "creative compromise." Rather than assume there has to be a winner in every negotiation, if each of the parties gives a little, I believe we'll both be happy and will do business again. Since we're all in business to make money, and create relationships, why not do it with a smile? Remember, "The greatest success we'll know is helping others succeed and grow." When you've mastered the principles behind "Mentoring your way to Millions," you – and everyone who works for you – will love their job each day!

But there's more to life than work. "Mentoring your way to Millions" is also about giving back to the community and telling success stories to inspire others, especially the youth. Through public speaking and involvement with mentoring programs, you can teach the lessons you've learned, like the one you've just read, and encourage others to go after their dreams.

For when it's all said and done, "The truly rich have Hearts of Gold."

Greg S. Reid, "The Millionaire Mentor," began his company with one question in mind, "Why work hard, when you can Work$mart?" He created *Work$mart,Inc.* a custom imprinter of promotional items.
A dedicated mentor and frequent public speaker,
Greg can be reached at *(800) 924-7627*,
or visit *www.TheMillionaireMentor.com*

Working with People; Not Against Them

By Somers White

Many years ago, I came to Seattle, Washington as the youngest bank President in America for any bank located in a major metropolitan center and without nepotism. I had a lot to learn.

One of the Directors was reported to drive the hardest bargain in Seattle. His name was Josef Diamond. He was a Senior Partner of the law firm of Diamond and Sylvester. Later I learned firsthand he was an absolute teddy bear filled with integrity. He always took the high road and the tough reputation was developed from his ability to win by working with people, not against them.

As I was walking out after my first Board of Directors meeting, Joe said to me, "Until the bank opens, you are going to need an office and as a newcomer you will need to meet people. I will be pleased to give you at no charge an office in my law offices." My office was next to the restrooms. Joe said, "You will meet all the members of the firm. Don't talk to anybody going in. On the way out, they will be more interested in chatting with you."

Every day, for six months, seven days a week, I had one meal with him. It was the greatest learning experience in my life.

When You Receive a "No"

In one of her columns, Ann Landers wrote this story about Joe Diamond. At the height of the depression, he went to every law firm in Seattle looking for a job. Everywhere he was told, "We are not hiring lawyers, we are letting them go." He went in to see the Senior Partner of one firm and said, "To get the experience, I would like to spend a month working for your firm and I will work for no pay. " The Senior Partner agreed. Joe made a tremendous effort. When the month had ended, he stopped by the senior partner's office to say thank you and good-bye. The Senior Partner asked, "How much have we been paying you?" Joe replied, "You haven't been paying me anything." The Senior Partner then said, " Well, we are going to pay you now."

Learning the Nuances and Subtleties

Joe went to work at four times what any other member of his law class was making and by age 29 he became the youngest Partner of any Seattle law firm. He was with the firm his entire career. At 96 years of age, he has been practicing law longer than any person in the State of Washington and still goes to the office every day.

On the opening day of the bank, I was encouraging several employees to entice a man named Irving Anches to open an account. Joe put his hand on my shoulder and said, "Somers, you are a bank President now. You don't need to work so hard."

During the director's meeting, I had more and stronger disagreements with Joe Diamond than with any of the other Directors, but I never left a meeting without feeling that Joe and I were on the same team and without increased admiration for him.

I know of numerous instances where Joe Diamond put other people's interests above his own. Joe had a piece of property in downtown Seattle. He leased it to two black men who wanted to start a business at one quarter the price of another offer he had. Joe said, "I want them to have a chance to succeed."

I talked to an attorney with another firm who said, "When I went around in the building to take a collection for the barber who had a stroke, Joe Diamond was the biggest single contributor."

When the bank had a disagreement with the owner a very small business, Joe Diamond told the bank Board of Directors, "I am sorry, but you will have to get another attorney for this case because this woman is my client and her relationship with me goes back further than that of the bank. She needs me more than you do."

Joe would never hire anyone who was working for another law firm. He did not feel comfortable about taking someone from another firm's team. Joe told me he was thinking about writing a book to be called "Worry Later." He told me again and again he saw clients spend too much emotional energy worrying about things, 90% of which never came to pass.

Accentuating the Positive

His wife told me that after the war ended, Joe came back from the Army as a full bird Colonel and went to rejoin a private club to which he had previously belonged. They told him that he could not rejoin because he was

Jewish. I never heard Joe complain about this or any other thing. He was always completely positive. I never heard Joe raise his voice, get angry, and say bad things about anyone or use one piece of profanity, not even a "darn."

Of all the business people I have ever met, Joe Diamond is the most intelligent, most capable, most generous, most modest, and has the most integrity. He made his money not by taking from others, but by giving to them. Joe Diamond told me his one simple rule, "I do not want to do anything I can't tell the world about." You can easily think of American Presidents from both parties and CEO's of large corporations who could have saved themselves from so much misery if they had only followed this concept.

Most people have trouble making decisions. With one simple idea, Joe empowered me to make rapid and good decisions. He said, "Somers, when you need to make a decision, go with your initial gut feeling. It usually turns out to be right. If you make the decision quickly and you find things are turning out poorly, you have the time to make changes." Wow! Has this given me power in my life!

In these couple of pages I have only given you a quick glance through the keyhole at 1/10 of 1% of what I learned from Josef Diamond and how he helped me grow. It would not have happened without his coaching and mentorship.

Joe was my mentor at the time when I did not know the word. Our relationship was unspoken and grew with the passage of time. Joe was both a mentor and a coach. Today when people talk of a "mentor," I find individuals who think a mentoring relationship is a one-way street where the individual wants to suck out the mentor's brain and never thinks what he or she can give back.

Fifteen years after I left the bank, I received a letter from Joe in which he wrote, "I miss your vitality, your smile, your excitement and your enthusiasm."

Joe calls me about once a month. When I left Seattle to return to Phoenix, I gave Joe a silver box with his name on it and a small inscription without my name. Yesterday, I received the box back from Joe. "Enclosed is the box that you gave me, which has been on my desk since you gave it to me 30 years ago. I am not going to be around forever, so I wanted you to have the box on your desk for the next 30 years."

The Coach/Mentor

For the very wealthy and at some renowned educational institutions, a tutor is sometimes used – an individual personal teacher. This started centuries ago. Then what we saw was the emergence of the coach for an athletic team. Today, with athletes that are paid millions of dollars, stars on a team have a personal coach.

Today a whole new world has emerged, one where CEOs and Rising Stars are hiring coaches to assist them with their businesses and careers. There are songs about seeking love and not finding it by design, but rather coming upon it by chance. So it is with mentors. Few will be as lucky as I was.

However, today you can hire a professional business or career coach. Mentoring and coaching are a matter of definition with wide differences. The same is true of consulting and coaching.

The Differences

I will give you what some strict interpretationists say. A mentor is a relationship where life experiences are shared with the intent to inspire. A coach provides guidance via client self-exploration and assessment. Consulting provides a solution; coaching focuses on aiding the decision-maker in finding a solution.

Therapy moves a client from dysfunction to function while coaching is fine-tuning for something that already works. Trainers are not coaches. Trainers use replicated materials to provide these solutions, and are usually not much better than the book from which they train.

Here is the way I work as a mentor/coach. After an initial two-day meeting, I usually meet with the client twice a month for 30 minutes for twelve months, with additional meetings in the first few months. If distance is involved, we meet by telephone.

Coaching aids decision-makers in finding solutions. It helps individuals to develop personal responsibility and develops clarity of who one really is. Coaches encourage people to act on this basis while managing paradoxes. The client gets better organized, more focused, and ultimately achieves greater results.

What, How, and Who

A client for whom I performed over twenty assignments told me, "Somers, you have been a mentor to so many by holding up a psychological mirror so that the individual can see what is the truth for him or her."

Coaching integrates the what, how, and who of a client. The *"what"* are a client's goals. These can only be achieved with a strategy, the *"how."* Once these have both been developed, they must fit with the client, integrating the *"who"* of a person into their goals and strategies.

Often times, my coaching involves managing contradictory forces that have no permanent solutions, or paradoxes. Using specific client-tailored coaching tools and methods, these contrary forces can be equalized, providing client balance.

Starting from Ground Zero

A classic case of what a coach/mentor can do for someone was Pamela Yellen. When she sought my help, she wanted to be a professional speaker and consultant, but she had no special background. She had had only one $250 speaking engagement. With coaching and mentoring eighteen months later, she was netting close to $250,000 after all expenses on an annualized basis and has gone on to have huge success.

If you get the right coach/mentor, make the right efforts and follow through, it can provide what one Indiana client called *"Successes beyond his wildest dreams."* Do not wait. Get the "right" coach/mentor. In time, it will not be seen as an expense, but as the best investment you ever make, one that will quickly pay for itself many times over!

A former bank President, State Senator and Harvard Business School MBA, Somers White, FIMC, CPAE, has spoken professionally / consulted / mentor-coached in all 50 states and on 6 continents. Somers White works as a professional mentor / coach and can be reached at (602) 952-9292 or *Somerswhite@compuserve.com.*

Looking at What Motivates People

Everyone is Motivated, But Not in the Same Way

By Zig Ziglar

How one person demonstrates motivation may be quite different from the next person. Some people are initiators, and others are "waiters." (Yes, even those folks who wait can be motivated.)

Everybody is motivated periodically or temporarily to do something worthwhile, to make a contribution, to be somebody, to move forward, and so on. The problem is that many people are motivated to do something so seldom or so sporadically that they take from society more than they contribute. The major difference between the givers and the takers is the consistency in their motivations. That consistency comes only with the development of the total person, starting with a character base.

All my life, I have tried to understand why people do the things they do. (And sometimes my greatest challenge is to figure out the motivating factors for my own behavior!) When I boil down all my observations into a couple of concepts that get people to do something, I come up with these two motivators:

- *The desire for gain.*

- *The fear of loss.*

All people have both motivators inside them, creating actions and reactions. One motivator may dominate some people most of the time – perhaps the difference is the "half-empty glass" or the "half-full glass" philosophy. But both motivators are valid reasons for actions and responses. For example, some people may take a job offer because of the travel involved, and others may reject the job for the same reason. Inside, they see either gain or loss as the outcome of the travel.

The Desire for Gain

According to Rabbi Daniel Lapin in his book *The Jewish Edge*, four basic desires exist to motivate people:

"Gold" or wealth: Nothing is wrong with wealth as a form of motivation, as long as it is a motivation and not the motivation. The desire for wealth is limiting in that if money becomes your major motivation, you fall short in many other areas of life. Wealth acquired as a result of your efforts and kept in balance with the rest of your life provides financial security and a certain peace of mind. Not having to worry about the bills and being able to enjoy some of the fun things in life is a good thing!

Power or strength: This motivating factor also gives you a feeling of security and helps you feel good about yourself – if you have acquired that power by playing the game in an ethical manner. Power motivates many people to do such things as build companies that employ others or achieve high political office so that they can do good for themselves, their families, their community, their country, and their fellow man. Properly used, strength or power motivation is basic and wonderful.

Wisdom: Wisdom is acquiring all the knowledge you can and then using that knowledge to make intelligent decisions. Because wisdom is the correct use of the truth in the knowledge you have, wisdom enables you to make good decisions and treat people in an ethical manner. Doing so gives you a legitimate chance to have plenty of friends, good family relationships, peace of mind, and the hope that the future is going to be even better.

Honor: Unfortunately, in today's world people often forgo honor, confuse popularity with notoriety, and work to get the latter, with disastrous long-term results. Taking the "service" approach and doing the right thing gives you a realistic chance of being recognized, rewarded, and honored for the right reasons. Check the records, and you find that people who occupy prominent places of honor are men and women who have lived their lives with integrity and have been servants to scores of other people. Many times these people are dedicated parents, school teachers, small business owners, ministers in small churches, government workers, farmers – anyone who has simply used the other three motivating factors of wealth, strength, and wisdom in a completely ethical manner. The bottom line is that people whose prime motive is contributing to others are able to do more for themselves with the extra energy and feeling-good-about-themselves attitude that results from helping others.

The Fear of Loss

During World War II, the United States government initiated a life insurance program stipulating that the beneficiaries of any U.S. service person killed in action would be paid a $10,000 insurance benefit. Although this insurance was a marvelous idea, the government still had to do a sales job on the policy. A young lieutenant presented the life insurance plan to the troops, giving them all the intricate details and encouraging them to sign up. Not one volunteered. Finally, an old sergeant who had been around for a long time said to the young lieutenant, "Sir, let me talk to the troops. I believe they'll listen." The young lieutenant objected, stating that he had explained all the details and that the men simply were not interested. The old sarge, however, persisted and finally persuaded the young lieutenant to let him have a shot.

The sergeant's sales talk was short and very clear. "Gentlemen," he said, "if you get this insurance policy and you get killed, the government is going to send your family $10,000. If you don't get the policy and you are killed, the government is not going to send your family anything. Now, my question to you is very simple: Which of you do you think the government is going to put on the front lines first? The ones who get killed and cost the government nothing, or the ones who get killed and cost the government $10,000? You think about that." Need I tell you that 100 percent of the troops signed up for the policy?

Whether the story is true or just another GI tale, I'll never know. But this I do know: Fear motivation *does* work.

In most cases, however, fear motivation is short-lived, because you get over your fear. The fear of losing a job if you don't perform is sometimes, at least temporarily, effective at making you perform. Telling a 5-year-old that you're going to deny him television privileges if he misbehaves works to modify his behavior – at least temporarily.

Legitimate Fear for Realistic Reasons

It's been said that you should base your actions on love and not fear. Theoretically, that's true, but in practice it does not always work out that way. There are legitimate fears. Fear of ignorance causes you to seek an education, and fear of poverty makes you work. Fear of disease motivates you to practice healthy and sanitary living. Fear of losing your job inspires you to show up on time and do the best you know how to do. Fear of failing a class drives a student to spend extra time with the books. Fear of losing your family inspires you to be faithful to them, work hard for them, and show them love on a daily basis.

From time to time, I use the acrostic FEAR for False Evidence Appearing Real. However, if the evidence is real, healthy fear is essential for survival. You should have real fear in walking across a busy street without going to the corner. A fear of driving your car at excessive speeds under any conditions, but particularly where the visibility is poor or the streets are slippery, is legitimate. Legitimate fear for realistic reasons is not only natural but also desirable. However, don't allow fear to run rampant through your life, to the point where it becomes so devastating that it produces failure. The problem isn't getting rid of fear, but using it properly.

You must be able to distinguish healthy fears from unhealthy ones (such as worrying every time you hear a siren that a loved one has been in an accident). When you can do that, fear is a friend. Until you can do so, however, fear can be an enemy. Figure out what you should fear, and approach the rest with confidence.

Zig Ziglar (Dallas, TX) is an internationally known authority on high-level performance. He is chairman of the Zig Ziglar Corporation, which is committed to helping people more fully utilize their physical, mental and spiritual resources. His *I CAN* course has been taught in more than 3,000 schools, and hundreds of companies use his books, tapes and videos to train their employees. Zig has traveled more than 5 million miles throughout the world as a speaker and lecturer. He addresses over 300,000 people every year at the Peter Lowe Success Seminars and at businesses, sales organizations, schools and church groups. He also reaches countless numbers through television and radio appearances. Zig is the author of several best selling books, including Zig Ziglar's *Secrets of Closing the Sale*, *Raising Positive Kids in a Negative World*, *See You at the Top*, which has sold over 1.5 million copies, and his two most recent books, *Over the Top and Something to Smile About*. He also develops and markets training audio and videocassettes and other motivational and selling tools for world-wide distribution. His works have been translated into 32 different languages.

The Ten Generalized Principles of
ACTIVE INVESTING

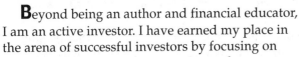

By John R. Burley

Beyond being an author and financial educator, I am an active investor. I have earned my place in the arena of successful investors by focusing on creating wealth through innovative real estate strategies. Over the past several years, I have closed deals on a weekly basis that have created tens of thousands of dollars of profit per deal. One of the keys to my success as an active investor has been following a set of ten generalized principles. By sticking to these principles in my investing endeavors, I have been able to consistently achieve personal success and financial prosperity. In this chapter, I would like to share those principles with you in the hope that you, too, will discover your own financial prosperity.

The Ten Generalized Principles of Investing

The 1ˢᵗ Generalized Principle of Active Investing is "Believe." After comparing those who are successful long-term investors with those who aren't, I discovered that successful people all started with, or soon gained, a belief that what they were doing would work. Belief is a key ingredient in stepping out into the world of successful investing. Belief precedes action. Investors pursue a course of action, because they believe that their actions will produce great financial results. Active investors are people who believe that they can reach their financial goals and experience the freedom that comes from controlling their own destinies. When it comes to developing an investment strategy, active investors believe in themselves and their ability to make it happen. As you take steps to become an active investor, let your first step be a step of faith. Believe in yourself and your ideas.

The 2ⁿᵈ Generalized Principle of Active Investing is "Do What You Love and Love What You Do." Ask yourself what area of investing appeals to you in a way that really grabs and keeps your attention. With very few exceptions, successful investors are very passionate about their work. They thoroughly enjoy their working hours and often treat their businesses and investments with the care they would treat a child who needs nurturing in order to grow and prosper.

The 3rd Generalized Principle of Active Investing is "Determine Your Niche." I cannot stress enough how critical it is that you do this. Without exception, every millionaire I know can tell you in a couple of sentences exactly what it is they do that has made them so successful and rich! Without a precise knowledge of what you do, your chances for success are greatly diminished. Keep in mind that your niche can always be adjusted. If you decide you don't like the "game" you are playing, you can change your niche and take your ball to a game you like.

The 4th Generalized Principle of Active Investing is "Become a Master of Leverage." You must leverage your own time and constantly focus on how you can access the skills, time, resources and money of other people. Leveraging resources is the most valuable tool available to the active investor for compounding investment returns and accelerating the process of wealth building.

Mastering your leverage of time will involve three main disciplines:

- Allocate at least 10 quality hours per week to concentrate on your investment strategies.

- Learn to prioritize your time in favor of the important and challenging tasks that bring you the most wealth. Remember that usually about 15-20% of what you do brings about 80% of your income.

- Learn the most efficient use of your prioritized time so that you get more important work done in less time. This will involve task delegations to other people who have particular areas of expertise that exceed yours, and systems streamlining.

Mastering the leverage of other people's skills will involve assembling a team of experts who support and counsel you to assist you in meeting your objectives. You cannot be a successful investor without the assistance and expertise of other people.

The 5th Generalized Principle of Active Investing is "Think Laterally." Lateral Thinking is the art of looking at things from different points of view. You can make a lot of money by doing very simple things that other people have overlooked. In simple terms, ask yourself how could something be done better or what do people want that they are not getting now?

As an active investor, I apply lateral thinking by providing the opportunity for the average non-home owner to own a home. I firmly believe that the best way to make a lot of money is to help a lot of people in a significant way. I do this without exploitation. Close to 25% of the population would like to own their own home but cannot do so using conventional means of financing. I relieve their pain by providing them with a housing opportunity. This is an example of lateral thinking within my niche of real estate investing.

The 6th Generalized Principle of Active Investing is "Do Market Research." As you progress in "The Game" you will become a master of your market. Keep in mind that, while market research is important, the only way to become a master of your market is to actually be in the market. Jump in and learn as much as you can while playing the game. Remember, if you need to know everything before starting, you will never get started. You must avoid analysis paralysis.

The 7th Generalized Principle of Active Investing is "Be Efficient." One of the hardest things for poor and middle-class people to understand is that hard work and money have very little to do with each other. Mastering efficiency depends very much on understanding the principle of leverage: having people, time, resources and money working for you and not against you.

All successful investment strategies feature streamlined systems that allow the investor to accomplish more with less effort and less time. Ideally they are run so efficiently that they continue to run whether or not the investor is directly overseeing them on a regular basis. I cannot stress enough the importance of systems. My business and real estate investing is designed so that an "average" person could come in and run it indefinitely. I do, however, continually improve my systems by engaging "exceptional" people to run the show.

The 8th Generalized Principle of Active Investing is "Let Lag Work." The time-honored principle of lag is best described by the biblical theme that *"you reap what you sow."* In other words, if you follow the principles outlined in this chapter and persist, you will be successful. The benefits follow the labor. The "reaping what you sow" theme has two implications. It refers not only to the effort you make, but also to the character or quality of the effort. An element of "what goes around comes around" is carried in the concept of lag.

When handed a setback, rather than giving into fear and quitting, bolster your determination to meet the challenge and keep going. If your principles are sound, then all you have to do is make minor adjustments until you find your own formula for success. Adjust your strategy until it is a good fit for the ten generalized principles. Lag guarantees your success if you will just get in the game and stay there. Keep the faith, persist and you will be rewarded.

The 9th Generalized Principle of Active Investing is "Understand Timing." Windows of opportunity exist in every market. It is just a matter of using lateral thinking and market research to locate and recognize them. So look around your market. Find the opportunities and jump in!

The key to proper timing is to ensure that your niche fits into the timing of your market – that you are not selling straw hats in the winter, only buying. Be prepared to modify or adapt your niche if the timing in your market is wrong for your first choice of strategy. Your market research will identify the timing issue for you. Do not get hung up on the idea that there is only one way to be a successful investor.

The 10th Generalized Principle of Active Investing is "Take Action." Rich people are masters of action. They understand that the only way to find the right formula for success is to participate in the game. Poor people are masters of excuses. They lay blame on others and on circumstances. Their fears provide them with an endless babbling stream of seemingly logical reasons why they cannot and should not act. This negative internal chatter is simply psycho-babble. You and only you are responsible for your success or failure. Take action!

These ten principles have guided my investment career. They have been major tools that I have used to carve out my personal financial freedom. My hope is that you will apply the *Ten Generalized Principles of Investing* to your investment strategies so you can enjoy the financial freedom that you deserve!

John Burley has completed over 1000 real estate transactions. John is a best-selling author, a sought-after financial educator and an internationally recognized authority on real estate investing.
To learn more about John Burley's wealth creating strategies, books, audio courses, and seminars, visit his Web site at
www.johnburley.com.

The Secrets To Success Discovered Through
Self-Promotion

By Debbie Allen

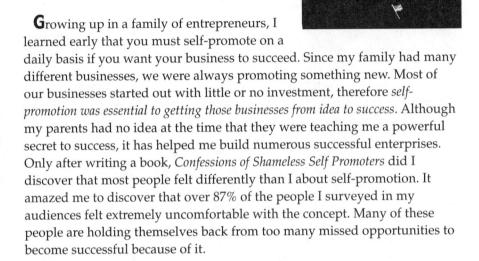

Growing up in a family of entrepreneurs, I learned early that you must self-promote on a daily basis if you want your business to succeed. Since my family had many different businesses, we were always promoting something new. Most of our businesses started out with little or no investment, therefore *self-promotion was essential to getting those businesses from idea to success*. Although my parents had no idea at the time that they were teaching me a powerful secret to success, it has helped me build numerous successful enterprises. Only after writing a book, *Confessions of Shameless Self Promoters* did I discover that most people felt differently than I about self-promotion. It amazed me to discover that over 87% of the people I surveyed in my audiences felt extremely uncomfortable with the concept. Many of these people are holding themselves back from too many missed opportunities to become successful because of it.

Where did the fear of self-promotion come from? Many learned the opposite from their parents as they were growing up. They were taught to believe that it was not polite to talk about yourself; that if you did, it would come across as pushy, rude or conceited. Your parents may have taught you that but they also said, "Go out in the world on your own and be successful." How can you be successful if you don't tell others what you do and how you can help them? You can't! If you don't self-promote, you are not going to achieve the success that you truly deserve! You already know how to do it. In fact, you were self-promoting in grade school, when you raised your hand in fervor to show the teacher you knew the answer. Right?

Undeniably, there is unethical self-promotion. We've all witnessed it, and maybe even lost business to it.

"Egomania is a strange disease – it makes everyone sick except the person who has it." – Zig Ziglar

But egomania is not what we're discussing. You can do successful self-promoting with class, ethics and truth. As Will Rogers said, "If you done it, it ain't braggin'." What have you done that has helped your customers? Why do your customers give you compliments about your service and/or products? They compliment you because they love you and want to support your success. But are you allowing them to offer you that support?

Another thing I discovered when surveying my audiences is that most people simply say "Thank you," when receiving a compliment and walk away. They are missing another big opportunity – an opportunity for their best customers to magnify their marketing. By adding just a few more words to the "Thank you," they could be receiving a lot more business. Take it one step further and *ask* customers if you could use the testimonial they just gave you in your advertising, web site and/or brochures. What your customers are saying is that they are your shameless fans and want to support your success. Third party endorsements are one of the most powerful marketing tools you could use to promote your business. And all you have to do get them is to *ask*.

If you still feel uncomfortable with the concept of self-promotion, I have another tip for you. Begin to look at self-promotion from this day forward as *serving others instead of self-serving*. I'm sure you are passionate about what you do and truly want to help your customers. If that is the case, don't you want to help more and more people who could use your services and/or products? You can't do that if you don't successfully self-promote and tell more people about what you do. Tell others why you are the expert and share success stories from your customers. Your self-promotion, when done well, helps people get what they desire.

The most successful people in the world are *all* self-promoters. These are the people that talk in elevators! In fact, behavioral scientists, George Dudley and Shannon Goodson, have made a career out of studying the science of self-promotion to prove it. Their assessment identifies the ways in which we unconsciously avoid self-promotion and limit our success. Their research studies discovered that *self-promotion is directly related to success.*

They also discovered that the most successful people all had the same three traits to help them achieve success from it. The first is *positioning*. They continually position themselves in front of people who will make a difference in achieving their goals. Who can you position yourself in front of who will help you and you can help them in return? *Ask* others how you can help them and how you may find a way to work together. Examples:

share numerous leads or customer database list, co-market with links online, create joint ventures, etc.

Too frequently we settle for working with the people who are the *easiest* to reach, not the most *effective*. And often we don't position ourselves to offer support to our competition. Yes, your competition! You may look at them as the enemy when they could actually be one of your best alliances. After all, you have one BIG thing in common with them – the same target market. Not only have I become the walking/talking *Rolodex* of my alliances, I believe in *never throwing business away*. Trust me – it has come back to me many times over.

For example: After I spoke in Australia, my client asked me if I knew of another speaker who lived in that country that I could refer to her. Now living on the other side of the world, I could have easily said "No I don't." But I don't believe in *throwing business away*. And I do *believe in looking for opportunities to position myself with competitors who want to build alliances*. I found my client the perfect speaker by doing a search online. I positioned myself in front of my Australian competitor by sending him the lead by email. That one email has brought me thousands of dollars in business. This newly discovered business alliance has referred me to dozens of leads in over five countries. The same opportunities are awaiting you too – simply seek them out and ACT upon them. Building strong strategic business alliances is like *networking on steroids*!

The second behavior Dudley and Goodsen discovered was that natural self-promoters had their own unique *style*. What makes you different from your competition? What makes you stand out and become memorable in a field of expertise? For example: I am called "The Shameless Marketing Guru." I had no idea that I would ever be called "Shameless" much less a "Guru," but it works for me. My books stand out in the marketplace. This tag is now a part of everything I do, including the license plate and the bumper sticker on my car. Shameless yes, but does it work at getting me noticed and support my style? You bet it does! It has even helped me to build my personalized brand. How will you get others to remember you?

The third attribute of natural self-promoters is *repetition*. Successful self-promoters don't ever give up. They keep going even after they have made big mistakes. They hit the wall, stand up, dust themselves off and move in another direction. Too many others give up way too soon. They throw their hands up in the air and stick with the limited belief system that they can't make it work. *But you are not going to give up!* Take one more step and keep going until you reach your goals and achieve your dreams. It's okay to make mistakes – every successful person has made plenty of them. In fact, they are constantly testing and adjusting their marketing efforts to see what works best. So, if you are not making mistakes, you are probably not stretching yourself far enough outside of your comfort zone. Just make sure that you learned from your mistakes, move on and keep on going.

How can you be successful if you don't believe in yourself and what you have to offer to your customers? You can't! Therefore the first step in successful self-promotion is to have a *strong belief system*. This positive belief has pulled me through many difficult times in my personal and professional life. When you have this inner strength, you can believe the universe will bring you many opportunities. Therefore only good comes to you in even the most difficult of times. It is powerful and it really works!

Debbie Allen is an international professional speaker and author of three books, including the best selling *Confessions of Shameless Self Promoters*. Download a free chapter, sign up for your free newsletter, visit the pressroom and view her dynamic presentations at *www.DebbieAllen.com*.

Allen & Associates Consulting, Inc.
PO Box 27946, Scottsdale, AZ 85255-0149
Toll Free: 800-359-4544
Fax: 480-634-7692
Email: *Debbie@DebbieAllen.com*

Awakening Your Creative Potential

By Kevin Eikenberry

After much thought and mental preparation, I sat down to write this chapter. While I knew what I wanted write, the exact words wouldn't come. After a few minutes of struggle, I decided to take a "power nap."

Often when facing a particular problem or challenge, I have found that if I sit or lay down thinking of this particular problem and take a very brief nap, when I awake the challenge is easily mastered, the problem quickly solved.

So I laid down, thinking about the title for this chapter and drifted off to sleep. I awoke with a solution, just as I had expected I would. You see the solution was inside of me; I just needed to find it. So it is with most people's creativity. We are born as creative geniuses; yet as adults, many of us can't seem to tap into this genius. We can find it if we know how to look. We can exercise our creative muscles, correcting the atrophy of inactivity. It is as if a part of us is asleep. We need to awaken our creativity!

You Were Born Creative

The first hurdle we have to get over in awakening our creativity is to believe that it is actually there! Howard Gardner of Harvard has spent his life learning about human intelligence. He has found that all of us are extremely intelligent, but that we aren't all intelligent in the ways we often think of intelligence (i.e. we don't all score high on an IQ test). He has identified seven different intelligences that we have in some combination. Gardner's research shows that we are most successful when we work from our strengths – reaching our potential by exercising those intelligence muscles that we already have.

Human creativity is like that. Most people have a personal definition of creativity and feel that creativity is reserved for "creative types"– artists, poets, musicians, actors, writers. (Feel free to add your personal descriptors to this list.) In reality, though, just like intelligences, there are different phases in the creative process and all of us have strengths among these phases.

Remember, the research says that we are all creative! What makes us have trouble believing it is other research which shows that much of our natural creativity has been stifled by the time we are 8 or 10.

The good news is that it *is* still there, and we *can* awaken it.

Awakening Our Creativity

How do you best like to be awakened in the morning? By a shrill, loud alarm? By your favorite type of music, softly played? Or do you prefer your body naturally awakening when it has received the sleep it needs?

My guess is that you prefer a gentler nudging out of sleep and back to consciousness. The techniques and tools in the rest of this chapter will help you start gently awakening your creativity. Think of these ideas and tools as fun and soothing ways for you to re-acquaint yourself with and start to gently exercise your creative muscles.

Observation

Noted biochemist Albert Szent-Györgyi said, "Discovery consists of seeing what everybody else has seen and thinking what no one else has thought." This is a powerful argument for the power of observation as a component of our creativity. Most of us think of observation as being a visual exercise. Upon more reflection, however, you would quickly recognize that all of our senses play into keen observation. When we notice smells and sounds, we are observing just as surely as when we are looking at something.

Here is a fun exercise to help you strengthen your powers of observation.

Look at a familiar object with a fresh perspective. You've probably looked at your television often, but have you really looked at it? Start this fun exercise by describing your set to someone or writing down a description. Then spend ten minutes really looking at your set (without it being turned on!) Look at it from different angles. Take note of the size and shape of the buttons. Run your fingers over the various surfaces. Now describe your set again (or write another description). Notice how different your descriptions are. You can do this exercise with any familiar item around you. Consider doing it often!

The skills developed through this type of exercise are invaluable when you are looking for new approaches or solutions. Take the time to observe (in new deeper ways) both the challenge you face and the solutions you are considering. You will be amazed at what you find.

Curiosity

Curiosity is important to our creativity and is linked closely to observation. If we don't notice or observe things, it is hard to be curious about them! While curiosity may have killed the cat (though I have never understood why), the lack of curiosity has severely stunted many people's creativity. One of the differences between kids and adults is their overall level of curiosity. Have you ever noticed how curious a preschooler is? Think about that level of curiosity compared to the curiosity of an early teen, compared to that of the average adult.

When you recapture your curiosity, you will further awaken your creativity. Here are several ways to invigorate your curiosity:

Do Puzzles. Whatever kind of puzzles you like! Crossword or other word puzzles are fine. Visual or mechanical puzzles work too.

Read a Mystery. Read a good "who done it" and put yourself in the role of the detective. Thinking like Nancy Drew, Sherlock Holmes or Columbo will help you work on your curiosity. You can watch a mystery movie as well, but reading allows you to exercise your curiosity more because it puts you more in control and you can manage the pace of the story.

Ask "Why?" Speaking of Columbo, asking "why?" is a great way to exercise your curiosity and learn a lot at the same time. Did you ever notice how successful Columbo was at asking questions?

As you look at the challenges you face, play the detective. Look for clues that may lead you to a creative solution.

Metaphor

When I woke up from the "power nap" mentioned earlier, I had more than a way to start this chapter. I had a metaphor. Tapping your creativity is a matter of awakening it! Having the metaphor of "awakening," helped me connect the dots to write this chapter (in what I hope is) a fresh way.

In school we learned about analogies, metaphors and similes, and the technical differences between them. They are all ways of comparing something to something else. For purposes of creativity, it doesn't matter what you call them. Think about how your situation, challenge, problem (or whatever you want to be creative about) is like something else. In fact, here is a unique way to do this.

Random Association Exercise. Create a random list of words. There are several ways to do this:

- Open the dictionary, and pick a random word.

- Use artifacts from a board game like Scattergories, Taboo, or Spinergy to provide random words or ideas.

- Email *metaphor@discian.com* to get a random word generator for use on your computer.

Once you have a word, ask yourself how your situation (or one or more of the general elements) is similar or dissimilar to the word/phrase/idea you randomly selected. Record all ideas. Use the words as a starting point. One word may not make a connection, but it might lead you to another word and a great idea. Let your mind go. Capture any and all promising thoughts. Be aware that the random word itself may be the key to your perfect metaphor!

Repeat the process of picking another random word, until you have one awesome "can't-miss" idea, or enough good ideas to move on in your creation or problem solving process.

Staying Awake

There are many great books filled with techniques to help you increase your creativity. I encourage you to follow up your reading of this chapter by going to the bookstore or library and finding some of them. Studying this subject is another way to awaken your creative potential.

I have shared just a few techniques. They are practical, but aren't a harsh alarm clock to your sleeping creative potential. Rather they are fun, gentle nudges that, while immediately applicable, are also meant to give you a glimpse into your creative potential.

You are creative. Your creativity may be in a deep sleep, but it is there. All you have to do is wake it up, and put it to use.

Pssst, it's time to wake up . . .

Kevin Eikenberry *(kevin@discian.com)* is Principal of the Discian Group, a Learning Consulting Company in Indianapolis, IN. For information on their services, visit *http://discian.com*. For more information on products and services to awaken your creativity and increase other life skills, go to *http://milliondollarskills.com*.

Taxes, the I. R. S. and You

By Bernie Gartland

Why would you possibly want to know what the I.R.S. knows about you? You *might* want to know if you fit the following profile.

• You have not filed tax returns for several years.
• You have filed tax returns, but you still owe the taxes.
• You have not filed the tax returns, but the I.R.S. says that you owe money.
• You owe a great deal of tax and you are wondering if you can eliminate those taxes without paying them.

With the Proper Request, Important Information (Called a "Blue Print") Can Be Obtained From the I.R.S.

This information can reveal all of the following:

• If you haven't filed tax returns in several years, which years are still considered open years by the I.R.S.?

• Has the I.R.S. had you under criminal investigation?

• If you did not file tax returns and the I.R.S. says that you owe taxes, for which years do you owe and how much is owed for each of those years?

• When did they make this assessment against you and on what basis did they make that assessment?

• What is the final date that the I.R.S. has the authority to collect these tax dollars from you?

• Does the I.R.S. have a refund waiting for you for which you have not filed?

• Has the I.R.S. done an analysis and placed you into an "uncollectable" category resulting in a stay of collection activity?

• Has the I.R.S. filed a tax lien against you?

• If you filed a bankruptcy, what was the date and discharge of each bankruptcy?

• If you filed an Offer in Compromise (OIC) did the OIC get recorded with the I.R.S.?

- Has the I.R.S. applied any kind of civil fraud penalty against you?

- What records does the I.R.S. have on your earnings for the past ten years?

When a person has a tax problem the initial step in solving that problem is to get the "blue print" of what the I.R.S. knows about them. By obtaining this information, and by working with a professional experienced in dealing with the tax code and the I.R.S., we can make a better determination of all possible solutions for any tax problem. If a person has not filed in several years, the information from the I.R.S. will tell us which years they are looking for, which years they are not looking for and how much the person has earned over the years. This gives us a starting point to get the tax returns prepared for the proper years. After we know exactly how much a person owes, we can then talk about options.

If the I.R.S. has indicated that the taxpayer owes tax dollars but the individual has not filed the tax returns, the information that we get from the I.R.S. will indicate which years the I.R.S. has prepared what is known as a substitute for return (SFR). The internal revenue code allows them to prepare returns on your behalf if you do not do so. The basis for the calculations is gathered from certain sources such as prior year tax returns, if any, the national labor statistics manual (that gives an average of the amount earned in each person's profession) or any W-2's or 1099's that the I.R.S. has received over the years.

It is very important to note what dates the taxpayer has filed any and all bankruptcies and when the bankruptcies were discharged. Likewise, it is important to note the OIC indicators. These indicators become vitally important when proceeding with a strategic game plan of how to resolve each persons tax problem.

Once all the information is analyzed, a game plan is developed as to which years need to be filed, and which years do not have to be filed. If the taxpayer has already filed the tax returns and simply owes taxes, we then come up with a plan to handle the amounts that are owed.

There Are Four Major Strategic Options That Are Available to the Taxpayer:

(1) Simply wait out the statute of limitations on collections. (ten years from the date of the assessment). The statute applies to both situations where the taxpayer has filed the tax return, or if the I.R.S. has prepared a substitute for return.

(2) Set up a payment schedule with the I.R.S. Interest and penalties continue to accrue.

(3) Develop an Offer in Compromise (OIC) which is the closest thing to a tax amnesty program that the I.R.S. has to offer.

(4) File a tax bankruptcy – either a Chapter 13 or a Chapter 7.

When we do an analysis of the options for each taxpayer, we always like to try to make an OIC work. Obviously, if you can offer pennies on the dollar to the I.R.S. to eliminate the entire tax debt (along with the penalties and interest) without having to go into a bankruptcy situation, then this is the method to utilize. Before an OIC is initiated, there should first be a complete analysis of the information we received from the I.R.S. to determine that all tax years have been filed and that the taxpayer is in total compliance. This is a requirement when submitting an OIC. Depending on the facts of the case, it usually takes anywhere from six months to one year to process the offer once it is determined the taxpayer qualifies and what the amount of the offer should be. Once the offer is accepted, the tax is abated and the liens are removed. Obviously no further collection activity takes place. There is, however, a contingency to this acceptance. The taxpayer has to be in compliance for the five years *following* the offer. This means that all tax returns, whether business or personal returns, have to be filed in a timely manner and be paid. If the person does not remain in compliance, the I.R.S. will default the OIC and collection proceedings will be initiated.

One of the most misunderstood options when taxes are owed is what we affectionately call the tax bankruptcy. Most professionals don't understand that taxes can be discharged or controlled in bankruptcy. Remember bankruptcy attorneys don't usually understand tax law and tax attorneys don't usually understand bankruptcy law. Therefore, confusion reigns.

When you read the sections of the bankruptcy code that pertain to whether or not taxes can be discharged, you will understand why most professionals have no understanding of the criteria. The sections are very confusing and speak in terms of what cannot be discharged. Because of the language, it is difficult to understand what *can* be discharged.

If a person has a tax problem, whether or not they filed their tax returns or the I.R.S. filed the substitute for return and there are taxes due, there are options. If the taxpayer's records are non-existent, there are ways to obtain an abundance of information from the I.R.S. We then analyze this information and come up with a game plan that is best for the taxpayer under the circumstances. There are clients that we commonly refer to as two-part problem solving clients. First, we get the information for the preparation of tax returns and prepare those tax returns to get the taxpayer in compliance. Then we look at all the options that are available to the client including, but not limited to, an OIC, an installment agreement, waiting out the statute of limitations on collections or declaring a tax bankruptcy, whether it be a Chapter 7 or 13.

Obviously there is not enough time to go into a detailed analysis of every single case. Suffice it to say that if a person has a tax problem there are many solutions to getting that person out of the "tax closet," back into compliance and beginning a new chapter in the taxpayer's life.

Obviously, this is something an amateur cannot do alone. It requires a person who is thoroughly familiar with the tax laws and the operations of the Internal Revenue Service.

At the age of 31, Bernie Gartland decided to go to law school where he graduated cum laude. After stints with the Attorney General's office and private practice in criminal defense and family law, he began focusing on the tax arena. His expertise in the areas of tax preparation, tax problem solving and tax bankruptcy are widely recognized, having lectured widely on the subjects, including a "road trip" with the I.R.S. He has authored a manual on federal tax liens. He is a frequent guest on TV and has had his own radio talk show in Southern California called "Taxes, the IRS and You." A CD from a recent show where he discussed the advantages of knowing what the I.R.S. knows about you and the basics to understanding the code sections involved in tax bankruptcy is available for of the price of shipping and handling. His Web site is *www.gartlandlaw.com*. and you can email him with your questions at *bernie@gartlandlaw.com*. A private, free consultation for any tax problem is available by calling *1-888-233-3313*.

Five Simple Reasons Most People Will Never Get Rich ...

and How To Make Sure You Do!

By Mike Litman and Jason Oman

What did I learn about getting rich by interviewing over 43 self-made millionaires? After interviewing one after another, I realized many of the secrets that make them rich while others continue to struggle. When you understand and do what self-made millionaires do, you get to become one of them. If you don't understand and do what they do, you don't get to become one. It's really that simple.

Here are five simple reasons most people will never get rich and how to make sure you do:

Reason 1: Waiting to Start

Most people don't want to wait for success. But, at the same time, they are willing to wait before getting started on the road to success. Do you see the problem here? The longer you wait to get started, the longer it will be before you get the money, success, and lifestyle you want. Many people are waiting for everything to be perfect before they get going. Therefore, they never get going and never get the rewards. No race has ever been won (or even finished) by someone who never left the starting line. Don't wait to get going. Start today on the road to success.

Reason 2: Being Financially Illiterate

The cornerstone of all wealth is understanding the difference between assets and liabilities. The difference is this: Assets put money IN your pocket. Liabilities take money *out* of your pocket. Most people think their home, car, and other possessions are assets. But, the truth is that in most cases those things take money out of your pocket. They *cost* you money. They don't *make* you money. Therefore, by the true definition above, those things are liabilities. They take money *out* of your pocket each month. When you have more money coming *in* from real assets than you have going *out* to pay for liabilities, you will be financially free.

There is only one way to do this. Which brings us to...

Reason 3: Focusing on Linear Income Instead of Passive Income

One of the millionaires I interviewed said it simply. He said, "If you're not making money while you sleep, you'll never be rich." Linear income is what you get from a job. You work for an hour and get paid only one time for that one hour's work That's it. Passive income is when you work once but continue to get paid over and over again from work you're no longer doing. Investing in or creating true assets that provide passive income for you is your ticket to wealth.

Reason 4: Not Understanding or Using Systems for Making Money

A system for making money is anything that allows you to make money without your own effort. In other words, it's an automated way to make money. All true assets are simply "systems" of one sort or another. Once you create or invest in a proven system for making money, there is no limit to the money you can make. Becoming a master of money systems can bring you riches beyond your dreams.

Reason 5: Not Being Persistent or Patient Enough

To finish any race, you have to leave the starting line and follow through to the finish line. Most people create their own failure by either not getting started or not following through, or both. To get rich, successful, and happy you must have the patience and persistence to cross the finish line. You must not only get started, but also follow through. This may sound obvious, but it's still the cause of most failure.

Only by joining the small percentage of people who are willing to do the five things mentioned above will you have the greatest chances for wealth and success. It's really quite simple... Decide to do these things and you can get rich too. If you don't do them, then – like most people – you may never get rich. Decide now to master the ideas mentioned above and begin your road to success now. Then follow through and watch the difference it makes.

Mike Litman is the host of *The World's #1 Personal Development Radio Show* and co-author of the #1 Best-Seller *Conversations with Millionaires*. You can visit him at *www.mikelitman.com*

Building a Successful Business

Aspirational Sales Planning

By Bryan C. Davis

Have you ever listened to a successful business person or colleague at a meeting or seminar and wondered quietly to yourself, "How have they become so successful?" This is normally quickly followed by, "He is no more intelligent or talented than I am, so why am I not as successful?"

If so, then this article is for you. But before I go on, let me just make a point. Success is relative; what we often don't see is the downside – the broken marriages, the debts, the ill-health. So the "health warning" on this article is to always strive to maintain balance in everything you do and strive to become successful without losing yourself. This advice is equally applicable to companies.

In my experience the single key differentiating factor between the meaningfully successful and the merely moderately successful and, indeed, the unsuccessful is related to two contributory factors: (1) a deep understanding of the reasons the person is doing what he does in the first place and (2) a laser beam focus on making it happen.

I know that this is something of a simplification but I stand by it nonetheless. Some may call it obsessive – I call it good business and life practice! Think about it – why do companies get into trouble?

More often than not they get into trouble because they take their eye off the ball, fail to understand the changing market place, or perhaps move away from their core reason for being in business in the first place. Often they replace their core reason with a much shallower thing called "greed." Greed is never good. It just makes you unpleasant. However, there is a very clear distinction between greed and selfishness; one is self-destructive and the other is self-serving.

M. Scott Peck puts it very well in his book *The Road Less Traveled and Beyond*. He describes how we are all basically selfish, always seeking self-gratification or self fulfillment as the end goal of all that we do. (This is probably more evident in business than in our private lives since businesses have many "self interests" to serve.)

That doesn't mean that we are all needlessly unpleasant or indeed that we are any less philanthropic, just that we tend not to do things if there is nothing in it for ourselves. The rewards may be as basic as just feeling good after we complete a particularly hard task or some form of community service, or as complex as creating a business to deliver the means to pursue our dreams!

The stress in life, as well as business, comes when we either don't understand or don't buy into the reasons for doing what we do but we have to do it anyway!

So let's start at the top. Why are you in business or working for someone else in the first place? What are your aspirations? Why do you get out of bed in the morning? There are as many reasons as there are people. For instance, some may want to just provide their family with a comfortable lifestyle; others may want to secure their financial future. The bottom line is that we're all motivated by some aspiration or other.

But let's be very clear about one thing. In business as well as in life "You can't have a bottom line without first securing your top line!" No amount of expensive consultants or business techniques or training courses will help you if your proposition can't open the door to opportunity.

Securing your top line is the key to the Aspirational Sales Planning (ASP) approach.

ASP is a three-stage approach that helps companies and individuals understand what, when and how they can realize their aspirations – be they life goals or business outcomes. It is not a quick fix, get rich quick system. It's a business life style based on an honest approach to business.

Stage 1 – Understand Why

Understanding your end goal is the starting point for planning how to get there. This is as true in life as in business but here I'll concentrate on the business application. Remember businesses are made up of people – decisions are influenced greatly by individual aspirations, as are customers, suppliers, employees and families. Stephen Covey puts it well when he says, "Seek first to understand and then to be understood." If you don't understand yourself and your reasons for doing something, then how can your business colleagues or partners possibly understand?

When I do an initial ASP consultation, very often I find that each member of the Board of the company has different aspirations and a personal exit strategy for themselves and the company or product we're discussing. It's amazing just how divergent these may be! For instance, in one company, all members of the board had such different ideas of what they wanted to achieve, it's a wonder that the company was able to do anything at all. So the first stage of the ASP process is to clearly identify what the key stakeholders want to get from their efforts or, more simply, what they want the product or service or business to deliver! For example, my Aspirational Sales Plan for the Longwater Network is orientated to helping me realize my life goal of financial independence within the next 5 years. I have clearly identified and discussed this with my business partners. Now it is explicit in everything I do.

But this isn't where Stage 1 finishes. Once you understand where you want to get to, the next and probably hardest part is to figure out how you're going to do it. Simply put, you strive to understand what you have and how to package it so that it becomes a viable proposition. A quick comparison between your aspirations and your plan will tell you if your original desires are realistic in the current market and with the current product. You will also have something that is linked to your personal motivations as well.

Stage 2 – Validate

What have we achieved thus far? We have a realistic aspirational plan. That's great, but it doesn't put food on the table. The second stage of the ASP model is to test whether the plan is indeed realistic. At Longwater, we do this by piloting the plan. We take a selection of our target client base and test the proposition. Not only that, we pre-set the success criteria and stick to them. It so easy to become seduced into the rationalization: "Well that's only the pilot – the real thing will be much better."

I don't mean spending vast amounts of money and resources on market testing or other such techniques, although these do indeed have their place. I mean getting out there and selling the proposition. If you can't get through the door with your proposition, what chance do you have of seeing if your product or service is viable? The end of Stage 2 will give you validation of the realistic outcome of your aspirational plan.

Stage 3 – "Walk the Talk"

Now comes the hard part – what if the pilot has not validated your aspiration? This is something with which individuals and companies alike can have difficulty. Rejection and failure are not something we like to experience. My own experience is that you can decide to quit or you can re-engineer the proposition or adjust your aspirations, i.e. go back to Stage 1 and refine your assumptions. This doesn't mean you have to change your aspirations. You just how you actualize them.

It's really a matter of personal choice. Each is equally good. The upside is that at least you have something tangible upon which to base your decision. In many cases it's better to walk away from a bad proposition than pursue it to ruin. What generally keeps us trying, and failing, is the false hope of success and the fear of failure. Remember fear is "false expectation appearing real" and is normally self fulfilling if you allow it to become so.

If, on the other hand, the pilot was a success, then you can transition to Stage 3, which is to implement your Aspirational Sales Plan.

Once you know that what you have is viable, then it is much easier to pursue the success that will certainly come your way. Note that here I said "easier," not simple! Don't be under any illusion that you will not need to remain focused and committed,. If you do, and your strategy is valid, you have improved your chances of realizing your aspirations many times more than those who have no such focus.

A business visionary, Bryan Davis has an international reputation gained delivering corporate transformation through the application of cutting edge business techniques. He is a regular speaker at international conferences covering a variety of business subjects and is a co-founder of the Longwater Network. He has developed Aspirational Sales Planning with his business partner, Brain Smithies, and now helps companies address the key issue of sustaining and growing their top line. He can be reached at *bryan@longwater.net*.

Purposeful Leadership

HOW TO TURN EMPLOYEES INTO PARTNERS

By Niurka

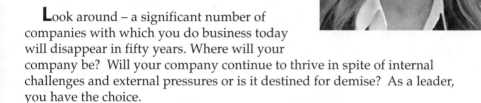

Look around – a significant number of companies with which you do business today will disappear in fifty years. Where will your company be? Will your company continue to thrive in spite of internal challenges and external pressures or is it destined for demise? As a leader, you have the choice.

Continually driving your organization toward uncharted levels of growth and development requires purposeful leadership. The terms "management" and "leadership" are often used interchangeably; however, the disparity between these two roles is vast. Management, although vital to an organization's existence, is only one piece to the complex corporate puzzle. Management is responsible for getting employees to commit to organizational goals while holding them accountable for achieving those goals. On the other hand, *purposeful leadership, is the art of inspiring people to make a total, enthusiastic, and voluntary commitment to achieving and exceeding organizational goals.* This form of leadership causes employees to embrace organizational goals as if they were their own.

Purposeful Leadership Key #1

Purposeful leaders align with their employees to discover and articulate a common vision. This is not a statement on a plaque. It is a shared vision ingrained in the hearts and minds of every partner. This shared vision acts as a beacon that shines brightly, guiding the moment-to-moment actions of every team member.

Far too many employees do no more than come to work, do their job, get paid, and go home. Their main motivation is making money, keeping their boss happy, having time off, and perhaps someday getting a promotion. Although there is nothing technically wrong with this motivation, it is vastly different from the motivation of a steadfast team of partners driven by a common vision. The lukewarm employee attitude conveys little or no interest in organizational growth, innovation, problem solving, or exceeding internal and external client expectations. With this attitude, work is a necessary evil.

In the absence of purposeful leadership, employees will react to external factors based on the dominating thoughts of *their* minds – which may or may not be consistent with your thoughts as a leader. This reactive state results from one of two triggers. Either the employee is reacting to avoid a situation he or she considers *painful*, e.g., placating an angry customer or making a sales call immediately after losing a sale. Or the employee is reacting by moving towards a situation he or she interprets as *pleasurable*, e.g., leaving early, taking long lunches, or engaging in extensive personal phone calls during business hours. Avoiding pain and moving towards pleasure are innate human needs. One key difference between employees and partners is that employees directly react to avoid pain and gain pleasure while partners proactively use pain and pleasure to drive themselves towards a compelling vision.

History reveals that premiere organizations like Disney, Johnson & Johnson, and Marriott that have produced outstanding results while withstanding the test of time have a very specific commonality – *they all have a steadfast corporate culture that is driven towards a collective vision and guided by core values.* Numerous organizations continue to operate in an environment devoid of a clearly defined and communicated ideology. The executives of these organizations often look internally and mistake symptoms for problems. They will see high turnover, low team morale and decreasing productivity. What they fail to understand is why these "symptoms" are occurring. They haven't yet noticed the inevitable connection between the organization's ideology and their teams retention rate, empowerment, and productivity.

Purposeful Leadership Key #2

Core values drive behavior. They are the foundation of an organization's success. Ask yourself, "If each employee within my organization were held at gunpoint and asked to define our core values, could they do it?" If the answer is yes, congratulations – your organization is part of an elite few. If the answer is no it is your duty to capitalize on the abundant resources readily available to you.

Core values answer the question, "What do we stand for when we are at our best? What principles and ideals depict us when we capitalize on our capabilities at the highest level?" These values are the foundation of your organization's success because they provide a clear benchmark for how every partner is expected to act. Core values drive behavior.

Many executives believe that they do not need to clarify the organizational values and vision because they once wrote a "mission statement" that they hoped would suffice for 2003 and beyond. Unless the mission (or purpose) is ingrained in the hearts and minds of every employee, it is worthless.

Purposeful Leadership Key #3

Ingraining core values into an individual's psyche is challenging. Purposeful leaders encourage and coach their employees to uncover their own personal values while developing their own personal vision. **Employees with a strong personal direction can align with their organization to create a powerfully synergistic relationship.**

Being able to continuously attract, develop, and retain partners is a result of creating an organizational culture that is grounded in a specific set of core values and driven by a shared vision. Once this ideology is defined, communicated, and lived you will find that it begins to positively impact your corporate culture.

Internally, each individual begins to realize the correlation between the organization's values and his or her own personal values. This link empowers the employee to take ownership for personal results thereby beginning the transformation process from employee to partner. When properly aligned, the individual can see that by achieving the organizational objectives, his or her own personal values will be met. Individuals who lack a strong sense of personal direction will miss out on the emotional juice that comes from taking continuous purposeful action towards a clearly defined and compelling vision. Once the employee realizes that the achievement of organizational objectives is completely aligned with their own personal vision and values, they begin unleashing their drive. This drive is apparent when individuals are willing to do whatever it takes to achieve and ultimately exceed the collective vision.

Externally, individuals with a strong sense of values and personal vision will feel attracted towards an organization that mirrors their ideology. This attraction allows the organization to implement a recruiting strategy that ensures new hires are "on the same page" with the other partners and the ultimate direction of the company. External clients will also feel more compelled to do business with an organization that reflects their core values. This association is so deep-rooted that the external client becomes a "raving fan" for the organization. Raving fans generate powerful word-of-mouth marketing.

A clearly defined set of values and a compelling shared vision begins at the very top of an organization. It is not possible to build a resolute culture without complete buy-in from key leaders and decision-makers. If the key leaders at the top of the organization do not grasp the power and importance of clarifying and continuously communicating and living the stated ideology, then it is better to not embark on this journey. The individuals within an organization will quickly begin to judge and evaluate whether or not they feel the leaders are congruent with the message they preach. When the leaders are *not* congruent, this process has the potential of creating a cynical culture. However, when the leaders *are* congruent, most employees will become inspired and therefore meet their own individual roles with a new found sense of drive and enthusiasm.

Purposeful Leadership Key #4

Be a positive role model. Executives and managers who display a "Do as I say, not as I do" attitude will not be effective leaders. To inspire employees, managers must be willing to do what they expect of their employees, do it right, do it better and do it consistently.

Purposeful leadership has the power to influence and ultimately change an organization's corporate culture. Shifting an organization's culture from that of a group of employees who are just "doing their job" to a team of partners committed to a shared vision is one of the most challenging yet worthwhile endeavors a company can face. High performance companies that have withstood the test of time while generating unprecedented results have a steadfast corporate culture that is aligned with core values and a collective vision. These outstanding organizations have eliminated the compliant employee mentality and replaced it with an environment that produces authentic commitment. These high performance organizations have turned their employees into partners.

Niurka is President of The Results Coaching Alliance, an elite coaching and consulting firm. The Results Coaching Alliance consults with organizational leaders in the areas of leadership, organizational behavior, team building, strategic action, and management by values.
You may contact Niurka at *949-252-0015* or at
niurkainc.com   niurka@niurkainc.com.

Surrender and Grow Rich:

On the Internet, The Customer Controls You

By Declan Dunn

I'm scared to write this article.

On one hand, I want to share with you an idea that may just save your business in the next five years. This secret will transform the Internet from a commercial village to a global marketplace.

The secret is *the customer*, but you've heard that before. For years the marketing gurus of the 20th century talked about this, talked about" following the customer," but, in the end, they made the same mistake everyone else did.

They began with a product, planned to control the audience with headlines selling the product, and hoped to sell it to customers they dreamed about.

I'm scared because right now I could read *Newsweek, Forbes, Fast Company,* and *Wired*, then present a calculated, compelling, influential and hypnotic view of the 21st-century personal Internet that would have you nodding your head and pulling out your wallet. This is because everyone believes the old gurus, and the old way of doing business. The new way requires a new point of view.

And that point of view is no longer under the control and direction of the company marketing the product. Online, the customer is in total control.

For instance, recently I wanted to buy a Windows computer to hook up to my phone line and get to work. My lack of knowledge led me to contact a friend who custom-designed these computers. I told him exactly what I wanted.

He warned me not to buy it from a big-name dealer. He also advised me that, since he is my friend, I could do it myself and save the $500 I would have paid him. So I looked around for the best deal, armed with my 1 GB Pentium/512 MB RAM/20 GB Hard drive/SoundBlaster/Warranty/fast modem schtick. I hadn't the slightest clue what I was talking about, but those were the words I would spout off to anyone who would listen. Then I browsed for the best price.

Good advice? I didn't think so when, after six weeks of searching, I gave my money to some guy from New York selling an Acer computer (with my entire schtick) for a good price. He sent me this cruddy-looking box that was barely held together by tape. I got scared reading about the BIOS threat on my warranty. (I think it is some form of germ warfare.) I knew it was a bomb when I plugged it in and that stupid monitor just kept blinking at me for two hours, while I plowed through manuals, confused and frustrated. Left with nothing but a dumb, gray box blinking at me, I returned it immediately.

I then went on the Internet and called Dell Computer, who listened to what I needed and recommended a custom system to fit my needs, with a guarantee and customer support. They solved my problem at an added cost to me, but it was worth it. Ready-made is much better than do-it-yourself.

Before the Internet, you really couldn't listen to your customer, you couldn't plan your business around their wants, their demands. Now you can, but it takes a shift of perspective, with the customer in control.

"Surrender" is the name of the game, and that game is scaring businesses worldwide, except for the ones who have learned to "surrender and grow rich."

Let Them Come and They Will Build It

In the movie *Field of Dreams*, a man builds a baseball field and prays that people visit, because of **his** love of baseball and a mystical connection! Why are so many on the Internet following the theme of this movie – build it and they will come?

Forget cyberspace; forget the information superhighway; forget all that jargon that impresses your friends at parties. Focus on making the audience the center of your site. **Let them come and they will build it.**

The time to surrender is now, before it's too late.

In the old model of publishing such as television, radio, and print, you risk an enormous amount of money and time to create a final product. You create the supply and hope to sell it to a mass audience.

This model leads to failure on the Internet. The Internet is about works in progress, built on what the audience wants. In broadcasting we have focus groups; on the Internet, we have people with a passion gathering because they are looking for sites to fulfill their needs, not because someone impressed them with an image. You have to engage this interest and bring it to life. You are the one responsible for inviting and inciting the audience's interest.

How To Get The Audience Involved: The 4 Steps to Surrender

Many businesses and people jump on the Internet with a traditional approach. Tradition tells us to work, sweat, and slave to produce a final product, risking a huge investment on the chance that customers will want it. If they don't, you lose. The Internet mixes the marketing with the creation of the product. The customer is involved in creating what they want. When they want, if you can listen to them.

Step 1. Let the Audience Control Your Internet Site by focusing on Feedback

Instead of spending your valuable time and money trying to convince the audience that your viewpoint is worth exploring, why not gather market research and adapt your content to what they have indicated they want? You have to define just what the customer's interest is, discover what others are doing, and develop a unique vision. You won't do this by sitting down alone in your room, planning and flowcharting your own imagination into an Internet site. Let the audience tell you what to develop.

What does this mean to you? Get your Internet site up and work it into shape. Start slowly, don't use the "Under Construction" con, and provide room for feedback while enticing them to come back for more. Let the customers control development, solicit feedback. Follow their wants, their demands. They know more than you do, online and offline, if you know how to listen to them.

Step 2. Reward Customers for Sharing their Feedback

If you want the audience to send you feedback, use email forms, not just an email address, and reward them for their feedback with free reports and savings. Give them a reason to share their ideas. Don't just use an email link, such as "email me at declan@adnetinternational.com." Remember that many people ask them for their contact information. The ones who win the game are those who reward them, giving them great value in exchange for their email address.

Step 3. Listen to the Audience, Use Email Wisely, and Create Requested "Opt-in" Email Lists

Treat your email responses like you would any business correspondence. If they ask a simple question, create a standard response that doesn't intimidate or antagonize. Invite them to participate and trust in their brilliance.

Ask visitors to indicate whether they would like to receive monthly newsletters, citing updates at a site. This is an excellent way to encourage participation and keep people in touch. More importantly, gain their permission and follow up in the first few weeks with more frequent communication via email. For example, you could give away a free series of reports delivered automatically (at a cost of less than $20 a month) which will build a bond with the customer and keeps you "top of mind."

Avoid calling them mailing lists, since people assume this means a large volume of email. Make sure you phrase it so they are excited about joining, keeping in touch with your site. Invite them to distribute it. I have one visitor who distributes my newsletter on news groups and to friends. He once wrote and asked if it he could forward it to 400 interested parties. Where else can you get this kind of support?

Step 4. The Power of Language: The Internet is part of an Ancient Tradition Built on Words, not Programming Codes

Wonder why seniors use the Internet so well? They were raised writing letters and adapt to this media quickly. A good writer is as valuable as a good programmer, a good graphic artist, or a good techie. When creating your Internet site, consider the text part of it as important as you do the graphics. If you need help, hire a professional or at least someone who can write well.

When using email as your tool for communicating to your audiences, be professional, keep it succinct, and – most of all – keep it fun. Don't take yourself too seriously.

When you surrender to your customer, when you trust them, you tap into the real genius – not you or your product; but your customer. Trust in that genius.

Declan is an Internet CEO, Svengali consultant, and performance marketer. He is the founder of the IMU (Internet Marketing University) based on real Internet business experience that launches a business from idea to online in 90 days. Author of seven books and an acclaimed international speaker, Declan is popular on radio, TV, and the Internet, putting tech marketing into plain, simple English for small businesses and Fortune 500 clients.

Contact: *declan@adnetinternational.com* or *530-342-7637*.

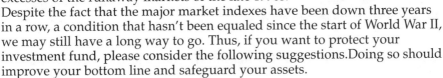

Five Tips To
Improve Your Market Performance

By Van K. Tharp, Ph.D.

Investors throughout the world are currently experiencing a down market that is correcting the excesses of the runaway markets of the late 1990s. Despite the fact that the major market indexes have been down three years in a row, a condition that hasn't been equaled since the start of World War II, we may still have a long way to go. Thus, if you want to protect your investment fund, please consider the following suggestions.Doing so should improve your bottom line and safeguard your assets.

1. Invest With the Current Trend of the Market.

Before you invest in the market you need to ask yourself, "What is the market doing?" Is it going up or down? Avoid having a major position in the stock market until you can safely say that the market is going up. But how do you determine that?

First, look at what the S&P500 index is doing. This index is a composite of the 500 largest companies in America. To determine how well it is doing, compare the close of the market today, with the average price of the market over the last 200 days. The latter is called a 200-day moving average. When the stock price is above the 200-day moving average, the market generally goes up about 12.6% each year. When the stock price is below the 200 day moving average, the market generally goes down by 1.6% each year. Isn't it better to have that average on your side?

233

To find the average, you can go to *www.bigcharts.com*. Plug in SP500 and click on the interactive charting button (at the top). You will then see a one-year chart of the SP500. On the left hand side you will see a set of buttons. Click on "indicators." The first indicator will be moving averages. Click on SMA and then fill in "200" in the space beside SMA. Scroll up and then click the red button "draw chart." You will now see a chart of the SP500 with a 200-day moving average, like the one below. All you have to do is ask yourself, "Is today's price above or below that average?" If the price is below the average, then don't buy any new positions. It is that simple.

In March 2003, the chart tells us that the price has been below the 200 day moving average since last May. This is a danger signal telling us to stay away from new market positions.

2. Never Enter A Position in the Market Without Knowing Where You Will Get Out.

Most people enter into a market position with the idea of holding onto it for a long time. However, the wisdom of that idea is strongly questioned when we enter down markets such as the current one. And even in the glorious markets of 1999, you still needed to protect yourself. For example, you could have purchased JDS Uniphase Corp (Symbol: JDSU) in early 1999 at a stock split adjusted price of about $8 per share. The stock then went to a high of over $140 per share around March of 2000. But today it is under $3 per share. That's a huge drop in price, the kind of drop from which you need to protect yourself.

A chart of JDSU is shown below. Notice how it had a huge gain, followed by a huge loss. However, a firm exit point would have allowed you to make a profit and protect that profit.

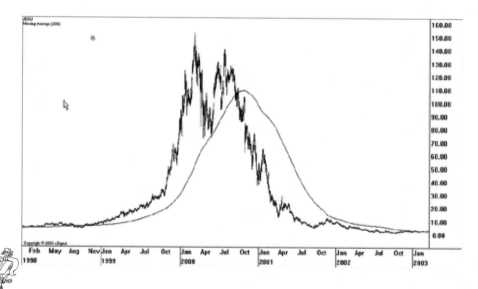

I recommend that you use a 25% trailing stop. Suppose you enter into JDSU at $8 per share in early 1999. You'd sell if it dropped 25% to $6 per share. In addition, the trailing portion of the stop means that when JDSU makes a new high, you trail the stop 25% from that new high. Thus, when JDSU moves to $12 per share, your new stop is $9. It's important to note that with a trailing stop, you only raise your exit point, you never lower it when the stock drops in price. Thus, when it moves up to $40, your stop moves up to $30. And when the stock hits its all time high of $153 in March of 2000, you would have a stop 25% away at $114.75.

Yes, you would have been able to ride the stock from $8 to $153 and would have then been stopped out of the stock at $114.75 for a very nice gain. The 25% trailing stop was far enough away to allow you to experience the entire gain, but more importantly, it got you out before the major fall started.

Notice that in our example, your initial risk was $2 per share (25% of the $8.00 entry). Your profit was $106.75 per share for a risk reward ratio of over 53 to 1.

3. Never Expose More Than 1% of Your Portfolio In Any Given Position.

Let's look at our example with JDSU. Suppose you started out with $25,000. Our rule says don't expose more than 1% of your position to any given stock. That means we cannot risk more than 1% or $250 on JDSU. However, our initial risk is only $2 per share. If we divide the total exposure we want (i.e., $250) by the risk per share of $2, then we discover we can purchase 125 shares.

Let's do a second example. Suppose you want to buy Microsoft stock today at $50 per share. Our second rule says "know when to get out" and we recommend risking 25% of the entry price. 25% of $50 is $12.50. Thus, we would enter a stop at $37.50 when we purchased and our risk per share would be $12.50. If our portfolio is worth $25,000 and we only risk 1%, then we can only expose $250 to the Microsoft position. And when we divide $250 by 12.50 per share, we discover that we can only purchase 20 shares.

Thus, in our first example, our risk per share was only $2 and we could purchase 125 shares. In our second example, our risk per share was $12.50, so we could only purchase 20 shares. However, in each case our exposure to the market if we are wrong about the stock is only 1% of our portfolio or $250.

And if you look at our example of JDSU, we sold at a profit that was 53 times our initial risk. That means that even though we only risked 1% of our portfolio, we made 53% on that one stock alone.

4. Continually Observe Yourself and Notice Your Patterns. Self-awareness of Your Patterns, Habits, and Emotions is the Key to Improvement.

I once asked one of the world's greatest traders, "What's your secret to handling your emotions and psychological problems?" His response was surprising at the time. He said, "I just notice that I'm emotional and then I continue to trade the system."

Most people allow their emotions to control them. They get caught up in those emotions and don't even realize what is happening. The great trader, in contrast, is simply aware of those emotions when they occur. Awareness is the key to change and it is essential if you want to improve. People who are not aware of what they are doing psychologically are victims of their own patterns and emotions. They are psychological robots.

Thus, a key step toward improving your trading is to become aware of what goes on inside of your head. Keep a diary of your trades and record what you are feeling and thinking on a regular basis. Look for patterns in your diary that might be self-destructive.

5. Take Responsibility for Everything That Happens to You.

One of the problems in today's down market is that everyone is trying to find someone else to blame. We can blame the market. We can blame corrupt CEO's and poor accounting practices for our losses. We can blame our broker or mutual fund manager for our losses. We can blame the analysts at the major brokerage houses. People who blame someone else are always repeating their mistakes. For example, someone recently sued a large mutual fund because his account went down 90%. However, this person got an account statement every month and watched his account drop. Only when his account was down 90% did he finally decide something should be done. Who was really to blame? The investor! He risked too much of his portfolio on one investment and he didn't have a predetermined exit point. Seeing that he is now suing the mutual fund, he still has no idea that he made those mistakes, so he'll probably make them again.

No matter what happens to you in the market, you must be accountable for the results. That way you can learn from the markets.

In the unique arena of professional trading coaches and consultants, Dr. Van K. Tharp stands out as an international leader. Helping others become the best trader or investor that they can be has been his mission since 1982. For more information go to *www.iitm.com* or call *1 800 385 4486*.

Could Understanding How Your Client Makes Decisions

Double Your Sales?

By Lynn Pierce

Understanding how your client makes decisions is the key to increasing your effectiveness in relating to people. Recognizing what type of personality you are dealing with could quickly and easily double your sales by allowing you to customize your presentation accordingly. Your powers of observation and a few key questions will immediately tell you which of the four basic personalities you are talking to.

Learning how each personality makes decisions using the YES System Personality Matrix is like money in your bank account. If your "client" consists of a couple or a group, understanding the personality matrix allows you to determine what the power relationship is in a matter of minutes.

Four Decision Making Styles

The YES System Personality Matrix is comprised of four basic personality styles: Driver, Analytical, Promoter and Amiable.

Drivers are self-assured and make decisions quickly. They want to get to the point and say YES or no and be done with it. You will most often ask a Driver to buy much quicker than any other style. Remember, bottom line results are their deciding factor.

Drivers know exactly what they want and easily say YES when they find it. They don't want to hear about all the options and everything the product will do. They will ask questions. When you've answered them, ask them to buy. Drivers appear to be difficult clients because they want to control your presentation, but if you give them information the way they best receive it, they will be the easiest to get to *yes.*

Analyticals want details. Stay on your written material until you have answered all their questions and have them totally involved. Analyticals are interested in saving time and money. They will say *yes* when you have satisfied their need for logic.

If you ask them if this makes sense and they say *yes*, the physical product demonstration is a formality. Quickly show the product to confirm what you have told them in your written presentation and then ask them to buy. Analyticals value their time just as much as the Drivers, so be aware of how you spend it. The easiest way to talk yourself out of getting to *yes* is to waste their time.

Promoters see this as a game; they love the excitement. They go along with the presentation and appear to be an easy *yes*. But they are playing with you. To really get to *yes*, get the promoter to stop watching the process and start listening to what you are saying about the product. Promoters want to know how you got your job instead of what the product will do for them.

If you can keep their mind on the product, they love to buy. They come to your presentation sure they aren't going to buy. They just want to see what you have to offer and play with you. Promoters want to be a part of a happy group. Emphasize any social opportunities that come with your product. Let them talk about all their accomplishments and you are listening your way to *yes*. The more impressed you are, the better. Introduce them to a person higher up in your company. They love to impress people.

Amiables take a long time to get to yes because they don't trust their own intuition. They need a lot of reinforcement. Tell Amiables stories about how people just like them have gotten involved and how happy they are they did. They are the most likely to have to think about it. Amiables love to shop, so you will have to convince them their shopping for this product ends with you.

Unless you make it easy for Amiables, decisions are just too difficult to make quickly. You need to be their rock. They will depend on you for leadership and guidance. Tell them you think they should say yes now. In their minds this takes the responsibility off their shoulders and they feel comfortable. Trust is most important to this group.

Now that you know a little about these personalities, let's look at how you implement the YES System Personality Matrix.

Customizing Your Presentation

Drivers and Analyticals want a short warm-up. Promoters and Amiables will have to be pulled away from the warm-up to get down to business. If you do a generic warm-up, you will decrease your chances of getting to yes by increasing their level of frustration.

When you deal with a Driver or Analytical type they are thinking, "What have I gotten myself into? This salesperson is an idiot!" They'll look for any opportunity to exit the presentation. You're finished before you've started. With a Promoter or Amiable you find yourself with the same reaction, but for a different reason. They feel like you don't care about them; you just want a paycheck.

In the survey process, spend time asking the same questions in several different ways to get the information you need from Drivers and Analyticals. They don't spend much time thinking from a feelings perspective. You can't get to desires without getting out of the head and into the heart.

Promoters and Amiables give you more than what you ask for, so rein them in while letting them talk enough to feel heard and understood. Evidence that you are interested in them would be using language like, "What I hear you saying is…"

In your written and physical presentations, Analyticals and Amiables need detailed facts to feel comfortable and to have sufficient time to absorb the information. Amiables want to see testimonials of people they respect and people just like them.

Drivers and Promoters are big picture people and want minimal facts and technical information. Once they tune out they may not come back. Pay very close attention to see when you are getting to the point of information overload with these types. If they are interested in further clarification, let them ask. You never run the risk of boring a client by giving them what they ask for.

Note: Clients can't digest information if you never stop talking long enough for them to think. When you present facts and new concepts, insert pauses and small silences. If you fail to do this, the only thing you will hear at the end of your presentation is, "I have to think about it." It's up to you. Give them the time now or they'll take the time later.

Closing the Sale

Drivers want to be shown measurable results. They understand time is of the essence and are quick decision makers when they see measurable results. Tell them what it costs and they'll gladly pay it if you've justified the value. Congratulate them on their boldness and decisiveness.

Analyticals want to feel comfortable with all the facts and technical information. Applaud their conscientiousness. Tell them how your product is an efficient use of their time and money. Make them feel their decision is a safe one. They need assurance that it's to their advantage financially. Let them know they have plenty of support material to take home.

Let Promoters know you are on their side and you are getting them the best possible deal. Promoters are proud of their negotiating ability. Make them feel like part of the team. Let them know this purchase is a feather in their cap socially. If you've made a friend, they'll buy from you.

Amiables want you to hold their hand and guide them to a decision. They are very price conscious and tend to want to shop around. Change is difficult for them. Unless you make it easy to say yes, they will want to think about it. Tell them you'll give them all the time they need to decide while they're there.

The way you ask each personality to buy is a highly individualized strategy. This is where you have to be most aware of who you are dealing with. Without having fully experienced the YES System Personality Matrix, these closing statements may seem simplistic, but it can be this straightforward. I've personally closed this way for over 25 years very successfully.

- Asking a Driver to buy can be as simple as an assumptive, "Would you like to use Visa or MasterCard?" or, "How do you want the name to appear?"

- With a Promoter it can also be very simple. You can say something like, "This is a great deal, isn't it?" as you fill out the paperwork.

- Analyticals and Amiables want an extensive review of everything you've covered before you ask them to buy. This takes patience and time. Guide them to yes by saying; "Based on what you've told me here today, I think you should go ahead with this." If you've done a good job gaining trust and establishing credibility this can be all it takes.

Lynn Pierce is America's Sales Therapy expert and is the Founder and Senior Consultant for *Change One Thing*. A full description of the *YES System Personality Matrix* can be found in the audiotape series, *Getting to YES Without Selling, The YES System* at *www.GettingToYesWithoutSelling.com*. To receive a free tip sheet on recognizing personalities, send a blank email to *matrixtips@GettingToYesWithoutSelling.com*. For more information email *lynn@changeonething.com* or call *480-242-5929*.

Does Your Lack of
Marketing Skills
Hold You Back?

By Denise M. Michaels

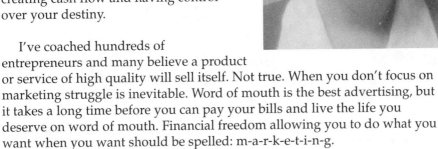

Effective marketing customized for your business is the most important factor to creating cash flow and having control over your destiny.

I've coached hundreds of entrepreneurs and many believe a product or service of high quality will sell itself. Not true. When you don't focus on marketing struggle is inevitable. Word of mouth is the best advertising, but it takes a long time before you can pay your bills and live the life you deserve on word of mouth. Financial freedom allowing you to do what you want when you want should be spelled: m-a-r-k-e-t-i-n-g.

In 1994 we were bombarded with 4,000-5,000 marketing messages daily. That number has skyrocketed to 13,000 messages daily. In this era of savvy consumers and advertising saturation an excellent product or service is the start. How do you break through the noise to present a message that will get ideal customers to happily say "yes?"

Even experienced business owners continue learning ways to dodge the time and money wasters that can gobble up a marketing budget. Often the expert guidance of someone who has cracked the code, willing to show you secret formulas proven in the marketplace can jumpstart success. Entrepreneurs want hands-on, concrete information that makes your life simple without putting demands on your time. You want practical systems that work automatically.

At the close of a large conference last year, I gave attendees a system for planning that was so helpful, I got a standing ovation. I thought, "What if I offered a workshop where people walk away with everything needed to create cash flow. Not just "great ideas" you must decipher later. You are in control. You put it out to the people who want it and are willing to pay for it.

One of the many marketing ideas I help attendees discover in my workshops is "The Five C's." No, these aren't the same five C's in diamond valuation but they will help you grow wealthier.

- Love Your **Customer**
- Be **Congruent**
- Have **Clarity**
- Do emotionally **Compelling** marketing
- Avoid **Confusion**

Love Your Customer

This means more than great customer service. Most people are so enraptured with their product or service; they never determine who their ideal customer is. They waste time trying to attract everyone, educating skeptics who will never buy, rather than focus on individuals perfect for your product or service.

When I ask, "What makes your customer or client tick?" they are often at a loss. After considering that question they realize their energy is going into learning everything possible about their product and almost nothing about the customer.

It's easy to get caught up in the passion of a product, process or idea. It's concrete and there is no risk of rejection. It takes vision to determine what you do and who you do it for. This helps you put out one message focused on the customers who are right for you.

Have a Clear Message That Makes it Easy for Customers to Say "Yes"

Be clear. Create a succinct, passionate message to share in one-on-one meetings such as at networking groups. Many people call this "an elevator speech." If you were riding an elevator and noticed you were with someone who could help boost your business, what would you say? If you can't sum up who you are and what you do in ten seconds, you're unclear. You're hoping potential customers will interpret and decide if it's right for them. Not good. Figure it out and offer it in a way they want to receive it. As you gain clarity you will attract more of the right people to your business.

Do Emotionally Compelling Marketing

The most valuable information you can share with people is about you. Your experience and how you overcame obstacles or challenges with your product or service can be compelling. People will see themselves in your story and feel, "Wow! If it worked for her maybe it will work for me, too." I believe in marketing that makes people say, "I gotta have that." It's emotionally compelling and tells a story about how you or others solved a problem with your product or service.

Most people teach that advertising should be brief – because people are in a hurry. That's what I learned in college. It's not always true. If people are interested in what you have you can't tell them too much. If they're not interested, it's impossible to be too brief.

Taking a fresh look at your customers and the problems your product or service solves as well as the benefits you offer can result in an exciting, compelling marketing message that will create the cash flow you deserve. This is what I help people do.

Be Congruent in Every Aspect of Your Marketing

In marketing, being congruent means more than integrity and "walking your talk." People sense when the smallest nuance is out of place. They can tell when you care less about them and more about selling your product. You may not be aware of it, but it's like trying to shove a square peg into a round hole. The energy isn't flowing effortlessly because you're wasting time attracting the wrong people. This creates a "disconnect" between you and potential customers because you don't understand them. You're incongruent. Get your marketing message flowing in one smooth direction towards the individuals who are ideal for you and it will become effortless.

Avoid Confusion That Results in a "No"

A confused mind always says "no." Because we are bombarded with so many choices we must say "no" to most of them. If your message is confusing people will say "no." You could have exactly what they want, but if they don't understand how it solves their problem the answer will still be "no." You have seven seconds to grab someone's attention. Keep checking to make sure your message is congruent, clear, emotionally compelling and avoids confusion.

I am a stickler about honoring my promises and I make sure the people who come to my workshops leave with what they've been missing. There are formulas that make it work, but they must be applied to your specific situation. That's what I help you do.

In a supportive environment with an expert to guide you, it can be done in three days. Here are some of the pieces needed to create *Five-C Marketing*:

- A mission statement that reflects your business, your way.
- A unique selling proposition that draws in new customers.
- A profile of your ideal customer and what it takes to attract them.
- A sales letter, Web site content and/or brochure that makes customers eager to buy from you.
- Internet strategies on a shoestring that draw in new business.

- Amazing ideas that will make customers eager to buy from you.
- Tips to help build your credibility, get free publicity and turn your business into a fun, highly profitable one.

These are just a few secrets to having a business in the flow of money and wealth.

Carpenters say "measure twice and cut once." Marketing is a lot like that. When you discover how your product or service is right for your ideal customer you will have cracked the code leading to greater success and more freedom and fun in your life.

Denise M. Michaels has shared the platform with Robert Allen and Mark Victor Hansen. She helps entrepreneurs create unique, emotionally-compelling marketing messages and a customized plan at her "No-Fluff Marketing Magic Workshop." For more information visit *www.denisemichaels.com*.

Why Struggle with Sluggish Sales and Why Settle for Average Results?

Give Your Business a Booster Shot!

By Robyn Levin

Top 9 Tips & Creative Remedies to Boost Your Bottom Line Quickly and Painlessly

How do you target and reach your most profitable prospects? This question is even more important in a difficult economy. As a Marketing Strategist/Business Consultant, I have always been passionate about connecting people to profits for mutual benefit. Often I work with fast-growing companies, women business owners, and experts in their field who are eager to make sales and increase visibility. But there is a difference between sales and **profitable** *sales.* In this article I have outlined 9 simple tips and money-making strategies to target, reach, and sell to better-qualified customers. A bottom line approach is presented, filled with "capsules" of ideas and inspirations from my new tips book located at *www.prescriptions4profits.com.*

1) Identify your specific target market and try to make sure it is not a moving target. Ask yourself who would ideally benefit from your products and services. You may target by: revenue, number of employees, geographic areas, women business owners, government, specific industry, teenage male golfers, etc. Dig a little deeper and try to understand their interests and buying habits. Show them how your products or services will benefit them and add value.

2) Capture a new market opportunity using industry knowledge and observation of trends that are related to your product or service. Recently there has been a lot of attention paid to a relatively new career, Executive Coaching, which is rapidly growing in California according to an article in the *San Francisco Business Times* of December 4th, 2002. In the fall of 2002 I began researching this field because I suspected a marketing opportunity to help coaches build a profitable business quickly and painlessly. Further research indicates that Fortune 500 companies are increasingly seeking this specialty for their rising star executives. So if your specialty is leadership coaching for emerging executives – you are in luck! This is an example of targeting **profit-rich prospects,** i.e., those that need you, want you, understand your value, and – most important – can pay you.

Another way to capture an opportunity is to sell your expertise and package your knowledge in an informational product. This is a smart way to add revenue and boost cash flow. Just make sure you have a captive audience.

3) Know your "Unique Value Proposition" so you can sell it to prospects. Ask yourself: what benefits do you provide that your competition does not? What unique value do you offer? Answer in terms of benefits – what's in it for them, your customers? Be very specific. Examples of differentiators:

- **Increased productivity**
- **Lower prices**
- **Higher quality**
- **Customization**
- **Fast, on-time delivery**
- **Simple and easy to implement**
- **Outstanding customer support**

The more time you spend clearly identifying the real value you provide, the easier your client will understand and the more he will want to conduct business with you. And remember: don't sell yourself short, charge what you are worth!

4) Determine where the profit-rich clients are hiding

A) Mine Your Own Business! Often the most lucrative opportunities are in your back yard, meaning existing clients. It is much easier to get more business from satisfied customers. They already know you, like you, and trust you. Statistics prove it costs five times more money to sell to a new customer than to an existing one. Why lose out to a competitor? Offer new or improved products and services. Probe top-level decision makers periodically to see if something has changed within their company like a management turnover or change in priorities.

B) "Big Brother" has bucks for you: Government agencies spend $200 billion according to the Small Business Administration (SBA) and *only 2%* is currently going to women business owners! Procurement Managers want and *need* you. Two programs available through the SBA are 8 *(a) Women and Minority Owned Business and Small Disadvantaged Business (SDB)* certification programs. Visit *www.sba.gov* to learn about the vast resources available. See *http://pro-net.sba.gov* to find out more about vendor/supplier opportunities from PRO-Net, (Procurement Marketing and Access Network).

5) Find the profit-rich candidates.

It is pretty easy to find winners and successful companies They are frequently in the news. You can perform a search on *www.google.com* and enter words and names that pertain to your industry or market. This is one of the best search engines. Other ways to find prime prospects:

- Networking in professional groups (mingle; don't just show up)
- Trade and business publications (a great way to find rising stars and new contacts)
- Speaking as a form of marketing
- Referrals – ask your friends, family and satisfied clients, "Who do you know that would benefit from my services?" Get testimonials; clients are impressed by good references. This really works!

6) How do you reach them? Directly!

There are several smart ways to reach your prospects.

- **Direct Contact** is one of the best ways and one of my favorite methods. You can find valuable key contact information in the book of lists published by regional business publications like the San Francisco Business Times. The list contains typically the fastest growing companies in select industries and usually includes the name of the CEO, revenue, number of employees, growth rate, profit margin, product mix, phone number, and address. Ask your local library to help you locate this resource or subscribe to the publication.
- **Direct Marketing** using email and/or direct-mail campaigns. Once you have identified your target-rich prospects, put together an attractive striking mailer that is brief, bold, and clearly describes your benefits. Stress how you can help your audience. Think benefits and value. Make sure to track results for effectiveness and to measure return on the investment. Hint: over-sized colorful glossy post cards are a great solution!
- **Listen to interviews from CEOs** on business talk radio. Two years ago I heard a CEO of a financial recruiting company interviewed on the radio. Based on something she said, I was able to land a profitable contract.
- **Speak at appropriate meetings, conferences, and events**. Educate your audience and distinguish yourself as an expert in your field You never know if prospective clients may be in the audience. This is a great way to earn name recognition and build referrals.

7) Use PR to promote your expertise without spending money.

Keep the press apprised of worthy news that would benefit their audience: new products, services, employees, contracts, etc., and become a contributing expert. Name recognition breeds success, credibility, and profitable sales. The secret to effective publicity is consistency – implement a

247

smart PR campaign using press releases to routinely spread your word so your stories will be told.

8) Close the sale by turning NO into YES!

- The first and most important rule learned from my years of corporate sales and training is *make sure you are speaking to the final decision maker(s).* To be sure, ask, "Who in addition to yourself will be involved in the decision making process"? This will save you hours of time and ensure you have the right names for your presentation. Why spend all your time and effort pitching to the wrong person? Also, ask early in the process if they have the budget this year for your valuable products/ services. Then, *ask* for the business – *close.*
- This tip is one of the easiest and most often neglected; *Make it easy for your customer to buy from you!* Why promote and advertise if they cannot reach, order and pay you easily? Accept as many forms of payment possible including: credit cards, checks, 800 number, fax, email, and mail. Accept online commerce and credit cards if you are marketing on the web. Visit *www.prescriptions4profits/ shoppingcart.htm* for easy payment and shopping cart solutions.

9) Follow-up fast

Execution is essential to succeed faster. Build and maintain quality rapport. Strike while the iron is hot. In other words, sell and close when the interest is high. So many sales are lost simply because the excitement and momentum waned. Your competitor might just sneak in ahead of you. Ask your client their preferred method of communication – email, phone, fax, mail. Make sure you note their preference and abide by it. You may never get a second chance to make a first impression but lasting impressions last!

For more information please visit *www.prescriptions4profits.com.* Featuring the new eBook, *Prescriptions4Profits for Women Business Owners, Entrepreneurs, and Professionals.* The book is packed with creative tips and proven strategies about boosting positive cash-flow, profitable sales, and visibility. Get your dose of ideas, solutions, and inspirations; short, sweet, and take them right to *your* banks.

Robyn Levin, Marketing Strategist/Author ©2003

Robyn Levin is CEO of *Robyn Levin and Company,* a strategic marketing company helping fast-growing businesses and experts in their fields create more wealth. She purchased a bankrupt ice skating arena in 1989 in southern Florida that became profitable a short while later, grossing over $1 million annually. Levin thrives on finding the edge. She can be reached at *1.415.383.IDEA (4332)* or *robyn@robynlevin.com.*

Awaken the American Dream

By Charlie Douglas

The American Dream is by no means behind us. We've just lost track of it. It is true that America was founded by settlers who heard that its streets were paved with gold. But more importantly, America also offered those gallant pioneers the freedom to worship their Creator in virtuous enterprise.

Over the course of time the American Dream came to represent a social ideal which stressed the importance of equality and material prosperity. The phrase itself became popularized in Horatio Alger's *Ragged Dick*, published in 1867. A-rags-to riches story about a poor orphan who made it big, Alger's classic puts forth the notion that the American Dream was available to anyone willing to work hard and to embrace noble values.

For most of America's history, the American Dream was seen as a by-product of a well-ordered and virtuous life, and not only the pot of gold at the end of the rainbow. The emphasis was on building spiritual capital with the belief that, through creative enterprise, our Creator would provide enough financial capital along the way. Since America's auspicious beginnings, the American Dream has meant different things to various generations. But our original concept of the American Dream is slumbering today — some say it has moved.

The #1 National Bestseller, *Who Moved My Cheese?* by Spencer Johnson, M.D., describes a world where mice and mouse-size humans react differently to change when the cheese they love is moved to another corner of the maze. As Ken Blanchard, Ph.D., describes in the forward, cheese is "a metaphor for what we want to have in life, whether it is a job, a relationship, money, a big house, freedom, health, recognition, spiritual peace, or even an activity like jogging or golf." Cheese to those made-up characters represents getting what you thought would make you happy. That is exactly what the American Dream is to us.

During the 1990s, millions of us aimed for the American Dream by trying to amass financial capital in a raging bull market, while refining spiritual capital oftentimes took a back seat. Yet, in many cases, amassing financial wealth proved to be fleeting and failed to enrich our lives by bringing about the security we thought it would.

Since the new millennium, our self-assurance has been badly shaken as our world changed. A brutal bear market, September 11th, "Enron-like" disasters, and indignities within the Catholic Church have pounded away at our already vulnerable institutional base. In our unstable world, we sought reassurance from unsteady institutions which in some cases only left us feeling more uneasy. As 2002 came to a close, Gerald Celente of Trends Research Institute in Rhinebeck, N.Y. had this to say: "We have never seen anything like this before. So many people have lost so much trust in so many institutions at the same time."

The dwindling spiritual capital and moral fiber being fashioned by our ailing institutions have caused some to question if we are still "One nation under God." Feelings of fear and envy, rather than love, often reside within us in an increasingly materialistically focused world. America is fast becoming a culture where accumulating monetary value is viewed as more important than developing meaningful values. Building economic assets is becoming more of a focal point than cultivating meaningful values and virtues.

Keep the American Dream Alive

If we are to keep the American Dream alive and awaken its greatness, we must rekindle the spirit of our nation's past. While many of the unalienable rights entrusted to us under the Declaration of Independence may be taken for granted today, that was not the case for the 56 men who signed that noble document. Overall, they were men of deep faith and many were prosperous members of the colonial elite. These noble patriots courageously signed the Declaration understanding that their property could be confiscated and, if captured, they could face execution.

Many paid a harsh price for their patriotism. Nearly one-third had their estates destroyed. Unfamiliar signers of significant wealth like Carter Braxton and Richard Morris supported the Revolutionary War with their own assets and died in relative poverty. Other men of financial means such as Richard Stockton and Arthur Middleton, who were taken prisoners by the British, likewise lost all that they had after their release. The price of the war forced John Hart to flee from the bedside of his dying wife. When he returned home after the war, he found his wife dead, his property destroyed, and his 13 children gone.

These brave signers lived with a spirit that transcends all religious faiths and carried out with honor the last line of the Declaration of Independence: **"And for the support of this declaration, with a firm reliance on the protection of Divine Providence, we mutually pledge to each other our lives, our fortunes, and our sacred honor."**

America became a great nation precisely because its early settlers exhibited great character. For them the American Dream was lived out seeking Divine Providence and pledging all that they had, believing that freedom and liberty were virtues worth living and dying for. They emptied themselves and, in many cases, laid down their lives and possessions for a neighbor they most likely didn't know.

Our Founding Fathers believed that the American Dream depended upon the strength of the character of its many diverse individuals. They understood that the Creator, who gave us our unalienable rights, requires virtue as the price for freedom and liberty. Liberty for them was not doing what they impulsively wanted to do, but finding the courage to do what they needed to do after careful deliberation.

For our Founding Fathers, America was an emerging market economy, and capitalism just a babe. If they could come back today, they most likely would be amazed by the financial capital that America has amassed in a little more than 200 years. On the other hand, it's hard to imagine that they wouldn't be troubled by the low level of spiritual capital found in the American Dream today.

Our Creator's Message to Humanity.

From our country's inception to this very day, our nation's republic depends upon virtue, both private and public, for its survival. But as both George Washington and Thomas Paine pointed out long ago, "virtue is not hereditary." Virtue must be taught, nurtured, and consciously passed on from one generation to the next.

In President Ronald Reagan's first Inaugural Address, he spoke of a man named Dr. Joseph Warren, and referred to him as "one of the greatest" among our Founding Fathers. Dr. Warren was a Harvard-educated medical doctor who became a Major General at the outset of the Revolutionary War. Instead of giving orders from a distance at Bunker Hill, he volunteered to fight alongside his men against the British onslaught. In doing so, Dr. Warren became the first high-ranking officer to fall in the war, when he was struck in the head by a musket ball and killed instantly.

The night before Bunker Hill, Dr. Warren, as the President of the Massachusetts Congress, said to his countrymen, "Our country is in danger, but not to be despaired of... On you depend the fortunes of America. You are to decide the important questions upon which rests the happiness and the liberty of millions yet unborn. Act worthy of yourselves."

The tragic events of 9/11, and the ensuing War Against Terror, awakened the greatness of that founding spirit and our slumbering sense of patriotism.

Our greatest challenge, however, is to hold onto that selfless spirit while the war persists, and long after it is over. Ultimately, we must find a way to live together as one human family with our brothers and sisters around the globe. The American Dream, grounded in love, is not America's message to the world; it is our Creator's message to humanity.

As we seek a life that is both rich and meaningful, we do so with the firm belief that we are our Creator's greatest creation, and that we are here to make the world a better place. Love is the power necessary to do that, and our Creator is the source of all love. Our life's mission is to stay connected to that source and make its presence felt throughout the world. Virtues keep us allied to our loving Creator, and despite all its shortcomings, religious faith is a tremendous teacher and guardian of essential virtues. I could write a book about the negative things concerning religious faith, but I could more easily fill a library with all the good it does for people.

If we are to achieve and pass on the American Dream from one generation to the next, it will be because of our commitment to virtues and the production of spiritual capital in a free market system. We don't really own the material possessions external to us anyway. We merely have use of them for a while.

We only have possession of what is found inside our souls, where the values that became our life's virtues were once conceived. And if we are successful in this regard, we will have left something dear for those who are living, and for those millions yet unborn. We will have acted in a manner worthy of ourselves and kept the American Dream alive for generations to come. No one moved the American Dream. It is still there right in front of us. Awaken it!

Charlie Douglas is an attorney, financial advisor, and author of the book *Awaken The American Dream*. Charlie has been counseling high-net worth individuals for almost 20 years. A frequent lecturer and keynote speaker, Charlie adds value by mentoring others to use values-based planning. Visit Charlie at *www.awakenthedream.com*.

Taking The "Heat"

A Powerful Tool for Dealing With Angry People

By Judy Hoffman

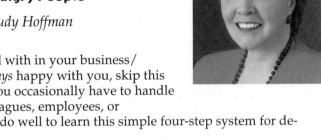

If everyone you deal with in your business/ professional life is *always* happy with you, skip this chapter. However, if you occasionally have to handle angry customers, colleagues, employees, or neighbors, you would do well to learn this simple four-step system for de-escalating anger.

Think back to the last time you had a serious disagreement. Did a customer feel she received less than expected from your product or service? Did you do something to an employee that left him feeling hostile? Does your operation annoy commercial or residential neighbors with traffic, noise, dust, etc.?

Whether it was a miscommunication, a mistake made by you or your staff, or a situation out of your control, it made someone angry. How well did you handle it? Was there a heated exchange? Did something that started out as a small disagreement grow into a much larger problem? Did it tear apart a relationship? Did you wish that you had known how to diffuse the anger and work through to a mutually acceptable solution? If so, read on.

I was introduced to this system by a friend and colleague, Dr. Judith Rosner, principal of The Rosner Group, a management training and consulting firm in Warwick, NY. Judy suggests this process to her clients who need help with customer service and stress management. I realized that it would fit well into the workshops I planned to teach on crisis management. Certainly, if something bad happens to an organization – whether a manufacturer, bank, hospital, utility, government agency, service provider, not-for-profit, etc. – there would likely be angry people.

A simple acronym to help you remember the four-step process is "HEAT." Let's go through each step.

Hear Them Out

Listen. Listen. *really* listen! Sometimes it is hard to make ourselves do this. People work to develop their speaking skills, but how many practice being a good listener? Being heard is a basic human need. It is one way we feel valued and respected. When we are angry, we need to "get something off our chest." Plainly put, we need to vent. When someone interrupts us – either trying to hurry us along by assuming he knows what we are trying to say or just to get us to stop "yelling" – it frustrates us; we tend to yell louder or longer to make ourselves heard.

Let me suggest that you practice the concept of "responsible listening." Assume the responsibility for truly understanding both what the person is saying and the emotions behind the words. Do not interrupt or contradict. Do not try to finish his sentences for him. Do not assume you know what he probably means.

Instead, *concentrate* on what the person is saying. Focus, giving the individual the respect he deserves and needs. Let your body language demonstrate you are paying attention. Some ways you can do this include:

(1) *Making eye contact.* Don't try to intimidate with a glare. Rather make sure your gaze demonstrates attention and concern. Do not get distracted by papers on your desk, your interest in what else is going on in the office, or your desire to glance at the clock.

(2) *Lean in.* You should be standing about three feet apart. Or sit down next to each other. (Being on opposite sides of a desk makes it more confrontational.) Leaning in shows interest. Leaning back signifies disinterest or that your wish to be disconnected.

(3) *Be careful of your facial expressions.* What we *really* think as we hear someone else talk is instantly communicated through frowns, grimaces, smirks, or the dreaded rolling of the eyes. We must consciously maintain an expression of caring and concern.

Empathize

This word is often misunderstood. It does not mean you have to agree with everything the upset person is saying. Constantly nodding your head while she accuses you of all sorts of things is not in your best interest.

Empathy simply indicates that you understand that the person is upset. Try to see the situation from her point of view. Steven Covey's statement in his book *The Seven Habits of Highly Effective People* emphasizes this point. "People don't **care** how much you **know** until they **know** how much you **care**."

Direct statements such as "I can see that you are quite upset about this. If such a thing happened to me, I would be upset too." Validate her emotions. It is counter-productive to tell an angry person, "You should not be upset."

One word of caution: be *very* careful not to say, "I know *just* how you feel." unless you have actually been in that position yourself. If the angry person is saying they have a child with a serious illness and they think your facility or your products are connected to that illness, you may think it would be empathetic to say this. It will most likely bring an angrier reaction,

"You do *not* know how I feel!" All you can do is empathize with how upset they must be, possibly indicating that you know how much parents care for their children because you are a parent (or grandparent) yourself. You acknowledge their powerful emotions and move on to the third step.

Apologize

It is hard to keep yelling at someone once they have said "I'm sorry." How many arguments could be dramatically shortened and soon forgotten if one of the parties could be persuaded to say this and mean it! (Remember, no sarcastic tone of voice or rolling of the eyes!) Sometimes an apology is all that is required. If you were raised to believe an apology is a sign of weakness, you've got a big hurdle to overcome. For people who feel they have been wronged, an apology fits into their concept of fairness. The more an individual tries to avoid an apology, the deeper he gets into excuses and defensiveness. This does nothing to move toward a resolution.

If you or one of your staff did something wrong, move quickly to apologize. Even if it was not *all* your fault, search for some part of the problem for which you can take responsibility. For example, "I'm sorry if we were not clear enough in our explanation of the terms of our agreement." would allow the other party to save face. If there is *absolutely nothing* in the situation that could allow you to take this step, the very least you can say is, "I am sorry that you feel that way…" and then move right on to the fourth and final step.

There are lawyers who will advise their clients not to apologize because they fear it signifies liability. Many companies and individuals have gotten themselves into deep trouble from a public relations perspective (and even later with the courts) because they refused to show some remorse. This stubbornness often convinces the angry person to take drastic action to MAKE them sorry. Work closely with lawyers to find appropriate wording to express regret without inviting a lawsuit. It can certainly be done and is worth the effort.

"TAKING THE HEAT"

H ear them out

E mpathize

A pologize

T ake action

Take Action

Now move toward reaching a solution. Let him get the monkey off his back and onto yours. You have several options.

(1) If solving the problem lies within your authority, take action quickly . "I am terribly sorry that we made this mistake of double billing you. I am crediting your account as we speak."

(2) If you need to appeal to someone with greater authority, let the person know that you have made notes and will take the matter to the person who can resolve the issue.

(3) If the matter is not clear-cut, assure the individual that you understand the problem so you can bring it forward to be discussed. Provide a time when you will get back to the individual. Then be sure to do it.

There you have it – four easy-to-remember steps. (HINT: Make a copy of this chapter's illustration on your copier and paste it next to your phone so you don't skip a step.) Maintain your composure. Don't get defensive. If this relationship is valuable, it is worth the effort to practice being a good listener, to exhibit empathy, to be the first to apologize, and to take some sort of action to allow you to mend fences.

People remember tense situations like this. If you decide you can do without the business of this one customer, remember that every unhappy customer tells between nine and twenty others. Unhappy employees can spread bad morale throughout an organization. Angry neighbors can bring regulatory authorities or investigative reporters or TV cameras to your door.

On the other hand, people who initially had a problem will remember that you treated them with respect and worked toward a resolution. Even better, they are apt to tell a number of other people how effectively you handled the situation. Using this process may take a little longer and require more patience on your part. The end result, however, is well worth it!

Judy Hoffman is a consultant, trainer, speaker and author who specializes in community relations, dealing with the media during a crisis, and handling angry people. To check availability/fees, call *1-800-848-3907 PIN 2145*, visit her web site at *www.judyhoffman.com*, or contact *jchent@fcc.net*.

Wealth Secrets of Millionaires

By Peter Lowe

Many people think that becoming rich is an impossible dream. When they picture millionaires, they think of big spenders living lavish, glamourous life-styles. The average millionaire is a very different sort of person.

According to financial consultant Todd Barnhart, the average self-made millionaire is a "middle-aged (or older) person who drives a moderately-priced car... Is married twenty years or more to the same person, goes to church... Owns or runs a business, has kids or grandkids, works ten hours a day and loves it." In other words, the typical American millionaire is an ordinary person who has achieved wealth and success over time by working, planning and saving for it. You can do the same!

Our free enterprise system creates opportunities and gives us the freedom to take advantage of them. No matter what your background, you can become a millionaire! These six secrets helped bring extraordinary success to seemingly ordinary people. They can do the same for you.

Secret 1: Treat Money as a Servant, Not as a Master

Jesus Christ said, "No one can serve two masters. You cannot serve both God and money." Money is a wonderful servant, but a terrible master.

Financial consultant Robert Ringer cautions in his book *Million Dollar Habits*, "Instead of possessing money, what happens when an individual's goal is money is that he becomes possessed by money. Instead of keeping money in perspective, it becomes an obsession."

An obsessive pursuit of riches can bring other problems. Far too many people have sacrificed their health to gain wealth, only to spend their wealth trying to regain their health. A proper outlook on money is needed to become – and remain – healthy, wealthy and wise.

Secret 2: Form Wealthy Habits

Have you ever wondered how some people become wealthy so easily? No matter what they do, money seems to gravitate to them. They have learned the millionaire's secret of making a habit of making money. They live in such a way that making money becomes as natural and habitual as eating or sleeping. Todd Barnhart wrote in his book, *The Five Rituals of Wealth*, "I've found one thing to be absolutely true of those who control vast resources: they don't just do wealthy things once in a while when they feel like it. They habitually live in a state of wealth... They save, dream, plan, invest and give in a never-ending cycle."

What are the habits of wealth? I'm going to share with you the three most important habits you can adopt. They are simple, timeless, and unchanging. And they are the foundation of building wealth and financial security.

I. Spend less than you earn. The first habit of wealth is to make the best use of the financial resources that you already have. No matter what your salary, you should make it a habit to spend less than you earn. Everyone can reduce their expenditures without making a significant dent in their lifestyles. If you doubt this, I challenge you to account for every dollar you spent last month. How much of it was necessary? How much was important? If you are like most people, doing a personal audit of your purchases for even one month will reveal that you spent a lot of money on things you didn't need, didn't really want, and may not even like.

II. Form a savings plan. The second habit of wealth goes hand-in-hand with the first. Once you get your spending under control, you can form a savings plan, and begin tracking your growing wealth. Wealth is measured by how much you keep, not how much you make. Every time you receive a paycheck, set aside a portion of it to keep – preferably, ten percent or more.

III. Invest your savings. The third habit of wealth is to make your money multiply by putting your savings to work through sound investments. Hoarding money will make you a miser, not a millionaire. The essence of investment is to generate wealth-creating opportunities for others and to share in the wealth created. The more, and more wisely, you invest, the more wealth you create for yourself and others.

Secret 3: Find Work You Love

I am convinced that the surest – and most fun! – way to succeed financially is to love your work. Most of America's millionaires made their fortune not by running after profit, but by throwing themselves into work they adored. They viewed their work as a mission, and riches became a by-product.

One financial expert did a study of self-made millionaires to find out what set them apart from others. He concluded that the single most distinct quality about these wealthy individuals was their love of and absorption in their work. He stated, "Long before they knew whether they'd be paid enough to support themselves, they were caught up in their work and doing far more of it than they realized."

Secret 4: Set Goals

The famous multi-millionaire Napoleon Hill, who wrote down Andrew Carnegie's secrets to wealth in his best-seller *Think and Grow Rich*, put it this way: "There is one quality which one must possess to win, and that is definiteness of purpose, the knowledge of what one wants, and a burning desire to possess it."

Conversely, the failure to set goals is the surest route to financial failure. Indeed, the refusal to set goals is the surest route to financial failure. Indeed, the refusal to set clear, specific goals is the most common feature of the bankrupt and broke. According to one study, more than 95 percent of the people who consider themselves financial failures lack a financial plan.

Secret 5: Shun Shady Schemes

The quickest way to destroy your fortune and reputation is to engage in unwise or unethical deals and practices. No matter how wealthy you are, your wealth is never secure unless it has been built on a foundation of integrity. Many of the richest men in America – Ivan Boesky and Michael Milkin, for example – have seen their financial empires disintegrate overnight because of unethical practices. To keep your wealth safe and growing, build on a foundation of integrity.

Secret 6: Invest in Yourself Through Education

Investing in yourself not only brings high yields; it is invulnerable to inflation, impervious to recession, and totally unaffected by stock market crashes. Material possessions, stocks and bonds, and liquid assets can be stolen, lost or destroyed, but the sum of your wisdom, expertise and abilities are yours to keep forever. As the great entrepreneur Henry Ford stated, "If money is hope for independence, you will never have it. The only real security that a man can have... Is a reserve of knowledge, experience and ability." Another way to say it is: to earn more, you need to learn more.

Peter Lowe and his *SUCCESS* seminars have been featured in *Time* magazine, *People* magazine, on the covers of *Selling!* and *Personal Selling Power* magazines, *USA Today*, on ABC's *20/20*, *CBS This Morning*, CNN and on the front pages of every major newspaper from coast to coast.

Keep Your Health...
To Keep Your
Abundance

The 8 Steps to Optimum
Energy & Vitality

By Brad J. King, M.S., MFS

My two-year-old nephew came for a visit the other day. The little guy didn't stop moving – walking, running, crawling, jumping, or bouncing – for five hours straight. When it was time to leave, his parents were less than thrilled. I had wound him up so much that he would probably need another hour or two to get back to "normal." (I love being an uncle!)

"All the wonders that you seek are within yourself." – Sir Thomas Brown (1605-82)

Watching my nephew got me thinking: When it comes to energy levels, what is "normal," anyway? Unfortunately, the majority of North Americans no longer know what optimum energy or vitality – true health – feels like. Worse, they probably don't know what they're missing. They think they're designed to feel the way they do – tired, listless, lethargic. In other words, they think they feel "normal!"

"In every moment, the quality of your life is on the line. In each, you are either fully alive or relatively dead." – Dan Millman

But lethargy and fatigue aren't "normal." Your body – like my nephew's – was designed to produce loads of optimum energy, at any age. If you're not feeling optimally energetic, chances are you've been gumming up the system and shutting down billions of your cellular engines for a while without knowing it. Fortunately, you can regain your lost energy potential.

"Oz never did give nothin' to the Tin man that he didn't already have." – America, Tin Man

We blame everything on our genes these days. As we learn more and more about the human body and its interactions with its environment, however, it becomes increasingly clear that our lifestyle and dietary choices are likely far more important to our health than our genetic makeup. In his groundbreaking book *Genetic Nutritioneering,* Jeffrey Bland, Ph.D., explains that our genetic inheritance is little more than a template upon which we build our unique life experiences. While our genetic codes may be fixed, their expression changes constantly, adapting to diet, lifestyle, and environment. To a very large extent, you choose whether you'll express your genes towards health or disease — towards vibrant energy or lack thereof.

"So often times it happens that we live our lives in chains and we never even know we have the key." – Eagles, *Already Gone*

It's never too late to teach your body how to be vital and energetic again. It's time to demand more than the "normalcy" of mediocrity. Accept nothing but the best from a body that was designed to take you through life at maximum capacity. In the following eight steps, I will guide you through the most important strategies for tapping into your unlimited energy potential and reawakening the energetic two-year-old within.

"The last thing we usually respect is the one thing we can't live without — our body." – Brad J. King

The 8 Steps to Optimum Energy & Vitality

Step 1: Believe You Can

Sir William Drummond said, "He who will not reason is a bigot; he who cannot is a fool; and he who dares not is a slave."

Are you a slave to your limiting self-beliefs?

We often limit ourselves with false beliefs that we accept as undeniable truths – for example, that we're too old, too out of shape, too far gone, too lazy or lethargic to experience optimum health. Many of us steer ourselves toward failure because of these beliefs.

In order to transform your life, you must first and foremost get rid of these false, limiting self-beliefs. Your self-image guides your habits, so if you see yourself as a lethargic, unhealthy person, then you'll be lethargic and unhealthy. When you consciously try to trade negative habits and ideas for positive ones, your self-image will eventually accept these habits and ideas as reality. Act as if you're already the person you want to be.

"Watch your thoughts; they become words. Watch your words; they become actions. Watch your actions; they become habits. Watch your habits; they become character. Watch your character; it becomes your destiny." – Frank Outlaw

Step 2: Drink More Water

You are mostly water. Water makes up 75% of the brain and muscles, 80% of the blood and lungs – even your bones are 25% water. Next to oxygen, water is the most important nutrient for sustaining life. It is essential to cellular energy production, slowing down the aging process, and helping us lose excess body fat. Studies show that for every pound of fluid lost, the body produces energy less efficiently – not good when we're trying to boost energy!

Yet many of us are dehydrated and don't even know it! Oh sure, we drink plenty of liquids all right – juice, coffee, tea and soda pop – but none of these come anywhere near the myriad health benefits associated with water. According to Dr. Batmanghelidj, the author of *Your Body's Many Cries for Water* and a world authority in the area of water biochemistry, many people overeat because they believe they are hungry, when in fact they may actually be thirsty and not even know it! As we age, the signals that are sent to the brain for both hunger and thirst often become mixed. This is one of the reasons I have my own clients drink a full glass of water approximately 20 minutes before each meal (in order to assure they don't overeat).

Do your body a favor and consume a *minimum* of eight full (8 oz.) glasses of water each and every day. Try carrying water with you wherever you go. Commit to drinking nothing but water for one full week. If you'd like, add lemon or lime (preferably organic) for taste. After a week you won't want to drink anything else.

"They suffer because they do not know they are thirsty" – Dr. Batmanghelidj, *Bio-Age: 10 Steps to a Younger You*

Step 3: Choose Food Wisely

Every minute of every day, your body rebuilds, replaces and replenishes about 200 million cells. And it gets the raw materials for this function from the food you eat. Every time you put something in your mouth, therefore, you choose your body's building materials. Junk food builds a junk body – period!

I could write (and have written) volumes about food choices. Suffice it to say that your diet should include a wide variety of fruits and vegetables (preferably organic), high-quality protein (game meat and organic grass-fed beef, organic free-run chicken and eggs, organic yogurt and fish), and "good" fats (organic butter, monounsaturated oils like olive and avocado, and omega-3 fats found in flax seeds and cold-water fish oils).

It's also important to realize the power of incorporating protein into every meal and eating smaller quantities of food at regular intervals (five or six times a day) throughout the day. By following this strategy, you will balance your blood-sugar levels (virtually eliminating cravings) and maintain an optimum hormonal profile for abundant energy.

Socrates once said, "Thou shouldst eat to live; not live to eat." Next time you sit down to eat, try giving your food your full attention. (Hint: turn off the TV for a change!) We should all learn to eat as though our lives depended upon it – because they do!

"Tell me what you eat, and I will tell you what you are." – Anthelme Brillat-Savarin, *The Physiology of Taste*, 1825

Step 4: Never Diet

One plausible reason that so many diets fail is that most of them focus on losing weight; not on losing fat. Too often, the lost weight comes from lean tissue or muscle. Since muscle is a key fat-burner (with the power to incinerate many extra calories in a day) and energy booster, dieting erodes a valuable source of energy and vitality. If would-be Fat Warriors focused on losing energy-sucking fat and preserving and building lean body tissues (especially muscle), there would be a lot more diet "success stories" out there – and a lot more energy and vitality to go around!

Dieting is a short-term solution to a lifelong problem. To lose fat and build muscle – and to look and feel great – you need to make wise eating and regular exercise part of your whole life, not just part of a two-week "diet plan." So get off the diet and get on with your life!

"All dieting accomplishes is turning you into a smaller fat person."
– Brad J. King

Step 5: Move Your Body

The human body is designed to move! Studies confirm that reduced activity levels strongly correlate to lost energy and strength and increases in body fat.

Don't worry: proper physical exercise doesn't necessarily mean hardcore sports or lifting mind-numbingly heavy weights. It can be performing moderate resistance exercises in a fitness centre or in the privacy of your own home two to four times a week for only 30 to 45 minutes. In a groundbreaking 1990 study presented in the prestigious Journal of the American Medical Association, even 90-year-old women showed greatly improved muscle size and strength after as little as eight weeks of weight training. And if nice little old ladies can do it, what's stopping you?

The message? Exercise is not optional if you want to experience optimum energy and vitality. Instead of parking it, take your body for a spin!

"People don't die of old age; they die of neglect." – Jack Lalanne

Step 6: Sleep More

Your lost energy potential might be a good night's sleep away. Proper sleep is essential to replenish energy reserves, rebuild and repair muscle tissue, re-energize the immune system, and cleanse the brain of excess cellular debris. Sleep loss has a cumulative – and disastrous – effect on the overall outcome of energy production.

All bodily processes revolve around the intricate timing of nature's clock – sunrise and sunset, or the circadian rhythms of nature. Staying up late or missing valuable sleep puts us out of sync with nature's clock, causing hormonal rhythms to run amok and energy levels to decline precipitously.

So start making a good night's sleep (at least eight hours) one of your highest priorities – your life depends on it.

"To achieve the impossible dream, try going to sleep." – Joan Klempner

Step 7: Stress Less

Many top medical researchers agree that stress may be the primary cause of many illnesses today.

During a stress response, the body produces powerful hormones designed to save your life in times of danger by increasing heart rate and muscle strength and heightening senses. But your stress response wasn't designed to stay on for extended periods of time. Constantly activated, it eventually destroys your cellular systems and depletes your body's energy potential – one reason why people tend to age drastically during short periods of major stress.

In the face of stress, perception equals reality. In other words, whether you're running away from an attacker or worrying about your unpaid bills, your body reacts the same way – by pumping out harmful, energy-zapping, illness-promoting stress hormones. In order to rebuild your energy reserves, you must learn to face stressful events with some degree of calm.

"I have been through some terrible things in my life, some of which actually happened." – Mark Twain

Step 8: Don't Wait

Johann Wolfgang von Goethe said, "Whatever you can do, or dream you can, begin it. Boldness has genius, power and magic in it." Don't put off change – life is way too short! Health is no different. If you constantly wait for the perfect moment to begin, you may never start.

"Why wait? Life is not a dress rehearsal. Quit practicing what you're going to do, and just do it. In one bold stroke you can transform today." – Marilyn Grey

Brad J. King, M.S., MFS, is a nutritional researcher, fitness expert, and author of the International best seller *Fat Wars: 45 days To Transform Your Body*. He has appeared as a leading expert on national radio and television shows, including the Today Show. For more information and to sign up for a free monthly *Fat Wars Chronicle* visit: *www.fatwars.com.*

One Minute to Health

By Gail Stolzenburg

There's a saying, *"If you don't have your health, you have nothing."* If the wealthiest person in the world were on their deathbed, they'd give up their fortune just to live a little longer. I know how they feel. Ten years ago I was in very poor health. I had respiratory problems – bronchitis, asthma and allergies. I lived on inhalers and I took steroids, which had terrible side effects. I couldn't sleep lying down, because I couldn't breathe. I slept in a recliner while my wife and children watched me to see if I would take another breath. It was not a good way to exist.

There Was No Other Choice

I had to find a solution so I wouldn't meet my father's fate. He died of respiratory problems at the age of 57. I began studying everything I could about nutrition and health. My library is filled with books on the subject. I took a year-long course from the *Life Science Institute* on all aspects of health. It was the same course taken by Tony Robbins, one of the top personal trainers in the world and Harvey Diamond, co-author of *Fit For Life*, the all-time best selling book on health. I studied the 31 needs of life including good air, pure water, internal and external cleanliness, adequate sleep, foods of our natural disposition, nutritional supplements, vigorous activity, sunshine and natural light, and rest and relaxation. Then, I began to change my lifestyle. *It was simple, but it wasn't easy.* But, the results were unbelievable – *for the past ten years I have not had a cold, the flu, a sick day, missed a day of work, or taken any medication, not even an aspirin.*

Paul Zane Pilzer, world-renowned economist, predicts the next trillion-dollar industry will be the health and wellness industry. It will surpass the "sickness" industry. (I know, you probably called it the health industry, but it's really about taking care of illnesses.) Based on what I've learned and experienced, I now conduct seminars on health and wellness. My mission is to help people be more productive by making a few simple changes to their lives. I'll tell you what I did to change my life, but first let's define health.

Most people would say, *"Health* is being without illness or feeling good." But, it's really a lot more. It can best be defined as "A condition in which we have complete function of our faculties." *Disease* is the body's way of healing itself, getting rid of toxicity. Did you ever wonder why you couldn't cure a cold? What's the reason everyone gets the flu right after the holidays? The experts tell us that most disease is caused by "free radicals" – unstable oxygen molecules that become oxidized. You know how an apple starts turning brown after it is cut open? That's oxidation. Dr. Ray Strand, a specialist in nutritional medicine, has written an excellent book entitled *BioNutrition,* that explains more on this subject.

The Myths About Nutrition

1. Eat lots of meat and dairy products. Meat contains a lot of fat and requires acidic digestive juices to digest. Dairy products are also high in fat and hard for the body to digest. We are the only animals who drink milk after 3 years of age and we don't drink our own milk. When a baby calf is 3 months old he will weigh 300 pounds; when he's a year old, he'll weigh 1, 000 pounds. Give me some more of that stuff! (Just kidding!) Some people take lactose pills so they can drink milk, can you believe it?

2. Eat a big breakfast: The bodies of most people have 3 cycles: intake - 12 noon to 8 pm; processing - 8 pm to 4 am; and elimination - 4 am to 12 noon. Your body's primary function is to digest food. During the digestion process, all of the other functions of the body are stopped or at least slowed. Remember how sleepy you feel after a big lunch? So, if your body is trying to eliminate all those toxins in the morning and you have a big breakfast, what happens? The body shuts down the elimination cycle to digest the food. Where do you suppose all the toxins, which should have been eliminated, go? Maybe the arteries, the colon, etc. I only eat fruit or fruit juice for breakfast and I find I have much more energy during the day.

3. All supplements are alike. I have a plumber friend who told me about pipes being clogged with nutritional supplements. I said I'd sure like to know what kind they were. He said, "No problem. I can read the names on most of them." You see the government allows 95% fillers in nutritional supplements. The government also only requires nutritional supplements to abide by the Good Manufacturing Practices (GMP) for food. An expert examined over 400 nutritional products and concluded the best supplements were manufactured by USANA Health Sciences. (See *Comparative Guide to Nutritional Supplements* by Lyle Mac William.) USANA uses the GMP for pharmaceuticals, a much higher standard than that for food. So, it's like comparing pizza to penicillin.

My wife and I have received so much benefit from using the USANA products that we now market these products as an integral part of our *Total Health System.* Here's what I did and what I ask other people to consider:

1. **Reduce meat and dairy products.** We know fat causes fat and fat comes from meat and dairy products. There is only one source of cholesterol outside of your body's production, and that is from animal by-products. Every time you look at food, ask yourself this question "Will it cleanse

me or clog me?" I eat 70% high water content foods, such as fruits and vegetables. There are 250 different kinds of fruit and 340 different kinds of vegetables. How can you ever get bored? I get plenty of protein from soy, beans and legumes. I also take nutritional supplements twice a day.

2. **Exercise every day.** Aerobic exercise is great, but it's not enough. You must do weight bearing exercises if you want your bones to develop and your food to digest properly. I use light weights with high repetitions. Using weights does not mean you have to be overly muscled. See *The New Nutrition* by Dr. Michael Colgan. Remember, exercising your eye muscles should be part of your program.

3. **Meditate, pray or practice yoga daily.** I was so impressed with Mark Victor Hansen when I learned he gets up at 4:00 AM and spends 1 hour meditating. What a great way to manage stress and to plan a successful day.

One of the side benefits to my daily regime is that I no longer use eyeglasses. I can read the Wall Street Journal stock market quotes without eyeglasses. My wife has reduced her eyeglasses prescription 5 times. We used a combination of special nutritional supplements and eye muscle exercises to accomplish the improvement. Others have used this method to improve their eyesight.

Did you know 17 million people died last year of circulatory problems? Millions more died from cancer, stroke and diabetes. Do you know anyone who doesn't have a relative or friend with health problems? Over 50% of our population is over-weight. 25% of the vegetable intake of teenagers is french fries that are 47% trans fatty acids. The water and air are polluted. For more information on this subject, read *A Diet for a New America* by John Robbins.

One Million American's Left the Same Suicide Note on Their Refrigerator Last Year:

Milk
Bacon
Candy
Coffee
Cheese
Soft drinks
Frozen pizza
Mayonnaise
Hamburger meat
Artificial sweeteners

So, what is the "**One Minute to Health**?" You've probably already figured it out. It's the minute you decide to change your lifestyle, the minute you decide to eat nutritiously, exercise daily and manage stress. It's the most important minute of your life.

My Challenge to You is to Make These 10 Daily Commitments:

I will "move my body" – walk, bike, or swim and use weights.

I will eat only fruit or fruit juice until noon.

I will eat 70% high water content foods.

I will combine my foods properly.

I will get 7-8 hours of rest.

I will take the best nutritional supplements.

I will relax – meditate, pray, or do yoga.

I will reduce my intake of meat and dairy products.

I will exercise my eye muscles.

I will write down and use affirmations.

The question I leave you with is: If not now, when? There is only one difficulty, if it exists at all, and that is taking the first step. Join me in helping America become the healthiest nation in the world.

This article contains excerpts from the soon to be published book *One Minute to Health*. If you'd like a copy of the 10 worst foods, the 10 best foods, the recommended daily regime or information on improving your eyesight, you can contact the author at his email address: *gail@freedomnow.net*.

Is Your Life A Sprint or A Marathon?

7 Vital Tips to Set Your Pace on the Journey

By Jacalyn Buettner, D.C.

You have just registered for the race of your life. The challenge is to become a successful entrepreneur. Have you prepared yourself for the tremendous amount of hard work that lies ahead, especially if you desire to be a top contender who can lead the way for others? America's legacy has been built upon the success, commitment and struggles of the pioneers who came before you. What is your strategy for success? Will you spring out of the box like a sprinter, with a burst of energy and short-lived brilliance and then fade? Or will you start off like a marathoner, off the block easy, setting a balanced pace, getting in the rhythm, feeling the natural high and staying the course for a lifetime of success? Here are seven tips to ensure you achieve your personal best in this journey we call Life.

Tip 1. Define Your Values and Live By Them

Define what is important to you what you value and believe in. This requires listening to your intuition, paying attention to your gut and following your heart. Create a vision and identify a purpose that will feed your soul and fulfill you at the deepest level.

Write down your five highest priorities in life. Do this now. You may value excellent health, work you love, loving relationships, spirituality, living an abundant balanced life, or achieving financial freedom. Once you have defined these, own them. Stay true to yourself by not compromising what you know is right. Don't let your need for recognition, achievement or approval override your top priorities. Once your values are clear, you will make a *life* instead of a *living*. Get ready. By defining your values, miracles are going to start showing up in the next two *weeks*.

Tip 2. Use Your Time Wisely: Set Goals

Are you always "busy" yet never seem to get anything done? There are 24 hours in a day, so use them wisely by setting long- and short-term goals.

What are your lifetime goals? How would you like to spend the next three years? No matter how busy you are, you must take time to plan and set goals. Ten minutes in the morning or evening will pay off greatly. You need to get used to planning and prioritizing what is important for you in order to move you closer to realizing your full potential. List your top five goals and post them on your bathroom mirror. Read them out loud daily. Take a few minutes every morning to write down your daily goals. This will help you stay focused and use your time more effectively as you move toward your dreams.

Tip 3. Take Care of Yourself

Grace was a 45-year old single mother with two young sons and her own business. Like many hard working, busy people, living on adrenaline became her drug of choice. When her feet hit the floor in the morning, she didn't stop until she collapsed in bed at night. Her body was in sprint mode "flight or fight" the entire day. She was running on automatic, driving herself internally to the point she became numb and disconnected from her body. She was always "busy" yet never seemed to get anything done. She lost her focus, became easily distracted and lost track of what her needs were. Eight months, four days and 15 hours later… Boom. She hit the wall – burned out from adrenal exhaustion. She couldn't get out of bed for days and it took her over a year to heal.

Don't sacrifice your health for success. You want to be able to enjoy the journey and a more abundant life. Taking a few time-outs during your day is a great way to adjust the speed in your life. Close your eyes; take a deep breath in and exhale slowly. Visualize your favorite place, breathe in and out again, letting go of all the tensions in your mind and body. Feel your shoulders begin to relax, stretch your legs out in front of you. Mini-meditations like this will refresh your body, mind and spirit.

Eating well will help you stay healthy and resistant to disease. We live in a country where 61% of Americans are overweight. Eat to live, don't live to eat. Eating healthier requires discipline – a determination to eat healthy foods.

Begin now; say, "No thank you," to sugar and fast food and watch your energy improve.

Rest will rejuvenate you so that you can accomplish your goals. Be sure to get enough sleep at night and consider adding a twenty-minute power nap in your schedule. Revisit your priorities. Get a massage, play with your kids, go to a movie, plan a date with someone you love – have fun.

Tip 4. Exercise, a Natural High

Exercise can give you a natural high that gives you a sense of peace and relaxation. Movement is power, power is energy, energy is productivity, and productivity is financial freedom and an abundant life. Stand up right now and begin moving your body… stretch. Take a thirty-minute walk at lunch, let those endorphins kick in, feel the energy. This will increase your productivity as you will be more alert, think clearer and feel more alive.

Exercise will also help you decrease anxiety and stress. How do you know if you're stressed? You will begin to experience muscles tightening in your neck and back, headaches, clenching of teeth and jaw, digestive disorders and shallow breathing. Stress can cause addictions to alcohol, drugs and caffeine. Behaviors such as irritability, anger, depression and sleeping difficulties are all signs that you are not handling stress effectively.

Other ways to release stress and tension include getting away on vacation, taking a day off, golfing, or running on the beach. Relax into your life. When you are relaxed you will be open to creative ideas. Find ways to replenish your tank, fulfill your needs and rejuvenate your mind, body and spirit.

Tip 5. Giving and Living an Attitude of Gratitude

"Giving guarantees receiving" is a well known principle of abundance. Give to give; don't give to get. Don't give with strings attached. Giving your time, love, and energy with a genuine intention expands your opportunity to receive, to increase your abundance. Giving of yourself makes you more productive and it feels good!

Start giving today. Get involved in community activities, join a club, share a carpool, volunteer, hug your child, tithe at church or support a charity either financially or with items from home you want to recycle.

Then be thankful – feel the gratitude in your heart when you give of yourself. Have an attitude of gratitude. Every night before you go to sleep, affirm out loud five things you are thankful for. Share this tip with your children; you'll be inspired how simple this process can be… by giving and living an attitude of gratitude.

Tip 6. Take Action Despite Your Fears

We all have fears. Fear can be a good thing. Fear creates a level of discomfort that will either incapacitate you or propel you to take action. A willingness to step into your fear is like bravely walking over hot coals. As in Tony Robbins "Firewalk Experience," walking on hot coals is a metaphor for turning your fear into power. You're not going to die. You may end up with a blister that is painful, but it will heal. The main thing is that you took action and action yields results.

One of my mentors taught me to do the "feared thing first." Whatever the fear is, be it making a sales call, firing a staff member, requesting a bank loan, or asking someone out on a date, handle the fear first thing in the morning.

Tip 7. Never Stop Learning

Affirm out loud, "Today, I commit to being a life-long learner." Say it again with enthusiasm. "Today, I commit to being a life-long learner!" Knowledge will help you in all areas of your life: operating a successful business, developing loving relationships and taking better care of you. This week visit your public library and continue your education for free. You can check out books and audio tapes on your favorite topics and exercise your mind by reading daily or listening to audio tapes on the way to work or while exercising your body. Begin by checking out *Think and Grow Rich* by Napoleon Hill or the *One Minute Millionaire* by Mark Victor Hansen and Robert Allen.

As you continue on your journey and apply these seven tips along the way, focus on the joys and miracles, not the obstacles and disappointments. Where your energy goes, that's what grows. Embrace the marathoner mind set… come off the block easy, set a balanced pace, get in the rhythm, focus, feel the natural high and stay the course for a lifetime of joy and abundance.

An active leader in her profession, Dr. Buettner has been recognized in national media including *Good Morning America, World News Tonight* and *On The Money*. A sought- after speaker on motivation and stress reduction using posture and ergonomic techniques, she is the author of an upcoming book *Head, Hands, Heart – 100 Years of Women in Chiropractic*. Email *DrB@UnionSquarechiro.com*.

The Seven Cornerstones of a
Strong Body and Strong Mind

By Shawn Phillips

I was recently being interviewed for an article and doing what I often do: answering questions about exercise, nutrition and getting in shape. The questions are generally the same, and so are the answers (the truth never changes). However, about an hour in I was asked a question I have *not* answered 100 times. In fact, it was a question I hadn't really given much thought prior to the moment the reporter asked, "Shawn, in these troubled times – in this uncertain, downright frightening 'post-9/11 world,' why even bother trying to get in shape, much less build a strong, lean body?"

Typically I answer questions quickly, but this time, the answer didn't come right away. I took a deep breath, leaned back in my chair and gazed out the window. A few minutes in contemplation and I saw the "bigger picture" – the importance of fitness was clear, like I've never quite seen it before. So I leaned forward and, with clarity and confidence, shared how I see it…

First of all, taking care of yourself and doing what you can to become as healthy and fit as possible matters *now* more than *ever*. I believe a strong nation is made up of strong people. And one thing every person in this country can do to help strengthen America is strengthen themselves.

Next, there's the economical impact on our country. Each year, U.S. taxpayers spend over $100 billion caring for Americans who didn't take care of themselves. That money goes to treat people who are suffering from obesity (an alarming 67% of Americans) and its secondary diseases such as diabetes, heart disease, vascular disease, cancer and other debilitating diseases. So if you just look at it from a fiscal standpoint, you can see how vitally important it is to make sure we don't become a burden to our country.

Then there's the mental aspect. When you strengthen the body, you strengthen the mind. You strengthen individual character and courage.

Today, more than ever, people need a healthy way to deal with the uncertainty, anxiety, stress and confusion. Now consider the fact that it has been scientifically proven that regular, intense exercise, along with healthy eating, elevates energy levels, keeps the mind clear, reduces depression and stress. That, in turn, improves quality of life.

Now, I'm not saying we should become obsessed with fitness or building a muscular body. I *am* saying it's a worthwhile goal. When you look fit, lean and strong, you're also going to *be* healthy on the inside.

Over the last decade I've helped thousands of fitness buffs, athletes and celebrities build strong, lean, healthy bodies. And what I've discovered is that regardless of whether you want to trim down, build up or firm all over, it is very important to understand and accept that there is no "one thing," no magic potion, single exercise or diet that will allow you to sculpt a healthy, toned physique.

The simple truth is that the "one thing" many people seek is *"everything!"* How you feed your body, the way you think and even how you stay motivated has every bit as much to do with how you look as the exercises you do. The following "Seven Cornerstones to a Strong Body and Strong Mind" are the "everything": the fundamentals I've seen that produce remarkable results time and time again.

1. Train With Weights

I've no doubt that you're aware of how vital exercise is to your health. Unfortunately, far too many people who do exercise only exercise one muscle – the heart. I agree that maintaining a healthy heart is serious business. But if you're not paying the same attention to the other (700) muscles in your body, you're missing out on some of the most potent benefits of exercise.

The single *most powerful* way to build strong, defined muscles and burn more fat for a lean body is by training your *entire body* with weights regularly – with *intensity*. And as weight training helps build strong muscle and maintain strength and flexibility, it is even more vital as one ages.

2. Supercharge Fat Loss

You may hear a lot about "metabolism" these days. All you really need to know is that the "faster" your metabolism, the more energy (and fat) your body uses to sustain normal living. Contrary to what many people believe, there are simple things you can do to speed up your metabolism and create a more energized, healthier state and a leaner body.

To boost your metabolism, start eating smaller, more frequent meals throughout the day, increase the amount of protein in your diet, do high-intensity cardiovascular workouts and, of course, resistance train to increase your muscle mass. All of those factors combined can be a powerful fat burner on their own.

3. Get Clear

It has been estimated that 98% of people who commit to getting in shape each New Year fail to follow through. One reason is that they never set a specific goal. A goal of "getting in shape" is like a financial goal of earning "lots of money." Neither is more than a dream – not until you've made the goal explicit and put pencil to paper to record it.

Don't make the mistake of setting "fitness dreams." Yes, your goals should be lofty and the thought of achieving them should give you energy deep inside, but you should also be able to convince a jury you believe you can achieve it.

For the next 12 weeks, decide *exactly* how much muscle you want to gain and *exactly* how much fat you want to lose! "A few pounds" will not do.

4. Have A Plan

I'll bet you learned early on, like I did, that there are "no shortcuts" in life. Darn good advice, but unfortunately, many people have taken this to mean they must always find the hardest possible way to success. Please don't make this any more challenging than it already is. I learned long ago the wisdom of following in the footsteps of those who have succeeded before me. My advice to you is to take this "shortcut" and find someone who's achieved the results you would like to realize and do what he or she did. *If you follow a proven plan, you may very well achieve spectacular results as well!*

5. Measure Progress

Sustaining the motivation toward achieving your goal is without question one of the greatest challenges in all of fitness. It requires unwavering determination, discipline and faith *and* regular, consistent feedback on your progress. A simple method of measuring results will provide that all-important feedback: trust me, when you see real progress, it fuels a fire like nothing else.

Given that muscle weighs considerably more than fat, relying on the scale alone is a mistake. A simple cloth tape measure can be a perfect complement to a bathroom scale. Each morning I step on the scale, weigh myself and use the tape to measure my waist (where I collect most of my bodyfat). I then record this in my "Success Journal." I watch the weekly trends and adjust my plan accordingly until I am getting the results I want!

6. Aim High

In the last decade, I've meet thousands of people who need to "drop about 5 pounds." See the same people six months later, and, you got it, they still need to drop "five pounds." Why don't they get on with it? Simple, it's not a significant enough goal. Most people reach only as far as they know their arm will extend, setting goals that lack the "magic" to access the energy deep in their souls. Don't make this mistake. Instead, set your sights high, outside your reach. Allow yourself to imagine your body looking and feeling a way that ignites a burning desire inside. Shoot for the stars and enjoy the ride.

7. Get Focused!

If you find exercise "boring" or it's just not "stimulating enough," get "focused." Focus means you put everything you have into what you're doing at that very second – whether it's your work, workout or nutrition, or a friend, family member or loved one. Absolutely nothing else matters during that given moment.

The ability to focus the energy of your mind and body like the light of an ordinary fluorescent bulb to the concentrated intensity of a laser beam is a powerfully important concept and an absolute breakthrough strategy – for exercise and for life. And, in my mind, there's no better place to develop your ability to focus than during physical exercise – to train your mind along with your body.

Final Thoughts

I've discovered that people who succeed in dramatically transforming their physiques – those who build a strong, healthy body – become so empowered that they can change many other things in their lives. By building a better body, you'll have greater self-esteem, more confidence and a better attitude. So if you want to improve in any areas of your life, start by focusing on building a better body, and let that flow into other areas of your life.

Shawn Phillips is an innovator, speaker, expert coach and the author of *ABSolution, The Practical Solution for Building Your Best Abs*. For over a decade, Shawn's helped athletes, celebrities and fitness buffs build strong, healthy bodies with his commonsense approach to fitness. To receive Shawn's insightful tips for building your best abs and body, visit *www.BestABS.com*.

Remember Your Family!

©2003 Kim Muslusky

Keys To a Successful
Marriage
By David & Venus Dye

Your aspirations may be wealth or fame but if you are not happy with your home life, what do you have? Can you have both? The average millionaire in the United States is married with three children.[1] They would no longer be millionaires with their assets divided through divorce. If you are only searching for happiness in wealth and fame, in our opinion, you first need to refocus your search. Try to put as much or more effort into your family as you do you business and you will find something money cannot buy.

Your Best Investment

You need to invest in your marriage just as you would any type of investment. The difference is that your marriage comes before your business. Your marriage is the example you set for your children and community. Is it a good example or a poor one? A large part of building the marriage is building yourself and helping your mate grow. The building of a marriage does take work. However, as Dale Carnegie pointed out, "People rarely succeed unless they have fun in what they are doing." It is easier to rebuild a business than to rebuild a broken marriage and repair the damage to each other and to the children.

Although we cannot tell you how to find your soul mate, we can give you insight on how to make your marriage a healthy one. When you do find your spouse, start your marriage off by talking about and deciding how to grow together. Everyone grows and matures differently, but if you decide to grow and mature together, you will not grow apart. Rather you become intertwined like a vine which becomes harder to pull apart with age. We think very differently in many ways. However, we have found that neither of us is exclusively correct is either wrong; a middle ground is normally best on most issues. Rarely do either of us make a decision without consulting the other first.

How to Grow Together

Even after 15 years of marriage, people still accuse us of being newlyweds. Our success is not attributable as much to "the school of hard knocks" as it is to asking older, successfully married couples how to enrich our union. Most couples would benefit from obtaining a better understanding of what is involved in marriage before their wedding day.

We discussed everything under the sun before we got married. We did not limit it to the important issues like children, religion, and family values. We discussed every little detail we could think of, from specifics on how to raise children to which end we squeezed the toothpaste tube! Even if you have been married for a while, you could improve your marriage with just a few efforts at communication, like making simple adjustments to your car during a tune-up rather than conducting a major overhaul, perhaps after it has broken down along the road.

Dr. Nathaniel Branden is a psychologist in California who points out that those couples who stay in love:

- Never take their relationship for granted.
- Express their affection for each other daily.
- Frequently say, "I love you."
- Express their love sexually.
- Verbalize their appreciation and admiration.
- Share their thoughts and feelings, learning to self-disclose what's on their minds and hearts to each other, confiding in each other.
- Express their love materially, giving each other little gifts.
- Create time together.[2]

Practical Implementation

We have some practical things that we try to implement along with the above. For example, always let your spouse know where you are. This alleviates those little seeds of doubt. Small seeds can grow into giant trees. If you are a homemaker, make a conscious effort to be home when your spouse arrives home. Try to give each other a quick kiss before ever leaving anywhere. Never allow selfishness to overcome you. Do not think of what you can get out of this but what can you do for your spouse to make things easier. Men, open the car door for your wife. Women, let your husband do things for you (i.e. open the car door). Do not continue to be independent when he is around you (i.e. ask for help opening a tight lid, getting an item that is out of reach, or anything that will make him feel needed). Men and women know that they can get by without each other; nonetheless, it is nice to be needed.

The one word – commitment – covers a whole realm of problems in a marriage. There should be a commitment to communicate, to overcome difficulties and differences, to grow together, to be kind, to love, to share, and to give of yourself. All marriages will have some obstacles. That is just part of life. Whether one partner stays home to raise the children or both work, there will be struggles. Sometimes one partner will be preoccupied with a problem, sickness, or may just have a temporary bad attitude towards his or her spouse. If one partner cannot give 100%, then the other needs to take up the slack. When Venus had our first child, she had some complications afterwards and was not able to keep up with all her normal activities. David stepped in and picked up where she could not. You have to work together and be a support for each other; it is a team effort. If one is not being supportive, then the other must double their efforts. It has been proven through many marriages that when one person shows love and support, the other will respond in kind. It may not happen right away; some things take time. You are building trust between two people. Due to the fear of getting hurt, some people take longer than others to develop trust, especially when it involves revealing your emotions to someone.

Balance

Just as there are psychological advantages to having your physical life in balance, there is an advantage to balancing your emotions. As hard as you try, you never leave your problems at home; they affect every aspect of your life. Determine to face your problems and work through them together. No doubt, there will be some type of conflict. Use this to your mutual advantage. Try to look at every conflict as positively as you are able. Not all conflicts are negative. Remember, without the conflict of the wind against the eagle's wings, he could not fly. Sometimes you must just learn how to agree to disagree. Besides, if two people always agree on everything, one of the two is not thinking!

Psychology does play a part in commitment. For example, people see what they believe; they do not believe what they see. The same is found in getting what you expected. If you expect something and truly believe you will receive it, your mind will subconsciously map out a path to attain it. So, if you expect to see great things in your spouse, you will; and the reverse is also true. We suggest you ignore the latter and develop the former. The mind works in whatever direction you have trained it. You may not have realized you have trained it to see negative or positive, but the training is there. If you have trained your mind to see the negative, retrain yourself to see the positive. There are reasons you fell in love with your spouse. Something positive caught your attention. Keep looking for those initial reasons and you will find them – and more!

Submit One to Another

Many people today think the Bible is full of a bunch of outdated stories. The Bible has practical advice on finances, marriage, how to raise children, and general living. Most men know that the Bible says that a wife should submit to her husband but do not realize that it also says for the man to love the wife as Christ loved the Church, and gave of his life. It also says to submit one to another. If you take the time to look, you would find out that the Bible covers all areas of our psychological make-up. If you are having problems in your marriage, read the Bible verses that deal with those problems. Pray everyday that you will stay attracted to your mate, that you will love them always, even when they do not seem lovable. Be very specific in your prayers. If you always have these thoughts in the forefront of your mind and it is truly the desire of your heart, you will be surprise to find you are totally and completely head over heals in love with your mate.

David and Venus Dye have been married for over 15 years and are still accused of being newlyweds. This article is written in response to all those who have asked their secret to a happy, healthy marriage. Contact David and Venus via email at: *vmdye@yahoo.com*

(Footnotes)
[1] T. Stanley & W. Danko, "The Millionaire Next Door."
[2] Dr. Nathaniel Branden, "Advice That Could Save Your Marriage" Readers Digest.

Empowering Kids
for a
Healthy Financial Future

By Lori Mackey

There are two paths most people take when it comes to teaching their children about money. One path involves teaching the language of abundance, where children learn how to manage money so that the results are an ever-increasing amount of financial wealth and happiness. The other path involves the language of limitation, which results at best in children learning to "live within their means" and at worst creating a life filled later with financial debt and emotional distress. Are you teaching your children to lead a life of financial well being or financial difficulty, and where will it lead them?

Too many of our young people are graduating from high school with failing grades in Financial Education. In 2002, household debt increased more than nine percent, and more than a million families filed for personal bankruptcy.[o]

To combat this growing trend, Americans are taking a stand on the benefits of teaching money management skills in early childhood. The *Jump$tart Coalition* is helping schools adapt curricula to teach personal financial management skills throughout the K-12 education. And Federal Reserve Chairman Alan Greenspan has declared, "Improving basic financial education at the elementary and secondary school levels will provide a foundation of financial literacy that can help prevent younger people from making poor decisions that can take years to overcome."

The Buck Starts Here

It is even more important that we instill good money habits at home. Indeed, it is *critical* that we let children practice basic financial skills throughout their childhood. But how? Although we are our children's most significant money mentors, most of us are not trained in financial literacy. And it is difficult to find hands-on tools to guide young children.

That's why I started **Prosperity 4 Kids.**

I believe we can empower our children to have true wealth – the freedom to have jobs they are passionate about, the financial ability to support causes they care about, and the security to see themselves comfortably into retirement if – and only if – *they are taught by doing at a young age.*

Money Mom's Mission

I searched for the tools to teach my young children about true wealth and how to become economically savvy. But almost every resource for teaching financial literacy that was available skipped elementary and even junior-high school students and went straight to the high school level.

So I decided to create early financial education products that are fun, engaging and effective, as well as age- and skill-appropriate. Plus I chose to write companion books with action plans for parents, teachers and kids that capture the attention and imagination of children.

The premise of these materials is to *help children develop a positive attitude toward money and empower them to practice money management that leads to true wealth...* the same concepts that the world's wealthiest people apply and teach their own children. What came from nearly a year of research, including attending seminars and meeting with some of our country's most truly wealthy individuals, is the "10/10/10/70" philosophy that is central in all of my books and products.

That is, *for every dollar children earn, they Give 10%, Invest 10%, Save 10% and Spend 70% wisely.*

Beginning to instill this concept as soon as children understand that a dime is worth more than a nickel will prepare them to live abundantly from 70% of their income and use the rest to build wealth, control their financial futures and reap the rewards (of money and personal satisfaction) from their contributions to making the world a better place.

Sharing Prosperity

Like many of us, I was raised to save and spend. My "financial education" was to put money into a piggy bank until I needed or wanted something, and then take the money back out and spend it. I *thought* that the money was *mine,* without thinking much about the fact that it *really* belonged to whoever I gave it to: the store; the hair cutter; the restaurant. Even though it seems obvious, I didn't really comprehend that if I gave it all away, I would be left with nothing. I didn't learn about the value of charitable giving, and I had no understanding of how money can grow or how to save for a long-term goal.

When I thought about my own circumstances, I realized that the piggy bank itself is a key teaching tool for parents, and that's why the **Money Mama Piggy Bank** became my first product. It has four slots with their own compartments so children can easily use the "10/10/10/70" concept from an early age. It is a natural, hands-on way to help children develop an early understanding of how to live from 70% of their income, how to plan ahead and save for major purchases and how to make their money grow for them.

How do young children "earn" money? Allowance. I've tackled that much-debated subject with two books and a magnetized chart *(It's Only a Dollar... Until You Add to It!)* that helps parents organize and track daily chores and allows children to see how quickly they can *grow* their allowance. Of course, kids really love the idea that they can turn their allowance into even *more* money.

When you make the decision to educate your children about the "10/10/10/70" money principle, you can combat the "entitlement attitude" that is so rampant in our society today. You can help your children develop healthy financial habits that will be with them for a lifetime. And you can inspire them to have a positive outlook on what they can acquire and achieve.

If you raise financially literate children, you will surely give them the most valuable "real life" education possible.

Lori Mackey, an entrepreneurial wife and mother of two, is the founder of *www.prosperity4kids.com. Prosperity 4 Kids'* mission is to develop fun, engaging, early financial educational products and services that empower kids to create healthy financial futures. The company donates 10% of all proceeds to children's charities. Contact Lori via email at *Lori@prosperity4kids.com.*

How Do You Score on the Key Measurements of Your Own Success?

By Gary Vurnum

Is your life terrible? Mine is!

OK. I lied… it *could* be terrible – if I chose to let it be. If you had asked me five years ago, I would never have accepted that I could have been happy with my life as it is now.

Five years ago I was in the comfort zone. My career was doing OK, I had a beautiful wife, Lesley, and a cute little two-year-old daughter called Katie with another child on the way.

I was paid well… but I certainly worked hard for it. First in, last out. Weekends. You name it, I'd volunteer for it. Sound familiar? I struggled for years knowing deep down that I was good enough to work for myself, but I didn't have the guts to do it. I knew that there was something missing from my life, yet I never wanted to give up my "security" and make that jump.

I knew exactly where my priorities were: make as much money as I could so that I could give my family everything that they wanted. *Wrong!* It's taken me this long to work out that I was on the fast-track to misery. I didn't realize it at the time, but the very thing that was driving me forward would ultimately be my downfall.

I thought that being successful meant earning a nice salary, driving a nice car, working hard and playing hard. Then – after all that – came my wife and daughter. That's what being successful is all about, isn't it? The fact that I very rarely was home early enough to tuck my daughter into bed didn't bother me. I was on my way… and nothing was going to stop me.

Well, something *did* stop me. Dead in my tracks. Like being struck by lightning, my life was to change forever in seconds. At 5:25 a.m. on June 2, 1998, my son Connor was born, and all hell broke loose! He was born with severe mental and physical disabilities. I can tell you now exactly what it felt like in those seconds after he was born. What was meant to be a happy occasion turned into the worst day of our lives. We didn't even know if he would make it through the first hour of his life.

I could write an entire book about what has happened to us since. In his first two months he contracted meningitis, which, although not diagnosed by the doctors, we managed to catch in time. If you're a parent, you'll understand what an important event your child's first Christmas is. At 10 a.m. on Connor's first Christmas, he suddenly stopped breathing and we had to resuscitate him! I could tell you in detail about the number of times that Connor has been close to death... and about the broken bones, the pneumonia, and the chicken pox that kept him in the hospital for his second Christmas.

But This Isn't About Me. It's About You.

It took me another three years before I really understood where I was going wrong before. My entire definition of success was based on money and prestige alone. I thought that I was a success at what I did. I didn't realize that money is the last thing that you should consider when you are defining how successful you are.

"Now hold on," I bet you're thinking. "What is this guy talking about? Of course money is one of the most important things where success is concerned, right?"

Wrong!

Look at the following six statements, and prioritize them in order from one to six, based on how important they are to you.
– You see a child (especially if they're yours) give you a massive smile.
– You are the only person to get a difficult question right.
– You think of the best memories of your teenage years.
– You find some money lying on the floor.
– You get a new house... and take on a bigger mortgage.
– You take a loan out for a vacation.

So how did you rank them? Which one do you think came out as most important overall based upon the ranking by 276 people who read my on-line newsletter? Number 4? After all... money *is* important, right? Number 5? We are all prepared to "pay" for a little more luxury in our lives aren't we?

The ranking went like this: six points if it was ranked 1st; five points for a ranking of 2nd; and so on... down to one point if it was ranked last. Here are the results:

Most Important: A child's smile.	1,573 points.
2nd: Difficult question right.	1,152 points.
3rd: Teenage memories.	1,042 points.
4th: Money on the floor.	983 points.
5th: Bigger house/mortgage.	641 points.
Least Important: Loan for vacation.	504 points.

Surprised? Did you notice that the three most important things had *nothing* to do with money whatsoever? So what does that tell you about what should *really* be important in your life? It took me a fair few years before I made the distinction that money didn't equal success. I haven't looked back either personally or financially since!

If a child's smile rates as over 60% *more* important than purely getting money for nothing in the street, don't you think that it would make sense to build your "ideal" future around what is *important*? Whichever way you look at it, you can't take *anything* with you when you go. Why not fill your life with those important thoughts, feelings, emotions, and experiences?

When I was considering what questions to ask, I deliberately made sure that I didn't give you an option like "having lots of money" or "being rich." Why? Because I know that it would have won! It would have won because the vast majority of people blame lack of money as the main "reason" why they haven't succeeded. Their main target where success is concerned is making money. Which is fine... But if you remove "money" from this equation, you can begin to see what is *really* the main reason *why* people want more money in the first place. You can chase after money all of your life but, unless you aim to do something *important* with it, then you will never get it. I think you'll agree that this survey gave you an idea of why material possessions aren't as important as people think they are.

What does this mean to you in real life? Let's look at your day as a series of transactions. On that basis, are you getting sufficient *value* from your efforts? Just as importantly - are you giving enough *effort* in return for what you value? Just for a moment, let's move money out of the way. I know that may be difficult, but it is essential that you can see past judging your achievements in monetary terms alone. Money is the means through which you can acquire more possessions or a method with which you can buy more experiences, but, on a day-to-day basis it can't *buy* you what is *important*.

It doesn't matter how rich you are. You will never be truly successful if you live by the principles of how much you can earn or own. In order to have a successful life, you need to focus on what's important to you first, before money even enters the equation.

So... are you getting something important in return from your efforts every day?

- Do you feel as if you accomplish something important every day?
- Do you feel that you are making something of your life in general?

- Do you feel that you are happy with *who* you are?
- Do you feel appreciated for the efforts you put in?
- Do you feel that you have strong relationships with the people that you love?

Did you notice that the word "feel" plays an important part here? These are *the* key measurements of that thing we call success. It's not money. It's not a big house. It's not regular vacations.

So how do *you* measure up? Aren't feelings so much more *exciting* than a line of numbers on a bank statement? Isn't it more important for you to have a life to live than just an amount of assets on a balance sheet? What would it mean to you if you had no family to share your millions with? What if your children hardly recognized you yet had everything material they could wish for? Are material assets really *that* important?

Still not convinced? OK. Let me ask you one final question: Your house is on fire. You have a choice: on one side of the room sits a pile of photographs of your family. On the other is $500 in cash. You only have time to get to one before you have to get out. I'll leave it up to you to decide which one you think is the most important to you.

To Our Success!

Dedicated to my son, Connor Vurnum
(2nd June 1998 to 20th February 2003)

"How Can I Help You?" I'm a father, husband, author, coach and
marketer in that order. Please subscribe to my 4-part Special
Report *You WILL Succeed – When You Defeat Your 11 Demons*
by sending a blank
email to: *succeed@scienceofsuccess.com*

What Price Success?

By Larry McIntire

I worry when I see anyone in business run the risk of sacrificing their marriage and family in a quest to be successful. Having been devastated by two divorces personally, I know whereof I speak! As the founder of the Christian Singles Registry who has counseled thousands of men in the past seven years, I know a great deal about what it is like to find yourself at middle age without a lifetime partner. I've heard almost every story you can think of, but there are many recurring themes. In almost every case, the individuals were overcome with a great sense of loss, disappointment and regret. No doubt if I had been interviewing women, the findings would have been the same. Loss of a love is loss of a love, whether you're male or female.

You Must Be Willing to Step Out of the Box

We all buy books and tapes, and listen to speakers exhort us to pay whatever price is required to achieve success. There is no doubt that if you want to experience extraordinary accomplishments, you must be willing to step out of the box to make it happen. Unfortunately, many interpret this as a license to neglect spouse and family, coming to their senses only after it's too late.

Jesus taught us: "What does it profit a man to gain the whole world and lose his soul?" Of course he was referring to our spiritual condition, but I have always associated this teaching with the peril of being successful in business, but losing your family or health in the process.

When I was younger, I remember being told of a very successful businessman who made a weekly appointment with his son. At that appointed hour, it didn't matter what was going on. He would give his son the attention he would have given his most important business associate! I have heard similar stories about other highly successful men who take their wives out on a date every week. Just as they would not have let anything stand in their way before their wedding day, they have kept their wives their highest priority years after the wedding vows.

Recently my wife Beth and I were able to build a 2000 square foot office suite adjoining our home, and were able to design it just as we wanted. We laid it out with Beth's office next to mine, with a sliding glass window allowing us to see each other. Most of the time I forget it is there, but what a great comfort to know all I have to do is to look up and see her. From time to time I'll hear her laugh or she'll pop in and ask a question.

Without Your Family, What Good is Success and Money?

I know this isn't possible with everyone, but maybe you're getting the message. Without your family, what good is success and money?

As a result of my divorce in 1992, I lost a 4000-square-foot log home filled with museum-quality antiques on 40 acres overlooking a 2-acre lake. I moved to a little house one of my church friends rented to me for $100 a month. I lived there for a full year while I was trying to regain my senses. I never missed the log home like I thought I would, but I sure missed my wife and three sons! When the boys came to visit on weekends, I found I appreciated the closeness we shared in that little rented house.

During the four and a half years I was involved in Amway, we went to a major seminar and rally every three months. We never missed, managing to sometimes drive 1500 miles one way. Did we always have the money? No, but we always went. Did I always have the time to take away from my other business? No, but we never missed. I learned from those experiences that if you wait for all the stars to line up perfectly, you'll never do anything; if planned three months ahead of time, however, you'd be surprised what you can make happen!

Beth and I make it a point to disappear for a few days together five or six times a year. This past year we traveled to Cleveland three times to attend mastermind meetings with eleven other business owners. To have time together, we would go a day early and stay a day late. I was the only one who brought a spouse along. I wondered what some of them might think, but I really didn't care. We also take advantage of the closeout cruise prices on the Internet two or three times a year. Recently we celebrated our seventh wedding anniversary on a five-day cruise that only cost $229 each. Was it a good time to be away from my office? No! Did we enjoy going anyway? Yes!

Almost every year we spend a month in the Philippines at our seaside home. We ride our motorcycle hundreds of miles a week going everywhere,

I always come back energized and refreshed. Does being on the other side of the world for a month ever foul up some things in my office? Always! Will I do it again? Yes!

A Success in My Business

Don't get the wrong idea. I haven't given up on being a success in my business. On the contrary. My business and prospects for growth have never been better in my life. We have plans to do 20 times the volume in 2005 as we did in 2002. What good is the money if you're not happy while you're making it, or if you somehow lose your family in the process?

You may be thinking: "My business is different, I have to stay there or it'll go down!" That's not true, and I can prove it.

In our program of matching people, we require that our clients make a trip overseas to meet a prospective fiance face-to-face before bringing her to the United States. Of the thousands of guys we have helped in the past seven years, hundreds have told us in the beginning that because of their business they wouldn't be able to make the trip. Some have come up with some very convincing arguments. The best I remember was this guy who raised millions of dollars worth of tropical fish. If the water gets off 1% they will all die. He just couldn't risk it, no matter what. All of this rationalization was *before* he met his dream girl. Up until that point, he would have never left, but here is how he worked it out.

His older brother is retired, so my client brought his brother in and trained him for six weeks to run the farm. My client was gone for 21 days. Upon arriving home, he found everything in the best condition it had ever been! Now his brother helps him every time he wants to take a vacation with his new bride, something he hadn't done for over 20 years. In all the other cases we haven't had one guy lose his job over the trip – not one! We tell them to give their employer three months' notice. Somehow their employees manage to cover for them.

It is my belief if you're in a job or business that will not allow you to make God and family a priority, you need to sell it or quit! How much will you leave behind when you die? *All of it!*

With the increasing number of women now owning and starting businesses, this does not just apply to men. Recently a successful woman confided in me that in building her business there were times she wasn't there when her children needed their mother. There were other times when she was around but very preoccupied. As her children grew older, problems arose. There was a price that had to be paid! She told me she would do things differently if she could do it over. At least this lady realized the error of her ways. Unfortunately, there are many people who aren't even aware of the problem.

How Great a Price for Success?

It's great to have a dream, and to be willing to pay a price to see it materialize, but how great a price are you willing to pay for your success? No doubt you are doing some of the right things. Reading books like this is a good start, but don't forget the motivation for it all! Schedule quality time with your children. Get away at least every 90 days on a retreat. Take your wife on a date two or three times a month. Set aside at least one full day a week away from your business, the same day every week, one your family can count on. If your deal is worth its salt, the other days will provide plenty of time to make all the money you'll ever need, and without sacrificing the ones you love the most in the process!

For the past 7 years Larry & Beth McEntire have helped over 3000 American men find Christian wives from over 60 different countries. To receive a free copy of their book, *Your Princess Is Waiting,* call *800-600-9802* or visit to *www.WifePlace.com*

The Most Important Clients Are...

Our Children

By Rico Racosky

Cell phone numbers and Social Security numbers. Credit card numbers and lotto numbers. Of all the numbers we know, the two most common numbers to any of us in our hyper-linked lives are 24 and 168. Those numbers reflect the maximum number of hours anyone has to live each day and each week. No matter who we are, where we are, or what we do, 24 hours a day and 168 hours each week is all the time we have to get everything done – from client meetings to memos, dinners to demos, email to snail mail, phone calls to faxes. To keep our businesses vibrant and profitable, we must learn quickly to organize, customize and optimize our finite 24/168 hours.

While our daily/weekly time is finite, the demands on this time are infinite. We are passionate about our businesses and we want them to boom, so we do our best with our clients to efficiently allocate our limited time by following proven principles and practices that reap real results. We know that if we fail to set aside the time to meet the needs of our clients, they might soon look elsewhere to get their needs met. So we attend meetings, luncheons, or social gatherings, provide technical or non-technical support, and try to maintain clear written and verbal communication. So, if it is just common sense that failing to spend quality time, provide support, or clearly communicate with a business client could lead to losing that client, then it should come as no surprise that failing to do the same with a child could lead to "losing" that child. Children have the same need for quality time, "technical" support, and clear communication. In short, good business practices can also make good family practices – and our children *are* our most important clients.

We wouldn't dare think of canceling a couple of meetings with a client; they would begin to lose faith in us. Cancel a couple of "meetings" with our children and they, too, will begin to lose faith. We wouldn't think of telling a client who asks for technical support to "figure it out on your own." When we don't find time to answer our children's questions or give them support, aren't we basically telling them the same thing? We attempt to communicate clearly with a client because otherwise we might lose the sale. Do we share this same level of commitment with our children?

Again, good business practices can also make good family practices. The successful business techniques we use every day to build solid relationships with our clients have direct application to building solid relationships with our children. It all begins with observing how we allocate our finite number of hours – 24 each day and 168 each week. So, let's take a quick look at several ways in which time spent with our clients can correlate directly to time spent with our children:

1. Just as we make time to build a solid relationship with our clients – make time to build a solid relationship with our children.

2. Just as we commit time each week to meet with clients – commit time each week to "meet" with our children.

3. Just as we make and keep appointments with our clients – make and keep appointments with our children.

4. Just as we are patient with and respectful of our clients – be patient with and respectful of our children.

5. Just as we take the time to listen to our clients' needs – take the time to listen to our children's needs.

6. Just as we make time to attend our clients' activities – make time to attend our children's activities.

7. Just as we agree to follow up with our clients and plan on a specific time and date – do the same with our children.

8. Just as we respond to our clients' questions in a timely manner – respond to our children's questions in a timely manner.

9. Just as we make the effort to provide resources and contacts to our clients – make the effort to provide resources and contacts to our children.

10. Just as we keep records of our clients' needs and interests – keep records of our children's needs and interests.

You get the gist, and there are several more ideas that can be added to this list. From your personal experience, what other business-family correlations come to mind? The time that we spend with our children should be as measurable and definable and as it is in any sales report. It's very simple. From phone calls to e-mails to personal interactions, how many hours a day or week do we actually spend with our children? Do we give our children the same attention that we give our most important clients?

The old saying, "The best things in life aren't things—they're people" proves an excellent axiom for both children and clients. If we don't have time for our clients, our competitors will entice them away. Just so, if we don't have time for our children *someone else* or *something else* will. The media is full of stories about children who think adults don't have time for them who become involved in shoplifting, assault, sexual abuse, pregnancy, drugs, gangs, or even a Columbine High School incident. As business people with a passion for making our unique dreams come true, we sometimes find ourselves getting swept away in that enormous tide of enthusiasm and commitment to personal achievement. As a consequence, we can have the tendency to divert more and more of our time from those closest to us to those "things" around us. Although relationships with our families can have the elasticity of a big rubber band, eventually even that big rubber band can be stretched to a breaking point. We would never "stretch" our clients this way, so why should we "stretch" our loved ones?

Another case in point: in his international best seller *How to Win Friends and Influence People* (first published in 1936), Dale Carnegie masterfully outlines and details several sure-fire methods for beginning new relationships, or beginning old relationships anew. Mr. Carnegie's first step is showing sincere interest in our fellow man. As he states directly: "Why should people be interested in you unless you are interested in them? Do this and you'll be welcome anywhere." When we forget to show interest in our clients, we can lose them – and the same applies to our children.

Now to the heart of it all – this entire article relating good business practices to good family practices can be condensed into one simple success formula for living: *dreams + action = Reality*® (*d+a=R*). No matter what the dream or goal, large or small, client or child, the *dreams + action = Reality* formula applies and is always at work in our lives. In fact, we're "never not" using the *d+a=R* formula. Why? Because the "Reality" each of us experiences every moment of the day is based on our *dreams* plus the quality of *action* we take. Think about it. When we take half-hearted, lackluster actions with our clients or children, we get a half-hearted, lackluster "Reality." On the other hand, when we take enthusiastic and dedicated positive actions with our clients or children, we get a full-bodied, whole-hearted "Reality!" Feel the difference? Our clients and children certainly can!

Every action we take gets "crunched" through the *dreams + action = Reality* formula. Like a giant calculator, *d+a=R* continuously adds up all our actions at every moment in time and computes our Reality throughout the day, every day. As a result, each of our actions will take us to some degree either *closer to…* or *farther away from* our dreams or goals. This is why it's so important for us to think about the actions we take, because every action counts!

All of us have only 24 hours each day and 168 hours each week of time. Time is the yardstick we use to measure the effectiveness of our actions. Did we or didn't we do XYZ during today's 24 hours? What actions *did* we actually take? Did these actions move us *closer to* our dreams of success with our clients and children… or did they take us further away? Our daily actions create our lives.

Dentists like to say, "Only floss the teeth you want to keep." In the language of *dreams + action = Reality*, this equates to "Only take positive action toward the dreams you want to make Reality." Each of us must ask ourselves, "What are my dreams regarding my clients and my children?" Our children are our most important clients. Let's use our good business practices as good family practices so that both our business and family *dreams*, through our consistent positive *action*, will become *Reality*. Talk is cheap. Actions speak louder than words. Every action counts!

Rico Racosky is an author, motivational speaker, airline Captain, and former F-16 fighter pilot. He has written two books on goal setting: *dreams + action = Reality*® (for children) and *Go Vertical! Life Has No Ceiling* (for adults). Contact: *www.RocketfuelPublishing.com*.

Life is a Balancing Act

By Mark Victor Hansen

Life on a Tightrope

Imagine a tightrope walker in circus. He is on a rope suspended a few feet above the straw covered floor. His purpose is to walk the rope from one end to other. He holds a long bar in his hands to help him maintain his balance. But he must do more than simply walk. On his shoulders he balances a chair. And in that chair sits a young woman who is herself balancing a rod on her forehead, and on top of that rod is a plate.

If at any time one of the items should start to drift off balance, he must stop until he can get all of them in perfect alignment again. The tightrope artist doesn't begin until all the elements above him are aligned. Only then does he move forward, carefully, slowly across the rope.

I suggest that life is very much a balancing act and that we are always just a step away from a fall. We are constantly trying to move forward with our purpose, to achieve our goals. All the while trying to keep in balance the various elements of our lives.

Getting Out of Balance

Many of us get out of balance with regard to money. If we don't have sufficient money, then our lives become a money chase. We constantly devote our energies toward improving our finances. In the process we tend to take energy away from our family, our mate, our spiritual and mental needs, even our health. More importantly, we don't move forward toward our life purpose. We don't proceed along the tightrope. Only when we get our finances straightened out can we spread our energies to all the other aspects of our life and proceed with our purpose.

Other areas of our life could be out of harmony. It could be our relationship with our wife or husband. It could be a spiritual emptiness that is gnawing at our insides. It could be lack of appropriate social contract. It could be illness. If any aspect of our life draws a disproportionate amount of energy, we have to shortchange the other aspects. The throws us off and we are unable to move forward on life's tightrope until a balance can be reestablished.

www.mentorsmagazine.com

Getting in Balance

Our first priority, therefore, is getting our life in balance. We need to deal with any areas that are taking too much energy and put them in perspective align them so that we have energy available for all areas.

We need to create a balance of winning identities as father or mother, lover, husband, or wife, son or daughter, worker, participant, finisher and so forth. Only when each identity is fulfilled will that area be functioning and not overdrawing our energy.

But this doesn't happen by itself. Achieving a balanced life is a choice that each of is continually makes second by second, thought by thought, feeling by feeling. On the one hand, we can simply exist. But on the other, we can choose to pack out seconds and create valuable minutes in all aspects of our lives.

It's important to understand that others cannot do this for us. I can be me, and only you can be you. No one can think, breathe, feel, see, experience, love or die for either of us. Inside, we are what we are. We all come into life without a map, an operating manual or a definition of ourselves, other then male or female. It's up to us to balance all the different aspects of our lives. We can do to by pushing the "decide" buttons in our lives.

Making an Assessment

At first it's important to stop and assess how we're doing. We should look at all the various aspects of our life that we are constantly juggling, constantly trying to keep in balance. These include: marriage and family, finances, health, social contact, spiritual development and mental growth.

Are we able to devote ample energy to all areas? Or are we tipped off to one side, unbalanced in one direction?

Steps to Achieving Balance In Your Life

1. **Assess your life as it is now**. Looking at ourselves as we really are is the first step in re-creating our lives. Do you feel physically exhausted, mentally stagnet, or find yourself without close relationships? Would you call yourself a workaholic? Do you feel a lace of spiritual alignment? If you answer yes to any of these questions, your life is probably out of balance.

2. **Make a conscious decision to become balanced.** Choosing reality as our basis of decision, is the second step to becoming balanced. Achieving balance allows us to reach our goals and our purpose in life while creating less stress to do so. A conscious decision to change is now in order.

3. **Re-make that decision on a minute-to-minute basis.** We are all instant forgetters. Remember all those New Year resolutions? Renewing our decisions on a daily, minute to minute basis allows us to ease into change, instead of expecting things to change overnight.

4. **Set goals in every area of your life.** Set realistic goals in all areas of your life to assist yourself in remembering that your ultimate goal is balance. Your goal should cover:

   - Relationships, both at home and in the marketplace.
   - Physical beingness.
   - Spiritual alignment.
   - Mental development.
   - Your job.
   - Finances.

5. **Be willing to take the risk.** Being willing to assess yourself and take the risk to change will not only enhance your life, but you will feel more energy and an expanded awareness of what life is all about. Acknowledging that balance is essential, and recreating your life to encompass your decision is worth all the risk.

6. **Make time to re-assess yourself on a daily basis.** None of us can really know how well we are doing with change in our lives unless we are willing to re-assess our position. Don't feel that your decisions are made in concrete. If something feels that it isn't working, be willing to look at a new decision. Make time for yourself every day, in a quiet meditative state, to relax and "check yourself out."

Mark Victor Hansen is the co-author of the wildly successful *Chicken Soup for the Soul* series and his newest book, *The One Minute Millionaire.* He is also founder of the fast-growing internet-based *Goal-Mining Challenge,* a free resource for people to learn how to set goals in every facet of life for immediate, and amazing, improvement. To learn more, visit *www.markvictorhansen.com.*

Surprise Bonus...

Section 6

Rare Exclusive Interview

with

Brian Tracy

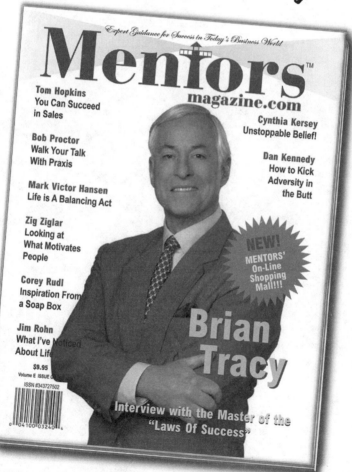

Expert Guidance for Success in Today's Business World

Mentors™
magazine.com

Tom Hopkins
You Can Succeed
in Sales

Cynthia Kersey
Unstoppable Belief!

Bob Proctor
Walk Your Talk
With Praxis

Dan Kennedy
How to Kick
Adversity in
the Butt

Mark Victor Hansen
Life is A Balancing Act

Zig Ziglar
Looking at
What Motivates
People

NEW!
MENTORS'
On-Line
Shopping
Mall!!!

Corey Rudl
Inspiration From
a Soap Box

Brian Tracy

Jim Rohn
What I've Noticed
About Life

$9.95
Volume E ISSUE

ISSN #343727502

Interview with the Master of the
"Laws Of Success"

Cover Story Excerpt from MENTORS Magazine

BRIAN TRACY

Laws of Success From a Master

Brian Tracy Interviewed by Linda Forsythe

Publisher's Note: This is an abbreviated excerpt from the original article which can be read in its entirety on *www.mentorsmagazine.com*. Read carefully and learn from this rare interview!

Recently I was honored to interview Brian Tracy and feature this discussion as our cover story in MENTORS magazine. Brian has motivated, inspired and educated countless individuals all over the world with his savvy, no-nonsense approach in what works to be prosperous. He is one of the world's leading authorities on personal and business success. His fast-moving, high-dollar, worth-while talks and seminars on leadership, sales, managerial effectiveness and business strategy are loaded with powerful, proven ideas. Brian teaches strategies that people can immediately apply to get better results in every area of their life.

Brian sits in front of me with his legs crossed, leaning back with an easy smile and relaxed demeanor. He exudes a powerful aura of confidence. We've just finished discussing the joys of living in beautiful San Diego, California and are ready to get down to business.

This wide-open transcript will give you some insight into the man who knows how to think and act in a way that has brought him millions of dollars. His passion is teaching others how to accomplish what he did in leading a fulfilled life.

Linda: *Brian... You have fans all over the world that flock in droves to learn your secrets of success. What first inspired you to do the work you do?*

Brian: Linda, first I want to thank you for choosing me as a MENTORS magazine cover story. I consider it a great honor! In answer to your question... Life has been very good to me, although I started off with no advantages. I did not graduate from high school or go to college. I worked at laboring jobs for several years before I got into sales. One day I stumbled over a concept that changed my life. It was the *Law of Cause and Effect*. What this law said for me was that there is a reason for everything that happens. It also said that if I could find out the reason for anything I wanted, and I duplicated those reasons, I would get the same effects each time. It was no miracle.

Although I first applied the laws to my sales career... they changed my life. I immediately began to ask other salespeople what they were doing that enabled them to be more successful than me. They told me and I applied it.

My sales immediately went up. Then I began to read books on selling and applied what I had learned from my readings and my sales went up even higher. I began to attend seminars and listen to audio programs. My sales went through the roof. My life went from rags to riches. I went from worrying about money to walking around with $1,000 in my pocket at any time. This was all because of the Law of Cause and Effect.

The reason that I do the work that I do is to share these same ideas about success with as many other people as possible. I want others to be able to enjoy the same blessings that I have experienced, but in a much shorter period of time.

My mission in life is to help people achieve their goals faster than they ever would without my help.

Ihe Law of Integrity

Great business leadership is characterized by honesty, truthfulness, and straight dealing with every person, under all circumstances.

Linda: *What, in your opinion, is the most important rule for success and how long did it take before people started to notice you?*

Brian: One of the most important rules for success is this: *Every great success is the result of hundreds and thousands of small efforts and accomplishments that no one ever sees or appreciates.*

I spent hundreds, and then thousands, of hours on the road learning how to speak and present my ideas. I napped in my car, slept in small motels, worked for almost nothing, lost enormous amounts of money and sometimes drove or flew overnight to get to a speaking engagement.

Meanwhile, I invested two or three hours each day in reading and learning more about my subjects for presentation. For the first few years, I lived on the edge. I almost went broke a couple of times. It was at about the five-year mark, after working virtually non-stop for the entire time, that my career began to accelerate.

Linda: *Just about every famous and/or self-made millionaire I know has gone through difficult circumstances or bankruptcy before they finally realized fame. Are you the exception or were there hurdles that you had to overcome?*

Brian: My life has been characterized by so many ups and downs that I can no longer count them. However, I have never felt that I have really *failed* at anything. I believe in what Henry Ford said, "Failure is merely an opportunity to more intelligently begin again."

After every setback, reversal, disappointment or loss, I have taken as much time as possible to evaluate the experience and to learn from it. Then I simply pick myself up and carry on.

Of course, I have been bankrupt or nearly bankrupt several times. I have lost enormous amounts of money and failed in a variety of ventures. I have had to sell everything I owned in order to raise the funds to continue onward. I have been betrayed by many people, and cheated by many others.

But this goes with the territory. This is all a part of living and learning. I just shrug it off and get onto the next challenge.

Linda: *I'm just curious... How did YOU overcome some of these hurdles to become successful?*

Brian: If anyone was to ask me the secret of success, I could sum it up quite simply. *Decide exactly what you want, but be flexible about the way you achieve it. Be prepared to work extremely hard, especially at the beginning of any new venture. And resolve, no matter what happens, to persist until you succeed.* These have been my guiding principles throughout life and they have enabled me to overcome any problem or hurdle that I have experienced.

Linda: *Where did you obtain the knowledge to teach what you do?*

Brian: Over the course of my lifetime, I have invested an average of 2-3 hours per day reading and studying in various areas. To date, I have probably spent 50,000 hours reading and learning. When I travel by air, sometimes to Europe or Asia, I will often read 8-10 hours on a variety of subjects, such as business, culture, psychology, current affairs, politics, economics and history.

By reading and studying eclectically and delving into a variety of different subjects continuously, I manage to develop a clear and better picture of a particular subject area.

In embarking upon a new subject, I start by accepting that I will have to invest 50-100 hours of reading and study to begin to understand that subject. If it is a language, like German or Russian, I expect to invest as much as 1000 hours to master the subject over the months and years ahead.

Once I have decided to invest a particular amount of time on a subject, I write it into my schedule and work on it steadily, day by day and week by week.

One of my mottos is, *"You can learn anything you need to learn to achieve any goal you set for yourself."*

Linda: *One of the things you do very well is telling motivational stories. Tell me a story to motivate or encourage me.*

Brian: Once upon a time, a 56-year old man died of a heart attack. He had spent 25 years of his life building a construction company to about $10 million dollars in annual sales. But he smoked too much, ate too much, drank too much and exercised not enough. It caught up with him and led to his early demise.

Meanwhile, his wife, who was about 50 years old, had taken care of the children and the home, and been involved with her church and community affairs. She did not know a lot about her husband's business, and it had not been necessary that she be involved.

But now the business belonged to her. After the funeral, she went into the business and sat the managers down. "Please tell me how this business works, and how we make money around here," she said.

The managers realized that she was serious. So they took her around the company and explained each activity of the company, how it worked, how successful it was, and how much it contributed to profit or loss.

Her management style was simple. She would simply ask, "What's working?" and "What's not working?"

If it was working – if it was successful and generating profits – she would encourage the managers to invest more time and people in that area. If it was not working; she would encourage the managers to discontinue that area of activity and reallocate the resources to the areas that were more profitable.

She then began asking, "Who's working?" and "Who's not working?" If someone was doing a good job, they were paid well and promoted faster. If they were not working up to standard, she would encourage them to go somewhere else.

This became her management style. She would come into the office occasionally during the week and simply ask, "What's working?" and "What's not working?"

Over the next ten years, using these simple questions and following where they led, she built the sales of the company to $25 million. She then sold the company and retired financially independent for the rest of her life.

The moral is this: In your life some things are working and some things are not working. Your job is to identify the things that are working and to do more of them. You must then determine what is not working, and then stop doing those things. *With this simple technique of sorting on the basis of what works and what doesn't work, you can transform your life!*

Linda: *Can you give me some of your hints to being a successful salesperson?*

Brian: Selling is a profession. All successful salespeople look upon it as a profession. Unsuccessful salespeople, on the other hand, look upon it as an occupation, something that they do during the day and forget about the rest of the time.

The Law of Courage

The ability to make decisions and act boldly in the face of setbacks and adversity is the key to greatness in leadership

If you want to move to the top of your field of sales, you must first of all realize that anyone can get into the top 10% of money earners in this field. It is simply a matter of applying the Law of Cause and Effect to selling, as I did at the beginning of my career. Find out what other successful salespeople do, and do more of it. Meanwhile, find out what unsuccessful salespeople do, and do less of that.

There are seven key result areas in selling. They are *Prospecting, Establishing Rapport, Identifying Needs, Making Presentations, Answering Objections, Closing the Sale,* and *Getting Resales and Referrals* from satisfied customers.

To move to the top of your field of selling, you must master each of these key result areas. Most of all, you must identify your weakest key area and work on that exclusively until you bring it up to the point where it no longer holds you back from using your other skills.

To be successful in selling, you should read 30-60 minutes each day in this area. You should listen to sales audio programs in your car when you drive around. You should attend sales seminars four times per year. You must get serious about your profession of selling if you want your profession to get serious about you.

Linda: *I notice that you speak all over the world. Where are some of the places that you speak?*

Brian: Over the course of a 24-month speaking cycle, I speak in about 24 different countries. Eight years ago, I made a decision to develop Europe as a major sub-market for my speaking, my books, my audiotapes and my video training programs.

Since German is the major language in central Europe, I learned to speak, read, write and communicate in German. Now, all my interactions in Germany, including telephone interviews with clients, radio and television appearances, magazine interviews and most of my seminars and talks are given in German. This German fluency has expanded my market in Switzerland and Austria and led to my giving regular seminars in Hungary, Poland and Slovenia.

The Law of Realism

Leaders deal with the world as it is; not as they wish it would be.

In Asia, I regularly give seminars in Hong Kong, China, Malaysia, Singapore, Indonesia, the Philippines and Taiwan. In addition, I speak quite frequently in Australia and New Zealand.

Linda: *Are the rules the same for selling or giving presentations in other countries? Sometimes culture requires the individual to act in a different way. Would you please give me an example?*

Brian: I have traveled or worked in 87 countries. I have spoken and given professional seminars to public and private audiences in 24 countries. In every case, my approach and my style is very much the same.

I begin with an overview of the subject, and the challenges and opportunities presented in the subject area, whether it is sales, management, leadership, personal success or making more money. I then teach an orderly series of proven, practical strategies, techniques and methods that have been used by other successful people (cause and effect!) in other situations, in other countries, around the world.

I do adapt my material to show how it is applicable to the current culture or country. But just as the laws of mathematics are the same worldwide, so are the laws and principles of success.

What works to build a successful business in Des Moines, Iowa will work to build a successful business in Stuttgart, Germany.

I feel in is important to do my homework and research on a country before I visit it. I study the culture, the language, the cultural norms and differences that my audiences may have from an American audience. I then adjust my talks and seminars so they are very much in harmony with the current country.

For example, my German audiences are made up of people who are logical and orderly in their thinking. This is not to say that they are not positive and optimistic and eager to learn. But they prefer that material be presented in such a way that it has a clear beginning, middle and end. I satisfy this need by designing my materials in this way.

In every case, in every country, my audiences appreciate it when I refer to the special qualities of the country, and of the people in that country.

For example, the Germans are extremely well disciplined. I explain to them that this national quality is one of the most important qualities they can have for success.

In Russia, the audiences are extremely persevering. They have endured enormous trials over the years and have developed a tremendous ability to withstand difficulty. I explain to them that this is a key quality for success in any area of business.

In China, I point out how entrepreneurial the Chinese are, everywhere in the world. I then illustrate how important an entrepreneurial attitude is to achieving success in their particular fields. In every case, I can support my observations with concrete examples drawn from natural experiences.

Linda: *You have mentioned the Laws of Success on multiple occasions. What ARE the Laws of Success?*

Brian: There are many laws of success. I have developed more than 150 laws that I teach in my various programs. Napoleon Hill had 17 principles. But I would say that you could summarize the laws of success in a single principle. It is this: Decide *exactly* what it is that you *really* enjoy doing, more than anything else. Throw your whole heart into becoming absolutely excellent in that particular area. Become the very best that you possibly can in your field. And when you earn a lot of money, hold onto it for the long-term.

Linda: *Have you noticed a common denominator for individuals who will never be successful?*

Brian: In Gary Zukav's book *The Seat of the Soul,* he says that positive thoughts empower; negative thoughts disempower.

Positive, optimistic people, with clear goals, who are working on them every single day, tend to accomplish ten times as much as negative, pessimistic people, with no clear goals, who live from day to day, without much thought of the future.

Perhaps the most important single principle for great success is called "Long Time Perspective." Successful people take the long view in their lives. They have 10- and 20-year goals. They then work back to the present and make sure that everything they do in the moment is consistent with where they want to end up sometime in the future.

Unsuccessful people, on the other hand, have little or no time perspective. They live in the moment. They eat too much, spend too much, and waste too much time in the moment, with very little thought to how this might affect their futures. And as my friend Michael Kami says, "Those who do not plan for the future cannot have one."

Linda: *What should the mind-frame or make-up of the individual be, in order to become a millionaire?*

Brian: I will use the more than five million self-made millionaires in America as an example. Each of them has a different story. But all of them have a central core philosophy that determines their success. First of all, self-made millionaires are hard, hard workers. They work an average of 60 hours per week, and they work hard while they work.

Self-made millionaires have a long-term perspective. One of their most important long-term goals is financial independence, and they think about it and plan toward it with every single financial decision they make.

Perhaps the most important inner quality of self-made millionaires is they are extremely honest. They are very family oriented, community oriented and committed to their businesses. But they have fine reputations for integrity and square dealing. This makes it easier and easier for them to do more and more business as the years pass. People come to rely on them and choose to purchase their products and services in ever greater quantities.

Linda: *Many people are complaining about not making enough money or being laid off from work because of the economy. What are your comments about that?*

Brian: The fact is that there are some people who are never unemployed. These people always have a job, sometimes two or three jobs. In any economy, including our economy, at any stage of the economy, there are endless possibilities for people to do valuable work and get paid well for it.

If a person is unemployed, it is largely a matter of choice. They are either demanding too much for their services in terms of remuneration, or they are looking for a job where there are no jobs because the industry has contracted or gone away, or they are looking for a job in a place where there is no employment.

The Law of Power

Power is the ability to influence the allocation of people, money and resources.

Anyone can get a job overnight if they will reduce their demands, change the work that they are offering to do or move to a place where they are more job opportunities. It is not complicated.

If a person is not making enough money, it is their responsibility to upgrade the quality and quantity of the work that they do so that they are worth more money. Another motto of mine is *"To earn more you must learn more."*

Whatever your level of knowledge and skills – even if you are a newly minted university graduate – your knowledge has a half life of two and a half years. That means that within five years everything you know will be worthless in the current marketplace. If you are not constantly learning and upgrading your knowledge and skills, you have no future. This is the major reason why people are not being paid the kind of money they want. They are not worth any more than they are getting.

Linda: *I love your stories. Please tell me another one!*

Brian: I have a friend named Igor who moved here from the Soviet Union a few years ago. He arrived in New York without the ability to speak a word of English. He had all his possessions in a cardboard box tied up with cord.

He took a bus into the center of the city and then began stopping people on the street and asking them, in Russian, "Do you know how I can get to Little Russia?" (Little Russia is the neighborhood where Russian immigrants tend to live when they arrive in the U.S. for the first time.)

Finally, someone responded to him in Russian and gave him instructions on how to get to Little Russia using the subway. When he came up off the subway, right in front of him, across the street, was a Dominos Pizza outlet. He went into the Dominos Pizza outlet

---

Leaders

Continually create situations that empower people, that make people feel stronger and more confident.

---

and spoke to the owner, who was also Russian. He got his first job, delivering Dominos pizzas to other Russians within the surrounding neighborhood.

But he was ambitious. He studied English night and day. He told me that he listened to my audio programs and read my books, and used them as his guides for success within the American economic system.

Within one year, his English was fluent enough that he got into sales, selling printing for a local printer. After one year, he started his own business, as a broker for printing services. He would sell printing services and then broker it out to other printing companies for a 20% commission.

In his third year in the U.S., he sold $500,000 worth of printing services, and earned $100,000 personal income. In his fourth year, he sold $800,000 worth of printing services, and in his fifth year, he sold over one million dollars worth of printing services, earned more than $200,000, bought a new Mercedes, tailored suits and moved to a beautiful apartment, which he could afford to furnish well.

When I last spoke to Igor, he had been in the U.S. for 8 years and was already a millionaire. He told me that all around him, people were complaining that there weren't enough opportunities for people to earn more money. He just laughed.

Linda: *This next question is for our American readers: What are your thoughts about those who live here and want to get into business for themselves but can't seem to get started?*

Brian: This is the very best time in all of human history to be alive and America is the very best country at this time to be alive in. It is more possible, for more people, to live longer and better today in America than has ever been dreamed of by man in the history of man on earth.

America has been rated as the "Most entrepreneurial country in the world." There are more people inventing more products and services, starting more businesses, and creating more wealth in America today, irrespective of the ups and downs of the current stock market, than has ever before existed. And if anything, it will be getting better in the years ahead. My biggest question for the reader who isn't moving forward toward success is "What are you afraid of?" It doesn't get much better than this!!! Our forefathers who started this country fought and died for your ability to live in prosperity. Many have done it and so can you. Move beyond your fear because it obviously isn't serving you well.

Do we have problems in America? Of course we do! Any society made up of individuals is going to have problems because individuals are imperfect. When you put 275 million freedom-loving, ambitious, individualistic people together in this vast country, you are going to have every kind of incredible event that you can imagine. There will be positive news stories and negative news stories. There will be terrorism and snipers. There will be courage and compassion. There will be incredible achievements, including stories of young men, like Bill Gates and Michael Dell, who have started from nothing and created some of the biggest fortunes in the world before they were 40 years old.

This is a great country. There has never been a better country in all of human history. And as my friends from overseas have told me, "If you can't be successful here, you can't be successful anywhere."

Linda: *Brian, in closing I'm going to ask you to give some of your laws for success in the 21st century.*

Brian: Here they are:

1. Your life only gets better when you get better, and since there is no limit to how much better you can become over time, there is no limit to how much better you can make your life.

2. It doesn't matter where you're coming from; all that really matters is where you are going. And since where you are going is only limited by your imagination, there are no limits.

3. You are only as free as your options. Your job, throughout your life, is to develop alternatives so that you always have a series of options open to you, if things should change.

4. You can learn anything you need to learn to achieve any goal you can set for yourself.

5. The only limits on what you can be, do and have in life are self-imposed. They exist in your own mind, not in reality.

6. Within every problem or difficulty lies the seed of an equal or greater benefit or advantage. Your job is to find it.

7. If you do what other successful people do, over and over, nothing can stop you from eventually achieving the same success that they enjoy. But if you don't do what other successful people do, nothing can help you.

Linda: *Thank you Brian for taking the time to join us today. Your words have been truly inspiring!*

To learn more about what Brian teaches or to purchase any of his products, visit: www.briantracy.com. The complete version of this interview is available on *www.mentorsmagazine.com.*

How to Master Your Time

(Includes six audio cassettes or CDs)

Brian Tracy gives you a concrete, step-by-step approach to making the best use of every minute of every day. Gain at least two extra hours every day with the techniques provided in this valuable program.

The Power of Clarity

(Includes six audio cassettes or CDs, plus workbook)

In this program you will learn how to develop absolute clarity regarding who you are and what you really want. The Power of Clarity is a synthesis of the best strategies on personal management in one easy-to-use plan.

Available at www.briantracy.com

INVEST IN
YOUR SUCCESS...

Tapes, Books, Boot Camps, Seminars,
Newsletters and Coaching from our
WALKING WITH THE *WISE*
contributors are available at
www.mentorsmagazine.com

WALKING WITH THE WISE
Contributors

Jay Aaron
David Adlard
Debbie Allen
Chris Attwood
Janet Attwood
David Baulieu
Kevin Brown
Jacalyn Buettner, D.C.
John R. Burley
Dawn Camilla Clinton-Jones
Keith J. Cunningham
Bryan C. Davis
Charlie Douglas
Declan Dunn
David & Venus Dye
Kevin Eikenberry
Gray Elkington
Dawne Era
Diane Fontenot
Linda Forsythe
Debbie Friedman, C.Ht
Bernie Gartland
Susan L. Gilbert
Louise Griffith
Mark Victor Hansen
Judy Hoffman
Dawn M. Holman
Tom Hopkins
Vic Johnson
Rebecca Joy
Marilyn Joyce, M.A., R.D., Ph.D
Dan Kennedy
Cynthia Kersey
Brad J. King, M.S., MFS
Dan Kuschell
Robyn Levin
Mike Litman

Eric Lofholm
Peter Lowe
Lori Mackey
Joanne Mansell
Larry McIntire
Denise M. Michaels
Julette Millien
Mandy Myles
Kim Muslusky
Niurka
Jason Oman
Luigi Peccenini
Susan K. Perry
Shawn Phillips
Lynn Pierce
Joe Polish
Bob Proctor
Rico Racosky
Edie Raether
Greg S. Reid
Wendy Robbins
Jim Rohn
Corey Rudl
Brian Smithies
David E. Stanley
Gail Stolzenburg
Bradley J. Sugars
Van K. Tharp, Ph.D
Brian Tracy
Gary Vurnum
Dottie Walters, CSP
Joseph B. Washington II
Somers White
Carol Young
Becky Zerbe
Zig Ziglar

Are
YOU
A Mentor?

We are conducting a search for individuals with the following qualities:

- Embody principles of integrity in life and business

- Possess expertise in a particular field with proficiency as a mentor, trainer, consultant or coach

- Possess unique information, inspiration or motivation

- Live according to the principles of true prosperity

- Have a passion to help and guide others

If you qualify, you may be eligible to become part of our team. We publish articles and books, host mentorsmagazine.com, sponsor live seminars, workshops, teleseminars, and more!

Contact Us!

www.mentorsmagazine.com
Possibilities@mentorsmagazine.com

MENTORS Publications, Inc.
10755-F Scripps Poway Pkwy. #530
San Diego, CA 92131

858-277-9700

www.mentorsmagazine.com

Move Forward with Boldness
on Your Quest
and Mighty Forces
Will Come to Your Aid

MENTORS Magazine Motto